INTRODUCTION TO THE ENGLISH EDITION

This translation of Dr. Werner Schlote's *Entwicklung und Strukturwandlungen' des englischen Aussenhandels von 1700 bis zur Gegenwart* (Jena, 1938) has been made by Dr. W. O. Henderson and Dr. W. H. Chaloner of the Department of Economic History of the University of Manchester. They desire to thank Professor Arthur Redford and Professor E. Devons who have read the translation in typescript and have made valuable suggestions and also Dr. G. Flack who made a preliminary examination of the German text. Dr. Schlote has kindly cleared up some of the more obscure points in the text. Our colleagues, Dr. T. S. Willan, and Mr. B. W. Clapp, and also Dr. F. V. Meyer of University College, Exeter, have examined the proofs of the translation and we are indebted to them for helpful suggestions.

The translators appreciate that Dr. Schlote's methods of statistical analysis as well as some of his conclusions may be subjects of controversy. They do not presume to offer a critical edition of Dr. Schlote's work in which such matters would be discussed. They have confined themselves to producing as accurate a translation as possible. A few phrases have been interpolated in square brackets in the hope of making the author's meaning as clear as possible. Occasionally a footnote has been slightly amplified, also in square brackets, and some information has been added about the research that has been done since 1938 on the history of British overseas trade.

W.O.H.
W.H.C.

NOTE ON RECENT PUBLISHED WORK

Since Dr. Werner Schlote's work appeared in 1938 several scholars have dealt with some of the problems that he discusses. The books and articles mentioned below—by no means an exhaustive list—may be of interest to students. Reference may also be made to the useful bibliographies on pp. 648-50 and pp. 669-70 of Professor Herbert Heaton's *Economic History of Europe* (revised edition, New York, 1948).

Paul Rousseaux, *Les Mouvements de Fond de l'Économie Anglaise*, 1800-1913 (Louvain, 1938).

E. E. Hoon, *Organisation of the English Customs System, 1696-1786* (New York, 1938).

G. N. Clark, *Guide to English Commercial Statistics, 1696-1782* (Royal Historical Society, London, 1938).

A. H. Imlah, 'Real Values in British Foreign Trade, 1798-1853, (in *The Journal of Economic History*, Vol. VIII, November 1948, No. 2, pp. 132-152), and 'The Terms of Trade of the United Kingdom, 1798-1913, (*ibid.*, Vol. X, November 1950, No. 2, pp. 170-194).

A. J. Brown, *Industrialization and Trade: the changing world pattern and the position of Britain* (Oxford, Royal Institute of International Affairs, 1943.)

E. Staley, *World Economic Development: Effects on Advanced Industrial Countries* (International Labour Office, Montreal, 1944).

A. O. Hirschman, *National Power and the Structure of Foreign Trade* (University of California Bureau of Business and Economic Research), 1945.

A. E. Kahn, *Great Britain in the World Economy* (London, 1946).

L. H. Dupriez, *Des Mouvements Économiques Généraux*, 2 vols., (Louvain, 1947).

League of Nations: *Industrialisation and Foreign Trade* (Economic, Financial and Transit Department, Series II, Economic and Financial, 1945, II, A 10).

W. W. Rostow, *British Economy of the Nineteenth Century* (Oxford, 1948).

A. Maizels, 'The Oversea Trade Statistics of the United Kingdom' (in the *Journal of the Royal Statistical Society*, Series A (General), Vol. CXII, Part 2, 1949, pp. 207-221 and bibliography, pp. 222-3).

NOTE ON RECENT PUBLISHED WORK

Commonwealth Economic Committee, *A Review of Commonwealth Trade* (H.M. Stationery Office, London, 1949).

H. Tyszynski, ' World Trade in Manufactured Commodities ' (in *The Manchester School*, Vol. XIV, No. 3, September, 1951, pp. 272–304.

*   *   *   *

Attention should also be drawn to K. Zweig, ' Strukturwandlungen und Konjunkturschwingungen in englischen Aussenhandel der Vorkriegszeit (*Weltwirtschaftliches Archiv*, Jena, Vol. XXX, Part 2, 1929), pp. 317–351 (Chronik und Archivalien) ; A. G. Silverman, ' Some International trade factors for Great Britain, 1880–1913 ' (in *The Review of Economic Statistics*, Harvard Economic Society, 1931), p. 114–124, and C. J. Fuchs, *The Trade Policy of Great Britain and her Colonies since 1860* (1905), esp. chap. iii, and the books and articles therein cited (*translation of German original published in 1893*).

PREFACE BY THE GERMAN EDITOR

Dr. Werner Schlote's book is the first of a series of studies concerning the quantitative development of the British economy which has been undertaken by one of the research departments of the *Institut für Weltwirtschaft* (Institute for the Study of World Economic Affairs at the University of Kiel). Research commenced during the worst stage of the world economic crisis [of 1929-33] when it was clearly urgently necessary to study the significance of crises in world economic development. It was desirable also to re-examine the modern theory of the trade-cycle with the help of quantitative material. The study soon broadened into the question of the reciprocal relationship of economic structure and trade-cycle. Eventually the author was drawn to the real heart of the problem, namely, the question of the long-term development of capitalist economy.

To gain a clear and really comprehensive statistical picture of the development of capitalist economy it is necessary not only to conduct an investigation over a long period of time, but also, if possible, to include in the study the most important industrial countries, namely, Great Britain, Germany, the U.S.A., and France.

A preliminary examination of the available literature showed that even the essential preparatory statistical work had not been carried out for any of these countries. So if the original plan had been pursued it would have been necessary in every instance for the research group itself to have obtained the required statistical material from original sources. Such an undertaking, however, would have been beyond the resources at the disposal of the Institute for purposes of research, even if there had not been numerous other enquiries which became more and more urgent in the course of the economic revival [of the mid-1930s]. Consequently we limited the investigation to the country which, owing to the predominant position it occupied as the leading industrial power in the nineteenth century, afforded the most satisfactory basis for an analysis of economic development.

We do not propose to write an economic history of Great Britain. Although we have limited our investigations to a single country, we have no intention of pursuing our enquiries beyond what can be discovered by statistical analysis. We have therefore refrained from

PREFACE BY THE GERMAN EDITOR

attempting any presentation of our results in the form of a synthesis of the material. What we do offer are individual reports on various aspects of the British economy. The present work on British overseas [1] trade will be followed by an enquiry into the development and forms of growth of Britain's industrial structure.[2] We believe that we can best serve economic science by presenting our results in this way. It will thus be possible for the material we have used to be presented in the clearest and most helpful manner both for the average student and for the research student who wishes to pursue the enquiry further. In this way the results of the research undertaken by an Institute can be made available to the widest possible circle of readers.

This is particularly true of the present work, which aims at tracing the development of British overseas trade and its changes within as long a period as possible. In view of the fact that we have limited our studies to quantitative statistical material, this book falls into two main parts. The first deals with the sources and methods of the research and tabulates the results. The second part (based upon the evaluation of the statistical material) shows structural economic changes by analysing the growth of overseas trade. These changes have affected both the composition of the goods entering into overseas trade and also the geographical complexity of British overseas trade during the last 120 years. This second part also attempts to justify the methods used in the first part of the work by showing that our results can be used to solve actual economic problems.

The serious student will readily appreciate the wealth of statistical material and theoretical ideas on which the present study is based. We hope that this book will substantially advance our knowledge of the factors involved in economic growth far beyond the specific case of Great Britain. The book attempts to do more than clarify the past. It claims to contribute to the live economic issues of the day—not by encouraging any fatalistic belief in the existence of iron economic laws, but (by giving a clear picture of industrial structures of the past) to help those who are planning the framework of our economic and political development.

---

[1] [Dr. Schlote includes both Britain's foreign trade and Empire trade in the word *Aussenhandel*, which has been translated by 'overseas trade', although between 1696 and the Union with Scotland (1707) an insignificant fraction of England's external trade was 'overland'. For Anglo-Scottish trade in the seventeenth century see T. Keith: *Commercial Relations of England and Scotland* (1910).]

[2] W. Hoffmann, *Wachstum und Wachstumsformen der englischen Industriewirtschaft.* (Probleme der Weltwirtschaft, vol. 63, Jena, 1940).

PREFACE BY THE GERMAN EDITOR

The Institute thanks the *Deutsche Forschungsgemeinschaft* (German Research Board) for bearing the main financial burden both of research and publication. Our thanks are due also to the Rockefeller Foundation, without whose additional help the research could not have been carried out so intensively and thoroughly.

ANDREAS PREDÖHL.

Kiel, February 7, 1938.

LIST OF CONTENTS

	PAGE
Introduction to the English Edition	iii
Note on Recent Published Work	iv
Preface by the German Editor	vii
List of Contents	ix
List of Tables in the Text	xiii
Diagrams in the Text	xvi
Index	114

A. METHOD

		PAGE
I.	The Statistical Bases of the Enquiry	3
II.	Methods of Calculation used in the Investigation	10
	1. Classification by Commodities and Commodity-groups	10
	2. Calculation of the Volume of Overseas Trade	12
	(*a*) Preliminary Observations on the Volume of Overseas Trade and its Calculation	12
	(*b*) The Method of 'Official Values'	15
	(*c*) Method of Calculating Volume used in this work	26
	3. Calculation of Actual Current Values of Imports and Re-exports between 1800 and 1854	30
	4. Geographical Distribution of British Overseas Trade and Changes in the area covered by the Trade Statistics	34

B. ANALYSIS

		PAGE
I.	The Development and Significance of British Overseas Trade	41
	1. Periods of Growth	41
	2. Development of Overseas Trade in Periods of Boom and Slump	43
	3. The Prices of Exports and Imports in Relation to the Growth of Overseas Trade	46

LIST OF CONTENTS

		PAGE
4. Overseas Trade and National Income	... ...	47
5. Overseas Trade and Industrial Production ...	...	50

II. Classification of British Overseas Trade by Commodities
Preliminary Observations 51

    1. Imports 52
        (a) Classification by Commodity-Groups 52
        (b) Imports of Raw Materials 55
        (c) Imports of Foodstuffs 59
        (d) Imports of Finished Manufactured Goods ... 66

    2. Exports 68
        (a) Classification by Commodity-Groups 8
        (b) Exports of Foodstuffs and Raw Materials... ... 71
        (c) Exports of Finished Manufactured Goods ... 72
        (d) Exports of Finished Manufactured Goods and Industrial Production 75

III. Geographical Distribution of British Overseas Trade ... 79
    1. Distribution of British Overseas Trade by Continents 79
    2. British Overseas Trade with Industrial and Agrarian Regions 81
    3. British Trade with the Empire 88

Appendix of Tables 107

LIST OF TABLES IN THE TEXT

TABLE		PAGE
1	United Kingdom Imports of Textile Raw Materials in 1854 ...	21
2	Imports into the United Kingdom in 1854	22
3	Comparison of Official and Deflated Import Values of the United Kingdom, 1854–1869	25
4	Comparison of Official and Deflated Values of United Kingdom Re-exports, 1854–1869	26
5	Periods and Base-Years of Calculation of United Kingdom's Overseas Trade	27
6	Share of the Continents in Imports and Re-exports of the United Kingdom in 1854, calculated on Official and Actual Values (per cent)	35
7	Overseas Trade of United Kingdom in 1904 with Countries of Shipment and Consignment	36
8	Annual Average Percentage Increase in the Rate of Growth and the 'Rate of Expansion' of Volumes of British Overseas Trade, 1700–1929 (per cent)	42
9	Growth of Imports and Exports in Periods of Boom and Slump, 1816–1913	45
10	Total Overseas Trade and National Income, 1805–1933	49
11	Total Overseas Trade and Industrial Production, 1700–1933	51
12	Analysis of Imports by Commodity-Groups, 1814–1933	53
13	Net Imports of Raw Materials and Industrial Production, 1818–1933	57
14	Share of Different Kinds of Raw Materials in Total Net Imports of Raw Materials, 1827–1933 (per cent)	58
15	Home Prices of Wheat, Rates of Duty ruling and Imports of Wheat for Consumption, 1829–1868	61
16	Population, Prices, Imports and Wheat Harvests for the Period when Duties were being changed, 1825–1875	61
17	Cattle and Sheep imported before and after Exemption from Duty, 1841–1850	62

LIST OF TABLES IN THE TEXT

TABLE		PAGE
18	Imports of Ham and Bacon for Consumption, 1820–1860 (cwt.)	63
19	Imports for Consumption of Salt Beef and Pork up to 1849	63
20	Imports for Consumption of Butter, Cheese and Eggs, 1843–1865	64
21	Proportion of Net Imports of Foodstuffs represented by Essential Provisions and Luxury Foods and Drinks (per cent), 1820–1933	65
22	Net Import of Finished Manufactured Goods, 1858–1933 (Percentage by Value)	67
23	Net Imports of Finished Manufactured Goods 1833–1933	68
24	Analysis of Exports in Commodity-Groups, 1814–1933 (per cent)	71
25	Analysis of Exported Foodstuffs by Important Commodity-Groups, 1827–1933 (Percentage by Value)	72
26	Changes in Exports of Raw Materials classified by Commodities, 1827–1933 (Percentage Proportions by Value)	73
27	Changes in Exports of Finished Manufactured Goods classified by Commodities, 1827–1933 (Percentage Proportions by Value)	74
28	Changes in 'Export Proportion' of the Consumption-Goods Industry, 1815–1933	78
29	Percentage of British Overseas Trade with Europe and America, 1698–1929	80
30	Overseas Trade of United Kingdom with Africa, Asia and Australia, 1854–1929 (Percentage by Value)	80
31	Overseas Trade of United Kingdom with Industrial and Agricultural Countries, 1827–1929 (Percentage by Value)	82
32	Overseas Trade of United Kingdom with Industrial and Agrarian Countries, 1854–1929 (Volumes)	84
33	Britain's Imports from Industrial Countries, in Commodity Groups, 1854–1929	85

LIST OF TABLES IN THE TEXT

TABLE		PAGE
34	Exports of Home Products to Industrial Countries by Commodity Groups, 1827–1929	86
35	Empire's Proportion of Britain's Overseas Trade, 1909–1935 (Percentage of Total Trade)...	89
36	Geographical Distribution of British Exports, 1861–1879	92
37	Dominions' Share in British Trade with the Empire, 1814–1935 (per cent)	92
38	United Kingdom's Trade with the Empire, 1909–1935...	95
39	British Imports of Cotton, Jute, Wheat and Tea from India, 1854–1934 (Annual Average)	97
40	Empire's Share in British Imports of Foodstuffs and Raw Materials, 1854–1934 (per cent)	99
41	Empire's Share in British Imports of Important Foodstuffs, 1854–1934	100
42	Empire's Share in Imports of Important Raw Materials, 1854–1934	101
43	Empire's Share in Exports of Home Products, 1830–1934	102

DIAGRAMS IN THE TEXT

DIAGRAM		PAGE
1	English (later, British) Imports and Exports and the Tonnage of Shipping cleared outwards from 1696 to 1822...	9
2	Actual and Calculated Values of British Imports and Re-exports, 1854–1934 ...	34
3	Rates of Expansion of British Overseas Trade, 1700–1923 (per cent) ...	43
4	Volumes of English (later, British) Overseas Trade, 1694–1934 ...	44
5	Relation between Exports, including Re-exports, and Imports (by Volume and Price), 1814–1933 ...	47
6	Analysis of Imports in Commodity-groups, 1814–1933 (Proportions of total Volume in percentages) ...	54
7	Analysis of Imports in Commodity-groups, 1854–1934 (Proportions of actual value in percentages) ...	55
8	Net Import Volume of Raw Materials (Volume with 1913 as base-year) and of Industrial Production, 1814–1933	56
9	Analysis of Re-exports in Commodity-groups, 1814–1933 (percentage proportions by Volume) ...	59
10	Analysis of Exports in Commodity-groups, 1814–1933 (percentage of 'Volume') ...	69
11	Analysis of Exports in Commodity-groups, 1814–1933 (percentage of actual value) ...	70
12	Indexes of (a) Price Relation between finished goods and raw materials, and (b) 'Export-proportions' of British industry, 1814–1933 ...	76
13	Share of British Empire in United Kingdom Trade, 1814–1936 ...	91
14	Dominions' Share of Britain's Trade with the Empire, 1814–1935 ...	91

A. METHOD

I. THE STATISTICAL BASES OF THE ENQUIRY [1]

Systematic statistics of English overseas trade, tabulated by goods and countries, date from 1696. Previous efforts to ascertain the extent of England's overseas trade had merely been estimates derived from the annual customs revenue and no attempt had been made to find out the actual amounts and values of the goods involved. Since both import and export duties averaged about five per cent *ad valorem* the total value of imports and exports could be estimated at twenty times the customs revenue for any year. In and after 1696 however the customs authorities at the ports required the recipient, sender or carrier of all dutiable commodities to complete certain forms. The type and quantity of the goods as well as the country of origin or destination could be ascertained from these so-called Entries which became the basis of the statistics of imports and exports compiled by the Inspector General. The value of overseas trade was ascertained by multiplying the quantities of goods year by year by fixed prices that had been permanently allocated to each type of commodity. These prices had been ascertained very carefully. They were the average prices prevailing in 1694 for all goods entering into England's overseas trade.[2] By this calculation so-called ' official values' of the country's total overseas trade were obtained. A detailed examination of the significance of these official values will be made later and it will be shown that there are serious practical difficulties to be faced when analysing commercial statistics of this kind. Nevertheless we could have used these statistics as a firm basis for an analysis of England's overseas trade had they not, in all probability, been destroyed in the two fires at the Custom House in 1718 and 1814.[3]

[1] See S. Bourne, *Trade, Population and Food* ... (London, 1880), especially the three essays on pp. 1—75; R. Giffen, *Economic Enquiries and Studies* (London, 1904), Vol. I, p. 282 ff; F. Lohmann, ' Die amtliche Handelsstatistik Englands und Frankreichs im achtzehnten Jahrhundert' (in *Sitzungsberichte der Königlich Preussischen Akademie der Wissenschaften*, Berlin, Vol. 54, 1878, p. 859 ff).

[2] See below, pp. 16-18. [Dr. G. N. Clark points out in his *Guide to English Commercial Statistics 1696-1782* (1938), pp. 10-11, that ' many historical writers have indeed stated that it [i.e. the list of prices] continued in use unaltered from 1694 to 1870; but that is an error . . . the fossilisation of the list was a gradual process . . . Culliford [Inspector General between 1696 and 1703] as part of the routine of his office made changes from one year to another in the values of some of the commodities. Neither of his two immediate successors seems to have been aware of this '. See also A. Maizels's article in the *Journal of the Royal Statistical Society*, Vol. CXII, part ii, 1949, p. 211].

[3 Dr. Schlote gives the date of the second fire at the Custom House in London as 1813. The correct date is February 12, 1814].

The only statistics that have survived are those giving the total value of imports and exports (ascertained as we have described) and those giving the geographical distribution of foreign trade—both expressed in official values. There is also some information available concerning overseas trade in one or two important articles in the eighteenth century.[1] The surviving information, however, is not at all adequate for a reconstruction of total trade statistics.

It was only because no periodical publication [of British overseas trade statistics] took place—such as is done as a matter of course to-day—that the extensive statistical labours of an entire century could be so completely lost.

The Inspector General was only required to submit regularly to the House of Commons an annual survey of overseas trade. We have not seen copies of these reports[2] and therefore we cannot state whether they give sufficient information for a reconstruction of the overseas trade statistics. The reports are however unlikely to provide such information since Sir Charles Whitworth and George Chalmers,[3] who carefully collected information about the total value and geographical distribution of English overseas commerce in the eighteenth century, did not attempt any analysis of foreign trade by groups of commodities.

The statistics of overseas trade which we have used for this period are based upon those compiled by César Moreau who made some corrections in the statistics given by Whitworth and Chalmers.[4]

[1] See, for example, J. Marshall, *Digest of all the Accounts* . . . (London, 1833); E. Baines, *History of the Cotton Manufacture in Great Britain* (London, 1835); D. Macpherson, *Annals of Commerce, Manufactures, Fisheries and Navigation* (London, 1805); A. Anderson, *A Historical and Chronological Deduction of the Origin of Commerce from the earliest Accounts* . . . (London, 1787-89); J. R. McCulloch, *A Dictionary . . . of Commerce and Commercial Navigation* (London, 1834); J. Bentham, *Observations on the restrictive and prohibitory Commercial System* (London, 1821); W. Smart, *Economic Annals of the Nineteenth Century 1801-20* (London, 1910); A. Moreau de Jonnès, *Statistique de la Grande Bretagne et de l'Irlande* (two volumes, Paris, 1837-8); and *Customs Tariffs of the United Kingdom from 1800 to 1897 with some Notes upon the History of the more important Branches of Receipt from the Year 1660* (Cmd. 8706 of 1897).

[2] [Dr. G. N. Clark states in his *Guide to English Commercial Statistics, 1696-1782* (1938), p. 30, note ii, that he has not seen any printed annual copies of ' the annual Accounts given in by the proper Officers to the House of Commons ' to which Sir Charles Whitworth refers in his *State of the Trade of Great Britain in its Imports and Exports* (1776), preface, p. 2].

[3] G. Chalmers, *An Estimate of the Comparative Strength of Great Britain* (London, 1794).

[4] See C. Moreau, *State of the Trade of Great Britain with all Parts of the World* (London, no date of publication). [The catalogue of the British Museum library lists a copy of the French edition—*État du Commerce de la Grande Bretagne avec toutes les parties du Monde* (Londres)—and 1822 is suggested as the date of publication. A copy in the Bibliothèque Nationale, Paris, is dated 1824.] The official statistics of exports used by Whitworth and Chalmers include precious metals

Moreau continued the statistics to 1822. The statistics refer only to the overseas trade of England and Wales until 1754. Statistics of overseas trade for Scotland date from 1755 when a special Inspector General [for that country] was appointed.[1] Not until after this date were there statistics for the overseas trade of the whole of Great Britain.

It was not until 1798 that any reform of trade statistics was undertaken and then only two changes of any importance were made. In the export trade a distinction was made between the export of home products and the export of foreign and colonial goods. Henceforth exports and re-exports were recorded separately—a procedure that has been followed to the present day. Even at the end of the eighteenth century it appears that re-exports were defined as commodities which were re-exported in the exact form in which they had been imported—or, at any rate, had merely been packed, repacked or mixed. The second significant change was that henceforth exports of home products were priced according to the values declared by exporters as well as according to the official values [at prices ruling in 1694]. Imports and re-exports, however, were still assessed as before—that is to say, on the basis of the prices of 1694. Further, in and after 1800, Ireland was included in the trade statistics. From then onwards there were returns for the overseas trade of the whole United Kingdom.[2] Before 1820,[3] however, no systematic record of the overseas trade of the United Kingdom with details for separate commodities appears to have been made. If such an analysis exists —and for the period following the fire at the [London] Custom

which had been imported—though they were not recorded in the statistics of imports—and were then re-exported. Moreau made allowance for this error. Moreover, he also included the exports of those goods—for unknown destinations— on which a bounty had been paid. Such exports were at that time entered separately in the records. This accounts for the main discrepancies—which are only of minor significance—between the statistics of Moreau and those of Whitworth and Chalmers. Reference may also be made to the official report issued in 1897 by the Statistical Office of the London Custom House entitled *Customs Tariffs of the United Kingdom from 1800 to 1897* ... (*loc. cit.*). This records English imports and exports (excluding trade with Ireland) between 1779 and 1800 and United Kingdom imports and exports between 1801 and 1853. Until 1853 imports and exports were given in official values. Between 1854 and 1896 they were given in actual current values (p. 46 ff). No attempt was made [in this official compilation] to analyse foreign trade by countries.
[1] See F. Lohmann, *loc. cit.*, p. 867.
[2] [In a letter to the translators Dr. W. Schlote explains that this means that after 1800 there are available *separate trade statistics* for (i) Great Britain and (ii) Ireland. But in and after 1805 (see below, pp. 16-17) there are *joint trade statistics* for the United Kingdom as a whole.]
[3] A really adequate classification of exports is possible only after 1827. [See also below, p. 29.]

House (1814)[1] it would have been possible to have made such an analysis—it is not known to the author. Only for one or two of the more important categories of commodities could trade statistics be drawn up. They apparently relate to the whole of the United Kingdom and they go back to 1801.

The official tables of revenue, population, commerce, etc. have been used as data for the overseas trade of the country between 1820 and 1853. These tables include statistics of overseas trade in a fairly standardised form. For the five years before 1820 we have used the overseas trade statistics given in Marshall's *Digest*.

Trade statistics—independent of other statistics—were issued in 1853 for the first time as a separate annual publication.[2] The second volume of this series introduced an important change in the method of presentation. From 1854 onwards the prices of 1694 were no longer used for calculating either imports or re-exports. The old official prices however continued to be used for calculations which appeared in the Finance Accounts until 1869. [In the overseas trade statistics] commodities were now calculated by ' real values ' [*i.e.* by actual current prices] ascertained each month by experts. Thus arose trade statistics based upon ' computed real values ' [current values] for imports and re-exports and on ' declared real values' for exports which had been produced at home. In and after 1871 declared current values were introduced for all commodities entering into foreign trade and this practice has continued to the present day.

The last change of any significance that was made in the entries concerned the designation of countries of origin and destination. Until 1904 the country of origin recorded was that containing the port from which a commodity had been shipped to Great Britain. Further, the country which was regarded as the final recipient —provided that it possessed a port—was the ' country of destination ' of exports. If the importing country had no coast the decisive factor was—to which country did the port of destination belong ? Countries such as Switzerland and Bolivia could not appear at all in British overseas trade statistics until 1904 since they did not have a coast. In 1904 this was changed and the term ' country of consignment' came into use. The ' country of consignment ' was either the country from which a commodity had been sent to Britain or the country in which the firm ordering the commodities

---

[1] [See above, p. 3 note.]

[2] *Annual Statement of the Trade and Navigation of the United Kingdom with Foreign Countries and British Possessions* (London, 1853 onwards). This series is subsequently cited as *Annual Statement*.

was situated. It is hardly necessary to add that the actual producing or consuming countries would not be accurately determined by this method. No attempt has yet been made to do this in British statistics of overseas trade.

The statistics of overseas trade since 1853 which have been described have served as the basis for the researches of this section. Changes in the method of presentation also placed considerable difficulties in the way of drawing up comparable chronological tables. It must be emphasised that the degree of reliability of these sources of information varies considerably.

When the trade statistics were begun in 1696 the State was vitally interested in finding out exactly what quantities of goods were being imported and exported since nearly all goods entering and leaving the country were liable to duty. By 1700 however the export duties on all English woollen manufactures—and by 1722 the duties on many other exports of native origin—had been abolished. Of course quite a number of exports were still liable to duty[1]—for example coal, lead and tin—but the most important exports were already free from any official assessment [concerning the amount of goods leaving the country]. An exact determination of the actual quantities exported is possible only for those goods on which export-bounties were paid. Such commodities were the products of the woollen and cotton industries and, as time went on, certain other industrial products earned bounties. On the other hand those goods on which no duty was paid or on which no export-bounty was paid were—during the whole of the eighteenth century—only declared voluntarily at the discretion of exporters. Such declarations of the quantities of goods were often exaggerated for motives of commercial prestige. Although import duties were slightly reduced at this time the most important commodities continued to be subject to duty so that here, on the whole, the State continued to have a financial interest in finding out exactly what quantities of goods were imported. Under Pitt's Consolidation of Duties Act (1787) there were 1,200 articles liable to import duty as against 1,700 articles listed in the tariff of 1660. The number of goods liable to export duties had declined from 550 in 1660 to 50 in 1787.

When trying to ascertain the country's total import trade we have to consider another source of error. This is the large amount of smuggling that occurred. Smuggling was greatly stimulated by the

[1] See W. Vocke, *Geschichte der Steuern des britischen Reiches* (Leipzig, 1866), p. 307.

ever-increasing severity—and the entirely illogical nature—of the duties on imports. Because of smuggling the customs revenues in 1783 yielded only about half what they should have produced. Before Pitt's tariff reform the number of people associated with smuggling—in a population of some thirteen millions (for the British Isles)—has been estimated at about two millions. The trade in smuggled goods must have been extensive at that time.[1] The import statistics for this period are therefore somewhat inaccurate.

In the nineteenth century more reliable estimates of the volume of imports are possible—particularly in view of the decline in smuggling. The statements of importers and exporters were now checked by the Customs officials, though this inspection was often not carried out so carefully with regard to the importation of duty-free goods as with regard to the importation of dutiable goods.[2]

The basis of valuation chosen is of great significance when assessing the usefulness of foreign trade statistics. This is particularly true of the eighteenth century when normally the so-called 'official values' are the basis for tracing the development of overseas trade. The question of the reliability of the values assigned to commodities is important and will be discussed later.

It is possible to make a rough check of the (official) overseas trade values used in the eighteenth century by comparing them with the tonnage of shipping leaving the country.[3] Tables of shipping tonnages were drawn up independently of foreign trade statistics and they may presumably be considered reliable.[4] Since all Great Britain's external trade is sea-borne and therefore needs shipping-space, it may be assumed that a definite relationship exists between shipping tonnage and overseas trade.

On the other hand in making the comparison it should be noted that shipping-tonnage statistics include ballast-tonnage—and the relation between ballast-tonnage and shipping-space varies considerably.[5] Secondly, tonnage statistics were not obtained by actually weighing goods but overseas trade statistics were based on

---

[1] See F. Kilian, 'Die Pittschen Finanzreformen von 1784–92' (in *Jahrbuch für Gesetzgebung, Verwaltung und Volkswirtschaft im Deutschen Reich*, Leipzig, Year VI, 1882, p. 1282 ff).

[2] See S. Bourne, *loc. cit.*, p. 13 ff.

[3] Statistics of shipping tonnage entering British ports virtually show a parallel development to statistics of shipping tonnage leaving British ports.

[4] It is easier to calculate shipping tonnage than foreign trade. It is moreover unlikely that the figures of shipping tonnage were manipulated for the sake of any private interests.

[5] Net tonnage 'with cargoes only' is not indicated in addition to gross tonnage until after 1840.

genuine weights [or quantities]. Consequently any correspondence between the two can only be accidental and this proves nothing about the reliability of the statistics of foreign trade, even assuming the shipping-tonnage statistics to be accurate. It is therefore desirable to compare only the characteristic upward trend of the two sets of statistics especially in those periods during which this trend is particularly irregular. In the circumstances even an approximate correspondence may be regarded as satisfactory.

Diagram 1. English [later, British] Imports and Exports and the Tonnage of Shipping cleared outwards from 1696 to 1822

1791–1800 = 100

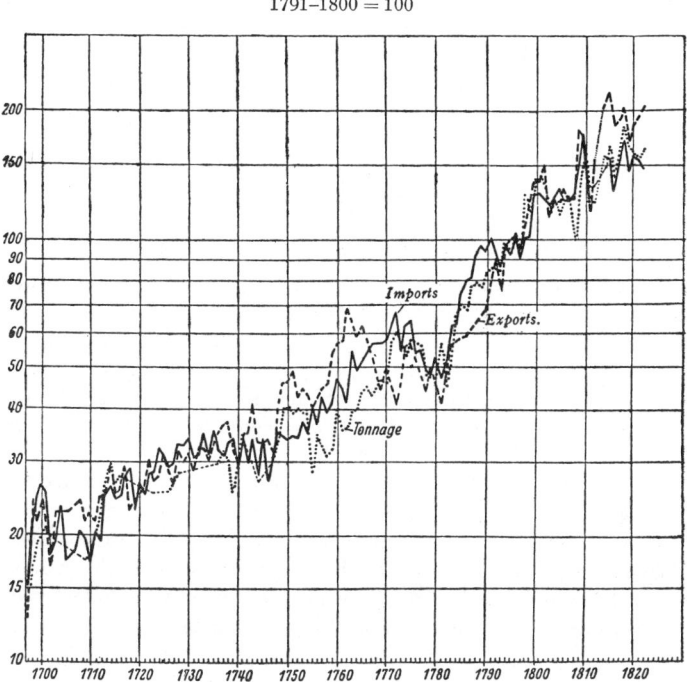

Diagram 1 is based, as far as overseas trade is concerned, on Moreau's statistics (including overseas trade with Ireland), which are shown as indices with 100 representing the average annual value for 1791–1800. The tonnage of outgoing ships is shown on the same basis but these statistics are unfortunately incomplete.[1] The comparison shows that the characteristic upward trend of all the curves is fairly similar. The correspondence is far closer than might have been expected when allowance is made for the technique and methods of compiling British statistics of overseas trade.

The rates of growth of overseas trade and of shipping tonnage show a close correspondence even if a comparison over an entire century is made. If 100 represents the average for 1791-1800 in each case the corresponding figures for 1697-1702 are : imports 21.4, exports 20.4, and shipping tonnage 18.5. Thus during the eighteenth century the tonnage of outgoing ships increased more rapidly than the volume of foreign trade but the difference is within the limits of error which might be expected. More far-reaching conclusions cannot reasonably be drawn from the mere correspondence of rates of growth over a century of statistics which are not really comparable.

II. THE METHODS OF CALCULATION USED IN THE INVESTIGATION

1. *Classification by Commodities and Commodity-Groups*

Our classification of British overseas trade according to groups of commodities is based on the schedule of the Brussels International Register of Commodities.[2] Following this Register, foreign trade is divided into (*a*) live-stock, (*b*) essential and non-essential foodstuffs, (*c*) raw materials and semi-manufactured goods and (*d*) finished manufactured goods. Every commodity entering into foreign trade is allocated to one of these groups.[3]

This classification does not correspond to the classification followed by the compilers of British overseas trade statistics, who—since 1899—have adopted a division into 5 classes of commodities,[4] I. Food, drink and tobacco. II. Raw materials and articles mainly unmanufactured. III. Articles wholly or mainly manufactured. IV. Animals not for food. V. Parcel Post goods not charged to Duty.

---

[1] Complete shipping tonnage statistics are available after 1747. Before that date they are available only for 1700-2, 1709-16, 1718, 1723, 1726-8 and 1736-41.

[2] Subsequently referred to as the Brussels Register. See the *Bulletin du Bureau International de Statistique Commerciale*, Brussels, 1922 onwards, for the division into the various groups of goods entering foreign trade.

[3] Certain arbitrary distributions cannot be avoided here, since the nature of the commodities recorded cannot always be definitely identified with complete certainty. This may explain the differences between parallel calculations elsewhere especially in those of the Brussels Committee itself.

[4] This classification first appears in *Annual Statement*, vol. I (1903).

The most significant difference is between the ' Raw Materials ' and ' Finished Goods ' in the Brussels Register and Classes II and III in the British overseas trade statistics. In the British list, for example, coal and briquettes, unworked metals, chemical manures and refined mineral oils are classified as manufactured goods and are included in Class III whereas the Brussels Register regards these products as raw materials or semi-manufactured goods. Moreover Class I in the British statistics does not correspond to the ' essential and non-essential foodstuffs ' group of the Brussels list. In particular ' livestock for slaughter ' has to be abstracted from Class I of the British statistics. In these statistics ' livestock for slaughter '—as well as Class IV—make up the ' livestock ' group of the Brussels list. Further, tobacco leaf appears in Class I of the British list but is classified as a raw material in the Brussels list. Tobacco products, which also appear in Class I of the British statistics, have been allocated to finished manufactured goods (in the Brussels Register). Apart from these important differences the other divergences of the two classifications are less significant.

We have reconstructed the British overseas trade statistics—from 1814 onwards—on the principles of the Brussels Register. Since 1814 many important alterations in the nomenclature used in British foreign trade statistics have taken place. The last revision was in 1920 when a much more precise subdivision of the various sections was introduced. This has made possible a more precise identification of the goods contained in the British and Brussels classifications. Formerly [in the British classification] commodities belonging to different classes were sometimes grouped under one heading in the customs classification which covered both raw materials and manufactured goods. We have reclassified all the commodities under such a heading according to the presumed character of the majority of the goods included. Thus if a section is composed mainly of raw materials then the whole of that section has been included under the raw materials group. This may render difficult any comparison of individual commodities in the tables year by year but it does permit comparison of the total values for entire groups. These totals are comparable since—
—in view of the large number of commodities in each group
—the errors probably cancel each other out and they are in any event of no significance in relation to the total value. When articles are listed in the overseas trade statistics as ' unenumerated '—that is to say they have not been included in any group of [named]

commodities—they are of only slight importance and we have allocated them to the four groups in the Brussels list in proportion to their share of Britain's total trade. The error that results [from these transfers] is very small.[1] Many commodities may have changed their character in the course of centuries although their designation in the trade statistics has remained the same. Thus 'bar iron'[2]— worked or unworked—is always included (together with rolling mill products) as a finished commodity although bar iron may in the first half of the nineteenth century have been largely a product in which 'blooms' predominated which would be included in the raw materials group [in the Brussels Register]. Nor should we overlook the fact that commodities listed as 'unspecified goods, worked and unworked' [in the British statistics] are included with either manufactured goods or raw materials [in the Brussels register]. We have assumed that those postal parcels which were not dutiable contained mainly finished goods.

This reclassification according to the Brussels list has been made with actual current prices. Our calculations could only be made for the period for which such prices were available—that is to say after 1854 for imports and re-exports and after 1820 for the export of native products.[3]

2. *The Calculation of the Volume of Overseas Trade*

(*a*) Preliminary Observations on the Amount of Overseas Trade and its Calculation.

Our classification of overseas trade according to the principles of the Brussels list has afforded an opportunity for a useful preliminary analysis of Britain's statistics of overseas trade. Since these are only statistics of value, however, they have many disadvantages from the point of view of considering the *development* of overseas trade over a long period.

Since the values are obtained by multiplying quantities by prices they reflect those frequent and considerable variations in price which are particularly evident over a long period. Sometimes, therefore, there is an appearance of a rise or fall in overseas trade, when there

[1] In 1854 'unenumerated articles' accounted for 2.6 per cent of the imports and 2.8 per cent of the exports and re-exports. These percentages declined appreciably later. Before 1854 the 'unenumerated articles' accounted for less than 5 per cent of the exports. In 1827 for example the percentage was 4.2.

[2] The words 'bar iron' are in English in the original.

[3] [From 1820 onwards the calculations deal with the overseas trade of the United Kingdom while] for the period 1814-20 they cover Great Britain only.

are really only rises and falls in the price level, but no corresponding variation in the quantities of goods imported or exported.

The statistics of overseas trade also give information concerning the quantities [of goods entering British overseas trade] but they do not enable the growth of commerce as a whole to be calculated. Even if one could overcome the difficulties arising from the addition of different units such as tons, yards, pieces, gallons, etc. which really cannot be compared—and this is hardly possible in practice—we should still not be much further forward. The annual movements of total quantities of goods secured in this way enable us to judge the growth or decline of transport facilities rather than the development of overseas trade. Obviously, cheap and bulky goods which were handled in great quantities would have a dominant influence on the level of the aggregate tonnage. On the other hand the quantities of goods of high value relative to bulk which were handled in substantially smaller quantities would be ignored or would not receive sufficient attention. For example, a relatively slight drop in the amount of coal exported from Great Britain would mask a really favourable development in textile exports so that, on balance, there would seem to be a decline in Britain's total export trade at a time when her most important manufacture of finished articles was increasing its overseas sales.

The disadvantages of using statistics which are purely those of value or quantity can obviously be overcome if we make a calculation for each year using constant prices on each occasion. In this way values are obtained for each separate commodity which can easily be added up to make total annual values for imports and exports. Since these values are obtained from quantities of different goods entering into foreign trade calculated year by year by the same prices they clearly eliminate actual current price fluctuations. This procedure also avoids the possibility of important goods of low value in relation to their bulk acquiring a preponderance [in the statistics] out of proportion to their real economic significance. This is because their high figures of weight are counterbalanced by their relatively low prices. Again, the smaller quantities of goods of high unit-value are counterbalanced by their relatively higher prices. Pending the results of further critical investigations of this procedure and of the assumptions on which it is based we may conclude that a series of values such as have been described can give a useful indication of the development of overseas trade. These figures of values are called 'volumes' in this book. They are calculated on the basis of a year when these prices really represented the true average prices of imports and exports.

By choosing prices as constants for calculating the quantities of commodities with which we are concerned, the resulting ' volume ' becomes of real economic significance. What we are really doing in this calculation is to use a special way of arriving at the total of the quantities mentioned above. These quantities were expressed in physical units which are a crude measure [from an economic point of view], but—for the volumes—coefficients are employed for weighting which give what may be called an ideal economic significance. It is because of this that we are justified in economic studies in calculating volume by this method.[1]

We have in this connection an indication of the limits within which this technique can provide us with results of economic significance. Obviously whenever fundamental changes in the factors influencing business and prices result in the appearance of a completely new price-structure, then calculating by the prices of a more or less remote base-year has the same effect as calculating by arbitrary constants. In such circumstances the method of calculation can only indicate facts of real economic significance to a very limited extent. This is because a calculation by current prices is not being used. Hence the decisive theoretical drawback of this method of determining volumes lies in the fact that it eliminates not only those movements in prices which disguise the actual development of foreign trade but also those changes which reflect a change in the economic significance of commodities. It is characteristic of this second type of price movement that it does not represent any general rise or fall in the price level. It represents rather an altered relationship in the price of one commodity to the price of another commodity—that is to say it represents an entirely new price structure. This must be taken into account when calculating volumes over very long periods.

Moreover when we employ this technique we make a number of assumptions which in practice are of only limited validity. It is desirable that trade statistics should classify commodities in such a way that a common average price fluctuation may be assumed for all goods collected together in a particular group. The price

---

[1] A calculation of volumes can also be of economic significance when the quantities are not weighted by prices, but by some other coefficients, which have been chosen in order to provide answers to other questions. We chose prices in order to assist us in the task of eliminating price-changes from the development of foreign trade.

relationships in the base-year should be roughly typical for that period in history. In other words the price relationship of the base year should not be highly abnormal because of some temporary or fortuitous occurrence. The commodities with which we deal should be recorded in quantities for the entire period covered by our investigation so that we can determine their volume. Finally —and here we approach the long-term aspect of the problem—we should check the material identity of the commodities grouped in sections. This is necessary in order to make sure that the price obtained for the base year by our calculations is applied always to the same commodity. The continued use of the same name for a group of commodities in trade statistics by no means guarantees that all the goods listed in that section always have the same material identity. It would not in practice be possible to compile commercial statistics in such a way as to ensure this completely even if the most refined methods of classifying goods were employed.

In modern trade statistics the preliminary assumptions we have mentioned are normally fulfilled to such an extent that our technique enables us to calculate volumes over short periods. So our results can confidently be made the basis of economic analysis. When we are concerned with long-term investigations however we cannot be sure that these assumptions are valid. Our conclusions therefore can be given only with considerable reservations.

We propose to illustrate this from the older English [and British] overseas trade statistics. Before 1801 these statistics relied entirely upon the use of the technique we have described. And until 1853 they still depended upon this technique to a very considerable extent. We propose to examine this instructive example in greater detail since—quite apart from its interest as a criticism of a particular technique—it has some significance when we study the history of the [British] trade statistics.[1]

(b) *The Method of ' Official Values '*

The ' official values ' first calculated by English statisticians were based upon the prices actually ruling in 1694. Great care was taken in fixing them to eliminate fortuitous or temporary factors. The prices officially recorded represented the price system which at that time was regarded as ' normal ' or ' typical '.[2]

---

[1] Very little has been written on this subject. Only the essays cited below are known to the author [i.e. César Moreau and S. Bourne. But see also bibliography, above p.   ].

[2] See César Moreau, *État du Commerce de la Grande Bretagne avec toutes les parties du Monde* (c. 1822-4) (British Museum Library Tab. 597 a. (bb)) : ' . . .

For example, since Indian cotton was valued at sevenpence a pound and wool at sixpence a pound[1] it was presumably intended to suggest that the normal price-relationship of these two commodities in 1694 was 7:6. Any temporary factors influencing the market in the base year (1694) were ignored. Moreover the commodities were very carefully grouped so that only those goods were brought together under one heading for which the same sort of price could reasonably be expected. The subdivision of commodities was therefore sufficiently thorough to make possible a determination of 'volume' which had some economic significance. Provision was also made for the valuation of new kinds of goods which might in future enter overseas trade. Such a valuation was to be related to the existing official prices already fixed for similar goods. Actually, however, the price of the year in which the commodity first appeared in overseas trade seems generally to have been used for this purpose.[2]

It is clear that the official values do not rest solely on the prices of 1694 since the prices of other years were used for some articles. The prices for 1694, moreover, relate only to the overseas trade of England and Wales. When the statistics were extended to Scotland in 1755, the volumes of goods entering the foreign trade of that country were calculated on the basis of entirely different 'fixed prices'. When Ireland was included within the area covered by the trade statistics—British overseas trade statistics covered the whole of the United Kingdom for the first time in 1805—Irish imports and exports were also valued in official prices which were also very different from those which had been fixed for the overseas trade of either England or Scotland. There can be little doubt that the prices actually in force at the time of the introduction of the new statistics were used. In the overseas trade of Scotland the prices of 1755 were

Un comité de la chambre des Pairs, désirant en 1696, se procurer les valeurs réelles, envoya, dans tous les pays d'où l'Angleterre importait des marchandises, des agens spécialement chargés de recueillir et d'étudier la variation des prix de chacune de ces marchandises à différentes époques, de manière à trouver leur valeur réelle la plus rationelle. Les mêmes moyens furent employés dans l'intérieur de l'Angleterre pour les objets d'Exportation : Les articles divers furent ensuite classés avec le plus grand soin. On comprit dans une seule cathégorie ceux qui offraient le plus de similitude entr'eux, et il fut résolu que lorsque l'introduction d'une nouvelle marchandise aurait lieu (*ce qui est extrêmement rare*) on en établirait l'évaluation d'après celle déjà attribuée aux articles qui auraient le plus de rapports avec elle.'
[The translators have inserted the original French instead of the rather unsatisfactory contemporary English translation printed by Dr. Schlote].

[1] Except Spanish wool, the price of which was quoted separately at 1s. 2½d. a lb.
[2] See S. Bourne, *loc. cit.*, p. 17 '... the value was taken from fixed official rates, founded on the ascertained prices which all known articles bore in the year 1694; with the addition of such new articles as afterwards sprung up, at the prices they each bore in the first year of their introduction.'

used, while for Irish trade the prices of 1800 were used.[1] After 1805 the position was that the official[2] values were based upon the prices of three different base years each separated from the other by half a century. English imports of coffee were valued at £7 per hundredweight, Scottish at £2 16s. and Irish at £10. The calculation of official export values was affected in the same way so that different parts of the total quantity of a commodity were weighted by different official prices. The differences of these official prices were frequently very considerable.[3]

Finally, actual current prices[4] appear in British trade statistics as well as official values. This occurred when the peculiar nature of a particular group of commodities made an assessment by quantity difficult or even impossible. This applied to needlework, embroidery, haberdashery, millinery, writing materials and even to machinery.[5] The official total values of imports and exports are thus made up of values based on the actual current prices of 1694, 1755, or 1801. Goods which were not included in the overseas trade statistics of 1696, but were added subsequently were valued at prices current in later years. Occasionally the values were based upon actual prices.[6] In practice we can regard the official values for the total overseas trade as being approximately the volumes calculated on the prices of 1694 since England's overseas trade was far more important than that of Scotland or Ireland. The proportion both of new commodities and of goods with values re-calculated on actual current prices

[1] No references to this were found in the works consulted by the author. Doubtless the qualities of the imports received from the different territories had an influence on the differing values of commodities. These differences, however, were of only a minor character. Otherwise we should have to assume that the quality of the coffee drunk by the English was almost three times as good as that consumed by the Scots, or that the Irish drank coffee of a quality 50 per cent superior to that drunk by Englishmen. Again, one would have to assume that the quality of the oranges imported by the Scots justified a price more than four times as high (in the case of Ireland a price more than twice as high) as that customary in England. (See Table 1 of Appendix).

[2] Between 1801 and 1804 exports of home products were already given actual current prices but these statistics refer only to Great Britain [and do not include Ireland]. Between 1805 and 1809 the average value of exports from the United Kingdom was greater than that from Great Britain by 2.6 per cent.

[3] See Appendix, Table 1.

[4] [To avoid confusion between different meanings of the word 'real', the words 'actual' and 'current' are used when referring to the prices at which goods in fact changed hands at a particular period.]

[5] Goods which might on one occasion be classified in this way were not necessarily always given their actual current prices subsequently throughout the period under discussion. It seems as if the inclusion of these commodities in the statistics took place to an increasing degree in the first half of the nineteenth century.

[6] [i.e. they were originally 1694 prices and were subsequently adjusted to new actual current prices].

C

was not large enough to influence the total volume to any great extent.[1]

In the older English [and British] overseas trade statistics the determination of the prices for the base year and the classification of imports and exports by commodity groups were done in such a way that the statistical and technical assumptions necessary for the use of the method of calculation we have discussed can be regarded as virtually fulfilled. In addition the names of commodities changed little during the entire period so that continuous calculation is possible. We have seen that the calculating of quantities could not be done entirely on the prices of 1694 but in practice this inconsistency is of no great significance. It is however questionable how far the material identity of the goods listed under the various headings was preserved. It is also doubtful whether the prices of 1694—used for calculating quantities of goods during the whole period—continue [for any length of time] to have economic significance—that is to say it is doubtful whether these official prices are close to actual prices.

It is obviously unlikely that the last two assumptions are in fact valid. Perhaps they were to a great extent valid between 1696 and 1770 or 1780. Subsequently the Industrial Revolution was bound to have had an ever-increasing influence on production and consumption and so we must assume that there was then a radical change in price-relationships. We can illustrate this by comparing the prices of goods entering into overseas trade in 1694 with prices of a later date.

In making this comparison the prices of the base year (1694) have for the most part been taken from a report presented to Parliament in 1826.[2] The list of prices given there is indeed incomplete, so further prices were calculated from the quantities given and their official value in overseas trade.[3] Prices suitable for comparison are first available for 1854, because actual current prices were not officially recorded before that date for the most important foodstuffs and raw materials, which were particularly important in the British

[1] This is of course not true for every single type of commodity. Thus, if one tries to obtain the price of the base year by dividing the official overseas trade value by the quantity, one cannot be certain of obtaining the actual price of 1694, although this in fact is the result which is nearly always obtained.

[2] See Appendix Table 1 (note). [See *Accounts and Papers*, House of Commons, 1826, Vol. XXII, Part 1, Account No. 385, pp. 47–62].

[3] The prices calculated in this manner are given a special designation in Table 2 of the Appendix since, in view of what has been said above, it is not absolutely certain that the actual prices of 1694 can be obtained in this way. For most of the goods listed, however, it seems highly probable that a price approximating very closely to the true one has been given.

import trade. In order to eliminate in this comparison the accidental irregularities in the prices of a single year—and thus to secure, as far as possible, prices of a 'validity' similar to those of 1694—our prices were calculated on the average for 1854-60 and this average was compared with the prices of the base year, 1694.[3]

This calculation shows that the price-structure of the 1850s was substantially different from that of 1694. This can be seen clearly in the wide distribution of the percentage change of individual prices. It is characteristic of these changes that the prices of manufactured goods had declined considerably since 1694, while almost all the important foodstuffs and the majority of raw materials show increases in price as compared with 1694. Thirty-seven of the 56 finished products in the list had lower average prices in 1854-60 than in 1694. On the other hand, the prices of only 10 out of 45 imported foodstuffs, and the prices of only 12 out of 64 imported raw materials were lower in 1854-60 than they had been in 1694.

A similar striking contrast may be seen by comparing the considerable changes in the prices of certain types of goods which were grouped under a single heading in the statistics. In the foodstuffs group nearly all the characteristic tropical and semi-tropical products —such as rice, coffee, tea, cocoa and spices—had fallen considerably in price, while meat and dairy products and alcoholic drinks for the most part had increased in price. Tropical and semi-tropical products—such as natural dyes and plants for the manufacture of dyes and drugs—were the main representatives of the group of raw materials for which a considerable fall in prices was recorded. But the prices of other raw materials also fell—for example, products of such fundamental importance as coal and cotton. These reductions in prices, however, were partly counterbalanced by considerable increases in the prices of timber, wool, silk and most other raw materials. In the group comprising finished goods the fall in the prices of textiles and iron goods was especially significant. These last mentioned goods were, of course, the products of the most important British export industries.

Apart from the price-changes for goods listed under one heading, the table also records considerable price-movements for commodities listed under subsections. These changes are quite abnormal in relation to the average price-movement of other goods under the same sub-heading. Thus the products of saw-mills cost ten times as much in the middle of the nineteenth century as they had done in

[1] See Appendix, Table 2.

1694. Unworked timber, on the other hand, also showed a considerable increase but was only three times as dear as it had been in 1694. There were also abnormal price-rises for rags used in paper-manufacture, bristles, clover-seeds, maize, oatmeal, beans and butter, and, amongst manufactured goods: woollen and worsted yarns, linen-yarn, thrown silk, cordage. Unworked leather, hardware and cutlery, arms, flint glassware, candles, tobacco-products, and books also showed abnormal increases in price. On the other hand mixed woollen cloths, linen thread, linen-yarn lace, showed equally striking *falls* in price.

The various changes in prices, both typical and abnormal, cannot be examined in detail here. But they show that by 1854—60 the ' material identity ' of numerous goods can hardly have been the same as that of goods listed under the same names in 1694. Thus the marked increase in the prices of tobacco leaf and tobacco products was due to the fact that quite different qualities and types from those of 1694 were being consumed. Had those new types entered into commerce in 1694 they would have had a different price [from the types in fact consumed in 1694]. This is probably true to an even greater extent of such typical groups of goods as hardware, cutlery, flint glassware, cordage, and books. Other alterations in price seem to be due to a change in the ' economic significance ' of the goods. This occurred, for instance, with regard to cotton and cotton-goods. Their importance in the British economy was very much greater in 1850 than it had been a century and a half earlier, so that from the point of view of ' economic significance ' these products might be regarded as entirely different commodities. This is also true of natural vegetable dyes and dye-woods, which were to an increasing extent being replaced by chemical and mineral dyes and this led to a change in their ' economic significance '. Numerous goods entering into overseas trade, had lost simultaneously, both their 'material identity ' and their ' economic significance '.

This, however, means that—certainly after the change from official to actual values—we can no longer depend upon the validity of certain assumptions which are essential for the satisfactory use of the technique of official values for the purpose of drawing valid conclusions of an economic nature [from the statistics]. Imports and exports were weighted by constants that had, indeed, the true character of prices in 1700, but which had for the most part lost their economic significance by 1850, so that they then possessed a more or less arbitrary character. By 1850 the technique of ' official values ' could not give results which reflected the growth of British overseas trade in a manner that had economic significance.

It is nevertheless possible that this technique occasionally gives the same final result as a determination of volume by weighting commodities by constants which correspond partly or wholly with the actual price-structure. This is because if one uses official values many quantities of commodities are weighted by constants of no contemporary economic significance, which results in a relatively too high or too low weighting. But it is quite possible that the sum total of volumes secured by multiplying a great variety of quantities with many different constants—each individual constant being very different from the actual current price—may produce the same result as would be obtained by adding up the true current values. This may be illustrated by the following table of British imports of raw textiles in 1854—in quantities, in official values, and in actual values.

The two totals of value are almost the same, although the weighting of the prices is entirely different. Taking all raw textiles together, a 'compensation' has taken place. Raw cotton accounted for the greater part (396,000 tons) of the total of 576,000 tons and cotton was the only textile raw material which cost less in 1854 than it had done in 1694. So the value of cotton imports, on the basis of current prices, was approximately £8.5 millions lower than when calculated

TABLE 1

UNITED KINGDOM IMPORTS OF TEXTILE RAW MATERIALS IN 1854

Commodities	Import Quantities	Import Prices (£ per ton)		Actual Import Prices in percentage of the official prices	Import Values (in £1000s)	
	tons	official	actual		official	actual
Cotton	396,131	72.34	50.94	70	28,657	20,175
Wool (inclg. alpaca)	47,376	57.47	137.18	239	2,723	6,499
Silk (including waste)	4,338	791.48	1,245.60	157	3,433	5,403
Flax and tow (including hemptow)	66,232	41.86	51.60	123	2,773	3,417
Hemp, jute and other vegetable raw materials for textiles	60,328	18.20	39.52	217	1,098	2,385
Goats'-hair	596	42.02	214.68	511	25	128
Horse-hair	1,484	70.00	102.66	147	104	152
Total Imports of textile raw materials	576,485	—	—	—	38,813	38,159

by official values. All the other textile raw materials cost far more in 1854 than in 1694, so that their actual values are above their official values. These official values, however, were used to weight substantially smaller quantities of imports, so that as far as these textiles were concerned the actual current prices were greater than the

TABLE 2
IMPORTS INTO THE UNITED KINGDOM IN 1854
(in £1,000s)

Commodities	Import Values		Difference between actual and official values	
	Official	Actual	Positive	Negative
Coffee, tea, cocoa, spices	13,778	7,678		6,100
Sugar and molasses	14,458	10,775		3,683
Cotton	28,657	20,175		8,482
Indigo, cochineal, madder	4,743	2,853		1,890
Animal products	3,009	5,662	2,653	
Textile fibres (excluding cotton)	10,156	17,984	7,828	
Timber	2,295	11,600	9,305	
Total of above	77,096	76,727	19,786	20,155
Cereals and flour	10,139	21,760	11,621	
Other imported commodities	37,103	54,105	17,002	
Total Imports	124,338	152,592	48,409	20,155

official prices by between £7 and £8 millions. Hence the reduction in the actual current value of the imports of raw textiles, which resulted from the lower price of cotton, was 'compensated for' —except for the small sum of £700,000.

This 'compensation'—though not apparent at first—is of considerable significance. In Table 2, Britain's total imports for 1854 are listed and both official and actual values are given. If we take seven important groups of commodities in the table representing 50 per cent of Britain's imports by value, we find once more that the positive and negative differences between actual and official values again nearly cancel out. Despite the great differences in the factors[1] used to weight values and volumes, the totals for all imports vary by barely 23 per cent as between actual and official values.

It can easily be seen that such a 'compensation' must necessarily take place. If the constants we use in our calculations no longer represent a true price-relationship they will to some extent substantially reduce the economic significance of the quantities of the

See Appendix, Table 2.

commodities. The volumes calculated in this way are again partly more and partly less than the result would have been if we had used actual current prices for weighting. So to extent a certain degree of compensation is inevitable. To what extent the compensation will occur cannot, however, be estimated *a priori*.

Of course if the constants used for weighting happen to be *all* above, or *all* below, the actual prices, and differ from them by a fixed proportion—then the calculation of volumes eliminates only the change in the average level of price of goods entering foreign trade. In doing so the technique of calculation fulfils one of the purposes for which it was devised.

If the constants used for weighting differ year by year from actual prices in such a way that the difference is in one case a negative and in another case a positive one then our calculation of volumes would fulfil its other purpose—that of eliminating price-variations.

On the other hand if price-relationships undergo a permanent change and there has been an alteration in the structure of the whole price-system, the results obtained from our method of calculating volumes loses its economic significance. Then the final result would, at any rate to some extent, be corrected only by ' compensation ' of the kind to which we have referred. The extent of this compensation cannot be anticipated and is to that degree ' accidental '.

Regarding the official values, still in use in the middle of the nineteenth century, their economic ' correctness ' cannot be decided offhand. It might be argued that the structure of the price-system had undergone such marked changes since the base year (1694), that the results of the calculations were, from an economic point of view, *bound* to be incorrect. Nevertheless they *could* in theory be accurate because of the corrective influence of the 'compensation ' that we have mentioned.

A check that can be used for this purpose may be derived from the considerations already discussed. If all prices moved in the same direction and to the same extent, then the difference in movement between the actual values and volumes listed would always be uniform. If we deflate the [actual] values by a price index of the commodities entering into overseas trade—which could be found from the change in the price of a single item—then the figures of the deflated values and volumes would be identical. They cannot fail to coincide permanently if one assumes that the prices—although different originally—move always in the same direction to the same extent. Values and volumes would move in close association if common changes in the average level of prices were eliminated by a suitable price-index. The method of calculation already provides for this and the ' compensation ' (described above) has an influence in the same direction. On the other hand, if we assume the existence of a structural alteration in the price-system then there is obviously no reason to expect the two sets of figures [of deflated value and volume] to coincide. They *could* however do so owing to ' compensation ', so that the regular quantitative relationship of the figures of values and volumes would provide no more than an adequate (and not a necessary and inevitable) criterion for the suitability of our method of calculating volumes. If we can show that the volumes that we have calculated, differ over a long period from the appropriate values (deflated by a suitable price-index) we can conclude that they no longer give a ' correct ' picture—from an economic point of view —of the changes in the amount of overseas trade that have taken place since the date of the base-year.

The practical application of this test assumes that volumes and actual values are known and also that there is available an index showing the average changes in the prices of goods entering into foreign trade. These assumptions are valid for British imports between 1854 and 1869. We lack actual values before 1854 and official values after 1869. A suitable index for comparing the price-level for imports with that of 1694—constructed with the help[1] of the price-list given in Table 2 of the Appendix—gives 169 as the average figure for the period 1854-60 (when 1694—100). The price-indices for each separate year of the 16-year period under discussion can be obtained by linking our calculation with Sauerbeck's Index, and also (for 1854-65) with Jevons's index. Which ever index we choose, the difference between the deflated values [cols. 4 and 5, Table 3] and the official values [col. 6, Table 3] is considerable. The official values are roughly a third higher than the deflated values for 1854-60. In the years of high cotton prices (1862 to 1865)—in 1865 the price of cotton was three times that of 1694—the figures temporarily come close together because the actual values were considerably increased for the time being owing to this rise in price of Britain's chief import—a rise in prices not proportionately reflected in the price-indices. In the

[1] This figure is the geometric mean of the price indices of the 109 imports listed. We prefer to use the geometric, rather than the arithmetic, mean, because in the result it damps down the effect of the extreme changes in price. These changes are frequently ' unreal', i.e. not caused by changes in supply and demand. On the contrary they are to a great extent due to the fact that goods imported in the 1850s were given the same name as goods which in 1694 had a very different ' material identity '.   (See above p. 20 ff).

years 1866–9, the official values are on the average again considerably higher than the deflated values. It follows from this that ' compensation ' has been inadequate to rectify the result of the calculation of volumes by the technique of official values, values which in themselves no longer guarantee ' correct ' results from an economic point of view.

TABLE 3

COMPARISON OF OFFICIAL AND DEFLATED IMPORT VALUES OF THE UNITED KINGDOM, 1854–1869

Year	Price Index (1694 = 100) 1854–60 linked with the		Actual Value of Imports	Deflated Values i.e. Actual Values (Col. 3) divided by price index		Official Values (i.e. at prices of 1694)
	Jevons	Sauerbeck		Column 1	Column 2	
	Price Index		Millions of £			
	1	2	3	4	5	6
1854	179	179	152.4	85.1	85.1	124.1
1855	172	177	143.5	83.4	81.1	117.3
1856	176	177	172.5	98.0	97.5	131.9
1857	183	183	187.8	102.6	102.6	136.2
1858	164	159	164.6	100.4	103.5	138.2
1859	165	164	179.2	108.6	109.3	145.6
1860	171	173	210.5	123.1	121.7	164.7
1861	168	170	217.5	129.5	127.9	171.2
1862	171	177	225.7	131.8	127.5	160.7
1863	168	182	248.9	148.2	136.7	171.9
1864	168	183	275.0	163.7	150.3	174.0
1865	168	177	271.1	161.4	153.2	181.8
1866	—	179	295.3	—	165.0	201.2
1867	—	176	275.2	—	156.4	201.1
1868	—	173	294.7	—	170.3	220.9
1869	—	173	295.5	—	170.8	224.3

A similar check was also made of the official values of re-exports To simplify the calculations the Jevons and Sauerbeck indices were used to calculate price-changes between 1694 and 1858—the single year 1858 being chosen instead of the average of the 7-year period 1854–60, that was chosen in the case of imports. The result of the calculation for the years 1854 to 1869 is quite similar to that for imports so that here too the changes in volume are no longer given in a ' correct ' manner—from an economic point of view—by means of the official values.

The test cannot be applied to exports, since the average price-index for 1854–60 (based on the prices of 1694) cannot be linked with price-indices of raw materials of the type devised by Jevons and

Sauerbeck. Such linking would be permissible only if it could be assumed that manufactures and raw materials had parallel price movements, and this cannot be assumed without further research. Moreover, exports were recorded by actual values as early as the beginning of the nineteenth century so that a check of their official values is not necessary.

TABLE 4

COMPARISON OF OFFICIAL AND DEFLATED VALUES OF UNITED KINGDOM RE-EXPORTS
1854–1869
(Millions of £)

Year	Actual Values recalculated on the basis of 1694 deflated by the index of		Official Values (i.e. at prices of 1694)	Year	Actual Values recalculated on the basis of 1694 deflated by the index of		Official Values (i.e. at prices of 1694)
	Jevons	Sauerbeck			Jevons	Sauerbeck	
1854	20.2	19.8	29.9	1862	48.0	45.4	51.0
1855	23.9	22.6	31.5	1863	58.5	52.4	54.9
1856	26.0	25.2	33.4	1864	60.5	53.7	55.0
1857	25.6	34.8	30.8	1865	61.6	57.0	62.5
1858	27.6	27.6	33.9	1866	—	53.2	64.4
1859	29.8	29.4	37.2	1867	—	48.2	64.8
1860	32.3	31.4	43.6	1868	—	52.9	59.5
1861	40.7	39.3	50.2	1869	—	51.8	67.1

[Calculated in the same way as Table 3.]

In the following chapters we make use of this analysis of the validity of official values in proceeding to our own calculation of the volumes of British overseas trade. Our discussion of the validity of official values forms the basis of an attempt to find out approximately the actual current value of imports and re-exports before 1854 when they were recorded only in official values. We shall in particular find our discussion of the statistical relationship of volume and value has been of practical use.

(c) *Method of calculating 'Volume' used in this work*

The calculation of volumes by the method of official values is open to criticism mainly because of its systematic use for a period of no less than a century and a half—a period during which changes in economic structure of exceptional significance were taking place. Production and consumption in this period underwent a revolutionary change which necessarily had an influence upon the price-structure. Since in the old English [and British] statistics the amount of overseas trade was ascertained up to 1854 on the basis of the prices of 1694 this was bound eventually—despite the careful determination of prices in 1694—to become increasingly a mere weighting of quantities by arbitrary constants which lost to an increasing degree any true relation to economic reality. This naturally applies also to the results of these calculations—the volumes for imports and exports on the price basis of 1694—although (because of ' compensation ') this occurs to a considerably smaller degree. Arithmetical accuracy no longer guarantees the economic usefulness of the result.

We have attempted in our calculation of volumes, to rectify this error, at any rate in part. To do this the whole period under investigation (in so far as a classification of goods, at any rate according to quantities, is available) has been divided into shorter periods of time. For each of these shorter periods we have calculated separately volumes of imports and exports, each on a base-year of its own—as is shown in Table 5.

TABLE 5

PERIODS AND BASE-YEARS OF CALCULATION OF UNITED KINGDOM'S OVERSEAS TRADE

Periods			Base-Years		
			Imports	Exports	Re-exports
1820–1849 } 1849–1859 }	..	..	1854	{ 1840 { 1854	
1859–1869	..	..	1864	1864	
1869–1881	..	..	1880	1880	1913
1881–1902	..	..	1902	1902	
1902–1920	..	..	1913	1913	
1920–1934	..	..	1929	1929	

For 1920 to 1934 the quantities of goods have been weighted by the prices of 1929 and the volumes of imports and exports have been calculated on this basis. For 1902 to 1920, corresponding volumes have been calculated on the basis of 1913 prices, for 1881 to 1902 on the basis of 1902 prices; for 1869 to 1881 on the bases of 1880 prices and so on. As it is only after 1854 that we have statements of actual values for imports, the changes in volume for the long period from 1820 to 1859 can only be calculated on the basis of a single year (1854). Exports, on the other hand, can be subdivided into shorter periods of time. Unfortunately time has not been available for a similar calculation of re-exports. But the absence of such a calculation is of no great significance in appraising the development of British foreign trade as a whole, because re-exports are quite trifling when compared with imports and exports.

Our analysis is based upon a distribution [of goods entering foreign trade] according to the groups of the Brussels Register. The volumes for livestock, foodstuffs, raw materials and finished manufactured goods are thus calculated separately, so that the total amount of overseas trade is obtained by an addition of these individual calculations. Within these Brussels groups various commodities are further subdivided into subsidiary sections, in so far as such a subdivision appears to be useful from an economic point of view. In the foodstuffs group for example, the following subdivisions have been made : (1) Cereals, (2) Rice, vegetables and fruit, (3) Meat, (4) Processed animal foodstuffs. In the raw materials group the following sub-divisions occur : (1) Ores and scrap, (2) metals, (3) textile fibres, etc. In the manufactured articles group the sub-divisions are : (1) Textiles, (2) Leather and leather goods, (3) Iron goods, etc.[1] Volumes have also been calculated for the commodities in the sub-divisions according to the appropriate prices and so a picture of the evolution of British overseas trade in various periods has been obtained.

To make possible the linking of the results of these separate calculations over short periods into a continuous sequence we have made each short period overlap by one year. In linking all the shorter periods together we have selected the years 1902-1920 as our final base-period and here we calculate the volume of British overseas trade on the basis of the prices ruling in 1913. We propose to examine the fluctuations not only of British overseas commerce as a whole but also of overseas trade in commodities within the various groups in the Brussels List and even within some of the more important sub-sections. We have therefore linked not merely the grand totals of imports and exports but also the totals of all the groups for which we have calculated the volumes of overseas trade. In this way we have secured continuous runs of volumes for the sub-sections which—when added together—give us totals first for the main groups of commodities and eventually for all overseas trade.

These volumes must naturally be distinguished from those calculated directly on the price-basis of 1913—that is to say volumes obtained by weighting separate quantities with the appropriate average prices of this base-year. The former volumes are related to the price-level of 1913 only because of our system of linking. We propose to call them *volumes based upon value* to distinguish them from *volumes based upon price*. The two types of volume—' price-

[1] See Appendix, Tables 11 to 16.

basis' and 'value-basis' volumes—are naturally identical for the base-period 1902–1920. Before and after this period however, they differ wherever linking by groups has taken place.

Our calculations of the development of overseas trade for periods other than 1902–1920 are based upon the prices of base-years other than 1913. If, for example, a commodity (hitherto given a relatively high weighting in comparison with the other commodities in its group) is given a lower weighting, then the other commodities in the group have a stronger influence over the development of the volumes as a whole. The reverse also holds good. In this way account is taken of changed price-relationships in ascertaining volumes. In so far as changes in the material identity or the economic significance of the commodity have resulted in variations of price they have been taken into account.

In this way our examination of British overseas trade can start as early as the year 1820. The information concerning exports of home products for the period 1820 to 1827 is, however, so incomplete that the calculation for this type of exports begins only in 1827. We have already pointed out that Marshall in his *Digest*[1] gives data concerning the foreign trade of Great Britain according to commodities (omitting the trade between Great Britain and Ireland). In this work imports and re-exports are given only their official values but most of the quantities can be calculated from these values with the help of the prices of 1694. So for these years the volume of overseas trade for Great Britain may still be ascertained on the 'value-basis' of 1913 except for re-exports which are calculated on the 'price-basis' of 1913. The volumes for individual commodities imported or re-exported in 1820 (exports of home products in 1827) have been linked with the appropriate volumes for the whole of the United Kingdom and the calculation has been taken back as far as 1814. The results obtained in this way are, indeed, rather in the nature of estimates, since they do not include the trade of Ireland with countries other than Great Britain and since somewhat defective statistics of quantities have been used. Nevertheless, as approximate results, they may well—particularly the total figures—enable us to survey adequately the development of overseas trade.

Our calculations cannot be made before 1814 on the basis of the available statistical sources. There is indeed the possibility of linking [our results] with official values and this has been done in Diagram 4. We have adopted this method solely to secure a contin-

[1] *Loc. cit.*, p. 56 ff.

uous curve and we feel that we are justified in doing so, since the general tendencies of development of British overseas trade [as we have shown above],[1] are probably adequately indicated by the statistics of official values. It would be unwise to attempt to draw any more far-reaching conclusions.

3. *The Calculation of Actual Current Values of Imports and Re-Exports between* 1800 *and* 1854

We have attempted to show in the previous section the possibility of making an approximate estimate of the [actual] values of imports and re-exports for the United Kingdom for the period before 1854 when such values were not provided by the trade statistics.

There was a tendency among contemporary writers to regard the official values as an adequate approximation to the real values although we have no means of discovering why they made such an assumption. Whitworth and Chalmers, for example, calculated the balance of trade on the basis of the official values. So did Marshall,[2] whose formula for the balance of trade was : [i] imports by official values compared with [ii] exports according to their real value added to re-exports according to their official value. This would be sensible only if official and real values approximately coincided. This is particularly true of Marshall, who tried to use the trade-balance when examining the problem of the balance of payments. According to his formula he arrived at a substantial excess of exports for 1793–1816 and consequently asked himself the question :[3] ' How then . . . was the enormous excess of Export equalized or balanced ? ' If, however, official and actual current values, contrary to his assumption, differed substantially from each other there might well have been a problem of an excess of imports ! The information then available concerning the British balance of payments was too inadequate to permit a reliable conclusion to be drawn (even by an indirect approach) as to whether Britain's balance of trade was active or passive.

A direct comparison of the actual and official values of imports and re-exports is possible only in and after 1854 and it can easily be shown that Marshall's assumption would in fact lead to completely erroneous results. Imports officially valued at £124,000,000 in 1854 represented an actual value of £152,000,000. Re-exports

---

[1] See above p. 8 ff.
[2] J. Marshall, *loc. cit.*, part III, p. 120a ff.
[3] Ditto, part III, p. 120a, para. 4.

had an official value in 1854 of £30,000,000 and an actual value of £19,000,000. Since the actual value of the exports of home products was £97,000,000 we would obtain by Marshall's method an active balance of trade of £3,000,000, but in actual values there was a passive balance of £36,000,000. This calculation does not disprove the validity of Marshall's assumption for an earlier period but it does emphasise the need to check Marshall's method.

To ascertain the actual values of commodities for the period before 1854 we have acted on the assumption which we have already discussed—namely that the volumes which we have calculated are economically correct and stand in a definite relationship to contemporary actual values. If there has been a change in the average price level of the commodities with which we are dealing, the relationship [to actual prices] is not, of course, apparent, until we deflate the actual prices by an appropriate price-index to this new level. A series of volumes—which we believe to be accurate from an economic point of view—is given in this book for the period from 1814 to 1854. We must therefore decide upon a price-index which reflects in an appropriate manner the average movement of the price level of imports and re-exports. The actual values which we are seeking, or something very close to them, can then be calculated by multiplying the 'volumes' by this index adjusted to the same base-year (1913).

For the period in question, two indices of wholesale prices are available. They are those of Sauerbeck,[1] beginning in 1818, and of Jevons,[2] who covers the period 1782–1865, using 1782 as his base-year. The Sauerbeck index is based on the prices of 43 commodities between 1846 and 1854, and before that on 31 commodities. It is weighted only in so far as several price quotations are included for important products. With this exception the total index is the arithmetic mean of the separate price indices without any weighting. Jevons bases his calculation on the prices of 40 articles, of which again a few are counted more than once. Jevons, however, in contrast to Sauerbeck, estimates the total price movement by calculating the geometric (not the arithmetic) mean of the separate price indices.

With a few remarkable exceptions, the two indices agree for the commodities on which they are based. In particular Jevons's index

---

[1] A. Sauerbeck, 'Prices of Commodities and the Precious Metals' (in the *Journal of the Royal Statistical Society*, London, vol. 49 (1886), p. 581 ff).

[2] W. S. Jevons, 'On the Variation of Prices and the Value of the Currency since 1782' (*op. cit.*, vol. 28 (1865), p. 294 ff).

gives greater weight to tropical foodstuffs and tropical raw materials. It includes, for example, dye-woods, cochineal, some spices and alcoholic liquors, which are not included by Sauerbeck. Sauerbeck on the other hand includes coal (actually with a double weighting), which Jevons does not include. Consequently Jevons's index falls more sharply than the Sauerbeck index between 1818 and 1854. This is due principally to the disproportionately sharp fall in price of the tropical products we have mentioned.[1]

Owing to the important part which these tropical products played in British imports and re-exports in the first half of the nineteenth century Jevons's index undoubtedly reflects the structure of British overseas trade before 1854 better than that of Sauerbeck This is why we have preferred to use Jevons's index in calculating. our actual values. To do this we have had to adjust Jevons's index to the base year 1913 and this was done by linking it with the average annual price-index of imports or re-exports for 1854–60.

The results of this calculation are the 'actual [constructed] values' included in Table 3 of the Appendix.[2] How far they approach actual current values depends partly upon the economic 'accuracy' of the volumes upon which the calculation was based, and partly upon the degree to which the Jevons Price Index accurately reflects the average price-movements of imports and re-exports. A direct check of our results is possible for the period from 1854 to the present day for which actual values are given in the trade statistics. In Diagram 2 we show both the values given in the statistics, and also the values we have calculated by multiplying our 'volumes' with the Sauerbeck Price Index.[3] There is a remarkably close correspondence between the two values—especially the imports. Hence it is reasonable to conclude that the method of ascertaining volumes that we have used—certainly for the period from 1854 up to the present time—gives us economically 'accurate' results. We assume, of course, that the Sauerbeck index gives an adequate representation of changes in the average price-level of imports and re-exports. The correspondence is not quite so close for re-exports. The volumes

---

[1] The Sauerbeck index falls by 28 per cent between 1818 and 1854, the Jevons Index by 38 per cent.

[2] In Jevon's index dye-stuffs fall by 60 per cent, and tropical foodstuffs by 56 per cent. The difference is on the average 3.6 per cent for 1841–50, 6 per cent for 1821–40, 12 per cent for 1801–20. These differences are of no importance, since the calculation of values can only give us approximations and we must be prepared for this sort of discrepancy. We have decided not to use an average of the Jevons-Sauerbeck indices as our approximate estimate, both for this reason and for others.

[3] The Jevons index cannot be used here, because it stops in 1865.

of re-exports were calculated only on a price basis. One might be tempted to see in this less close correspondence [of the two values] a confirmation of the conjecture that the calculation of volumes on a 'value-basis' gives more 'correct' results than a calculation on a 'price basis'. The difference however is a relatively small one and the price-index we have chosen influences the result to an equal degree so that it is not possible to claim too much for this agreement in our statistics.

If we assume that the volumes calculated for the first half of the nineteenth century are just as 'accurate' as the later volumes and if we also accept the Jevons Price Index as a suitable multiplier then the values for imports and re-exports that we have calculated for this earlier period give a satisfactory estimate of the actual commercial values of that time. That certainly applies to the period from 1814 to 1853. The volumes for the years between 1801 and 1812[1] were calculated only as rough approximations by linking the volume for 1814 (calculated on a value-basis) with the official values recorded for the period between 1801 and 1814. Nevertheless the values we have calculated in this way certainly give us far more useful results than the official values employed by Marshall.

We may therefore almost certainly conclude that the British balance of trade was passive during the Napoleonic Wars. According to our calculation the surplus of imports from 1801 to 1812 was approximately £90 millions. Even if we use the Sauerbeck index as a basis, which reduces the import values by 11 per cent, the balance of trade is still passive to the extent of £20 millions. Further, immediately after 1813 the British balance of trade was generally—and after 1825 invariably—passive. Marshall's assumption, that the official values can be regarded as approximating to actual values, is therefore untenable and the 'enormous export surplus', which he calculated, is highly improbable.[2]

[1] [There are no overseas trade statistics for 1813 owing to the fire at the London Custom House in 1814].

[2] [Albert H. Imlah in his essay on 'Real Values in British Foreign Trade, 1798–1853' (in *The Journal of Economic History*, Vol. VIII, November 1948, No. 2, pp. 132–152) makes the following comments upon Dr. Schlote's calculation of actual current values :

'Schlote does not project his estimates beyond his base years (1854–60) to test them further against the real values. However, these seven base years offer some pragmatic test of the adequacy of his method. The results, though much better than the 'official' values, are only fairly accurate. The errors range up to 7.4 per cent on imports and up to 14.5 per cent on re-exports. Had he projected his estimates forward through the years 1861 to 1865 when the American Civil War brought a wild rise in cotton prices, he would have put his method to better test— a test much needed as a clue to the degree of probability attributable to his estimates

**Diagram 2. Actual and calculated Values of British Imports and Re-exports.
1854–1934**

(At current prices)

(Mill. £)

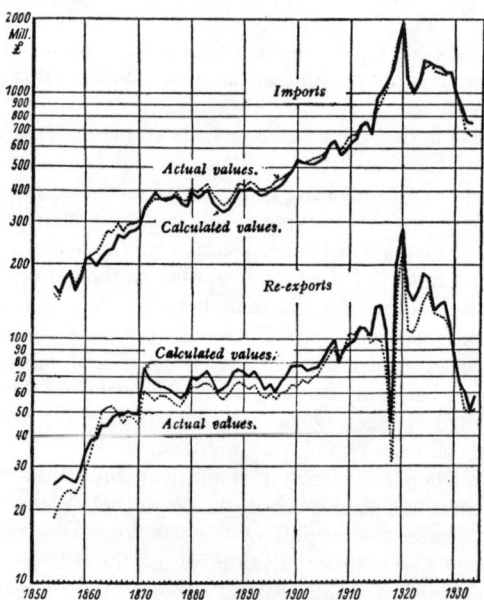

4. *The geographical distribution of British overseas trade and changes in the area covered by the trade statistics*

The geographical distribution of British overseas trade is analysed only according to value. This, however, is possible only after 1854,

for the years of rapid price change during and after the Napoleonic Wars. Had he done so, much larger errors would most certainly have shown up with the use of Jevons' general index.
'It is precisely this use of a general index with individual commodities that explains the size of the errors in some of the base years and that raises doubts about the reliability of the estimates for other years in the series. A general index—unless it is weighted—and here the weighting would have to be revised year by year—averages prices. Components of small quantity importance in the flow of trade have as much influence in determining the average as do commodities of large volume. If prices of all articles moved always in the same direction and at the same rate, Schlote's method would be a satisfactory one. They rarely do so. In this period prices sometimes varied as much in relation to one another as did the quantity imported or re-exported. To depend on a general price index, therefore, was to throw away a large part of the precision possible. Clearly, Schlote should have applied individual price series to each article whenever obtainable' (pp. 139–140).]

except for exports of home products. Before 1854 the classification of countries was only given for official values. The allocation of overseas trade to the different parts of the world—as calculated on official prices and on our estimates of value—differs considerably for the various continents and differs to an even greater extent for the different countries. This is shown in Table 6.

TABLE 6

SHARE OF THE CONTINENTS IN IMPORTS AND RE-EXPORTS OF THE UNITED KINGDOM IN 1854, CALCULATED ON OFFICIAL AND ACTUAL VALUES (PER CENT)

Continent	Shares of Imports based on		Shares of Re-exports based on	
	Official values	Actual values	Official values	Actual values
Europe	29.0	39.7	83.6	76.9
Africa	5.5	5.5	2.4	2.7
Asia	22.1	15.2	2.5	3.2
North America	26.0	24.4	5.6	7.0
South America	16.1	12.3	2.0	2.7
Australia	1.3	2.9	3.9	7.5

The possibility of making comparisons before and after 1854 is therefore considerably reduced. The official values of imports and re-exports are given separately and are used only to check general movements in this distribution of trade which occur before 1854. The allocation of countries to continents is that used in British foreign trade statistics. It should be noted that Mexico and the Bermudas are included with North America.

Before 1904 imports were shown only according to country of shipment. After 1904 the country of consignment was recorded. This was either the country of origin or the country from which the goods were actually sent to Great Britain. This change in the method of recording imports in the statistics might be an obstacle to comparison before and after 1904, but it is possible to classify the countries in such a way as to secure results which can be compared. As may be seen from Table 7 this can be done for (*a*) the continents, (*b*) the British Empire as a whole and (*c*) all the countries which can be jointly classified as Central and Industrial Europe.[1]

---

[1] Luxemburg has been included in ' Central Europe ' since the first World War. After the first World War the place of Austria-Hungary was taken by the ' Succession States '—Austria, Hungary and Czechoslovakia. For the term ' Industrial Countries ' see below p. 81.

TABLE 7
OVERSEAS TRADE OF UNITED KINGDOM IN 1904 WITH COUNTRIES OF SHIPMENT AND CONSIGNMENT (IN £1,000,000s)*

Area	Imports from		Exports to		Re-exports to	
	Countries of Shipment	Countries of Consignment	Countries of Shipment	Countries of Consignment	Countries of Shipment	Countries of Consignment
Germany	33.9	49.5	25.1	25.1	11.3	11.3
Netherlands	34.7	16.4	8.2	8.2	4.8	4.6
Belgium	27.5	16.7	9.1	7.9	4.4	4.4
Austria-Hungary	1.8	6.7	1.9	1.9	0.7	0.7
Switzerland	—	7.5	—	1.3	—	0.2
Central Europe	97.9	96.8	44.3	44.4	21.2	21.2
France	51.1	44.8	15.3	15.2	6.4	6.4
Italy	3.3	5.9	8.4	8.4	0.9	0.9
Industrial Europe	152.3	147.5	68.0	66.0	28.5	28.6
Agrarian Europe	87.5	88.6	36.3	38.3	10.5	10.6
Europe	239.8	236.1	104.3	104.3	39.0	39.1
Africa	27.4	28.0	34.3	34.3	2.6	2.6
Asia	61.2	62.2	74.1	74.1	1.9	1.8
United States	119.2	116.4	20.2	20.2	19.1	19.1
Canada	22.6	23.3	10.6	10.6	1.6	1.6
Rest of North America	1.1	2.3	2.6	2.6	0.3	0.3
North America	142.9	142.0	33.4	33.4	21.0	21.0
South America	43.0	45.8	30.8	30.8	2.7	2.7
America	185.9	187.8	64.2	54.2	23.7	23.7
Australia	36.6	36.8	23.8	23.8	3.1	3.1
Other Countries	0.1	0.1	—	—	—	—
Total	551.0	551.0	300.7	300.7	70.3	70.3
of which Brit. Empire	120.0	120.8	111.9	112.4	8.8	8.9

*See *Annual Statement*, 1904, Suppl. to Vol. I and II.

As far as exports are concerned, the two methods of recording give almost the same results, because even before 1904 the final country of destination was, if possible, invariably given although it had to be a country with a sea-coast. After 1904 the main change was that exports to countries in the interior of a continent are also given separately. Exports to Switzerland, for example, appear to have gone for the most part through Belgian ports. In and immediately after 1904 British exports to Belgium appear to have declined roughly by the amount one would have expected owing to this change from one method of recording to another. Another difficulty in comparing the figures of British overseas trade—which mainly affects the geographical distribution of Empire trade—occurs owing to the exclusion of the Irish Free State in 1923 from the area of the United Kingdom. There had been changes in the area covered by the trade-statistics as early as the middle of the eighteenth century and the beginning of the nineteenth century. Statistics which originally applied only to England (and Wales) were extended [in 1755] to cover the area of Great Britain and in 1801 to the United Kingdom. The incorporation of Scotland had little significance, as far as the amount of overseas trade was concerned, since the overseas commerce of that country was quite small. This is also true of Irish overseas trade in so far as it did not go to Great Britain. Trade between Great Britain and Ireland was, however, considerable. In 1801 it amounted to about 9 per cent of Great Britain's total trade. In order to make a comparison we must therefore deduct the trade of Great Britain with Ireland from the total British figures for overseas trade. This virtually preserves the continuity of the statistics.[1]

The omission of the trade statistics of the Irish Free State [now Eire] after 1923 is also of no great significance. Moreover, allowance can easily be made for the consequent change in the statistics. We have deducted the trade between Great Britain and the Irish Free State from the statistics of both countries and we have added their remaining trade.[2] We thus obtain the values for the overseas trade of the United Kingdom (in the area of 1801–1923), which are given in the general tables in the Appendix. The statistics referring to the new area of the United Kingdom since 1923 exceed the calculated values for the area of 1801–1923 by only 3 per cent for imports and 6 per cent for exports.

It is however more important to make corrections when we come to the individual groups of commodities. The increase in the value of imports of livestock into the United Kingdom (area since

---

[1] Our constructed volumes (on values for 1913) are calculated from the statistics of British foreign trade from which Anglo-Irish trade has been deducted.
[2] The total is reached by adding the foreign trade of the United Kingdom (deducting the trade with the Irish Free State) and the foreign trade of the Irish Free State (deducting the trade with the reduced territory of the United Kingdom —[i.e. the United Kingdom of Great Britain and Northern Ireland]).

1923), for example, is entirely due to the fact that livestock from Eire now forms part of Great Britain's overseas trade whereas formerly it did not. The same consideration applies to the imports of foodstuffs but as far as raw materials and manufactured goods are concerned the differences are insignificant. The differences are naturally more noticeable for Great Britain's exports—particularly exports of finished goods. Britain's exports of foodstuffs have also been affected by territorial changes since large quantities of hams, flour and tea—to mention only the most important exports—were sent from Great Britain to Eire. The differences with regard to re-exports are insignificant.

It is more important to take account of these territorial changes when considering the development of Britain's commercial relations with the Empire. Here the inclusion or exclusion of Britain's trade. with the Irish Free State [Eire] would make a significant difference A continuous survey of Britain's trade with her Empire is possible only if we take the appropriate measures to deal with the territorial change of 1923.

We need hardly stress the fact that the values for the area of 1801–1923 lack reality [after 1923]. Otherwise we should be assuming that the political separation of territories has no significance as far as their foreign trade is concerned, which is not true. So our calculations serve only to secure a continuous comparison and they have no other significance.

B. ANALYSIS

I. Development and Significance of British Overseas Trade

1. *Periods of Growth*

The growth and development of British overseas trade from 1700 to the 1930s were uneven. Before the War of American Independence Britain's foreign trade increased relatively slowly but there were considerable fluctuations—particularly in imports—and these changes were due to the numerous wars of the period.[1] After 1776–83 the rate of increase was much greater. Owing to the Napoleonic Wars and their aftermath the rate of increase was checked for a quarter of a century and then there was a further acceleration until 1860. Acceleration was subsequently steadily reduced and after the first World War only imports surpassed the level which they had reached in the years just before 1914.

It is however the 'rate of expansion' rather than the 'rate of growth' which enables us to appreciate these developments more adequately. We use the term 'rate of expansion' to indicate the growth of overseas trade in relation to the size of the population. We have calculated this 'rate of expansion' on the assumption that there is a genuine 'growth' of overseas trade only if such growth is greater than the growth of the population. Our calculation of the 'rate of expansion' of Britain's overseas trade turnover shows that the sharpest rise was between 1845 and 1855 when the average annual growth of imports was 4.4 per cent and of exports 7 per cent while the exports of home products alone [i.e. not including re-exports] actually increased by 7.3 per cent. If we observe the expansion of Britain's overseas trade for a hundred years or so we naturally see lower increases. Assuming that modern developments began in the 1820s our calculations show that the annual average rate of increase up to the outbreak of the first World War was 3.3 per cent while the corresponding 'rate of expansion' was 2.5 per cent. If we assume that modern developments began in 1780 then these rates are 3 per cent and 2 per cent respectively for the 133 years to 1913.

The main periods of development are clearly distinguishable from each other by political and economic events. At first the Industrial Revolution produced a swifter increase in the rate of foreign trade—which, of course, was not negligible before that,

[1] Between 1697 and 1783 there were forty-five years of peace and forty-two years of war. Between 1697 and 1815 there were fifty-five years of peace and sixty-four years of war.

although purchasing power and transport had been checked by long periods of warfare. In the last twenty years of the eighteenth century the vigorous growth of overseas trade was due to technical advances in machinery, which stimulated the expansion of overseas

TABLE 8

ANNUAL AVERAGE PERCENTAGE INCREASE IN THE RATE OF GROWTH AND THE ' RATE OF EXPANSION ' OF VOLUMES OF BRITISH OVERSEAS TRADE, 1700-1929 (PER CENT)

Periods	Rate of growth*				Rate of expansion			
	Imports	Exports	Re-exports	Turnover	Imports	Exports	Re-exports	Turnover
1700–1770	1.2	1.2	—	1.2	0.7	0.7	—	0.7
1780–1800	5.5	6.1	—	5.8	2.6	3.2	—	3.0
1800–1825	1.3	1.2	2.1	1.3	0.1	0.1	0.8	0.1
1825–1840	3.3	4.0	4.6	3.6	2.1	2.8	3.3	2.3
1840–1860	4.5	5.3	5.5	5.0	4.2	5.1	5.1	4.7
1860–1870	4.4	4.4	3.9	4.3	3.5	3.4	3.1	3.4
1870–1890	2.9	2.1	2.0	2.5	2.0	1.2	1.0	1.6
1890–1900	2.6	0.7	0.8	1.8	1.6	—0.1	—0.1	0.8
1900–1913	1.5	3.3	3.7	2.3	0.7	2.5	2.9	1.4
1913–1929	1.1	—0.5	—0.4	0.5	1.1	—0.5	—0.4	0.4
1700–1800	1.7	1.8	—	1.8	0.7	0.8	—	0.8
1800–1913	3.3	3.4	1.2	3.4	2.4	2.6	2.7	2.5

*We are concerned here with rates of increase in the literal sense and not with ' mean coefficients of growth ' such as Walther Hoffmann has calculated for British industrial production. See W. Hoffmann, *Wachstum und Wachstumformen der englischen Industriewirtschaft von 1700 bis zur Gegenwart* (Probleme der Weltwirtschaft Vol. 63). Hoffmann's figures are 2.8, 2.6 and 2.0 per cent respectively for the periods 1781 to 1913, 1819 to 1913 and 1855 to 1913. The corresponding calculation for foreign trade turn-over results in ' mean coefficients of growth ' of 3.5, 3.6 and 2.8 per cent, respectively. For the eighteenth century the ' mean coefficient of growth ' was 1.4 per cent, while for 1801 to 1913 it was 3.5 per cent.

markets. Under the protection of a powerful fleet there was an increased exchange of goods, principally with America. The Napoleonic wars did not cause any noticeable decline in either imports or exports but were followed by a long period of stagnation. In comparison with the first World War the retrogressive effects were slight although the world economic situation showed many similarities with that of the period between 1914 and 1918.[1] The main reason for this lay in the great strength of Britain at sea so that France was only able to injure British trade with the Continent. Even this interruption of trade was not complete, since Britain was able to exchange goods with Scandinavia and was

[1] See A. Sartorius von Waltershausen : *Die Umgestaltung der Zwischenstaatlichen Wirtschaft* (Jena 1936), p. 6 ff.

actually able to increase considerably her trade with Spain and Portugal. Nevertheless British overseas trade did not revive immediately after the downfall of Napoleon. Europe was exhausted after the long wars, while the United States had introduced high tariffs after its war with Britain (1812–14). Britain herself was suffering from the effects of a greatly increased National Debt and prices fell considerably. Not until the middle of the 1820s did trade again expand more vigorously. At the same time there began that gradual realization of Free Trade which powerfully increased Britain's capacity both to import and to export. After about 1860, however, the progressive industrialisation of the Continent and the United States gradually had a more powerful effect. Britian's competitive position became steadily more difficult, particularly as the newly industrialised countries soon showed that they had no intention of following Britain's example and adopting Free Trade. Then the first World War affected British foreign trade to a greater degree than had occurred in the whole of the previous two centuries.[1] In 1933 imports were only a little greater than in 1913 while exports had not reached the figure of 1913 even by 1937–8. In 1931–33 exports only reached the level of those of the middle of the 1880's.[2]

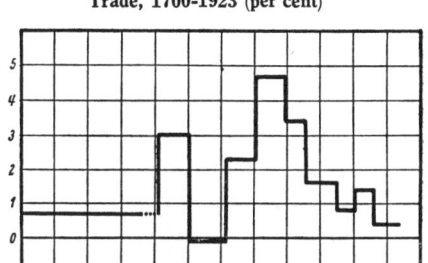

Diagram 3. Rates of Expansion of British Overseas Trade, 1700-1923 (per cent)

2. *Development of Overseas Trade in Periods of Boom and Slump.*

The rate of growth of British overseas trade in the [rather long] periods we have just described reflects only general trends of development. When we examine shorter periods the growth of overseas trade is subject to very considerable fluctuations and more detailed investigation shows a close connection between the rate of growth of overseas trade and the state of the trade cycle. Increases in imports and exports nearly always took place in years of general pros-

[1] See Diagram 4, p. 44.
[2] See Appendix, Table 7.

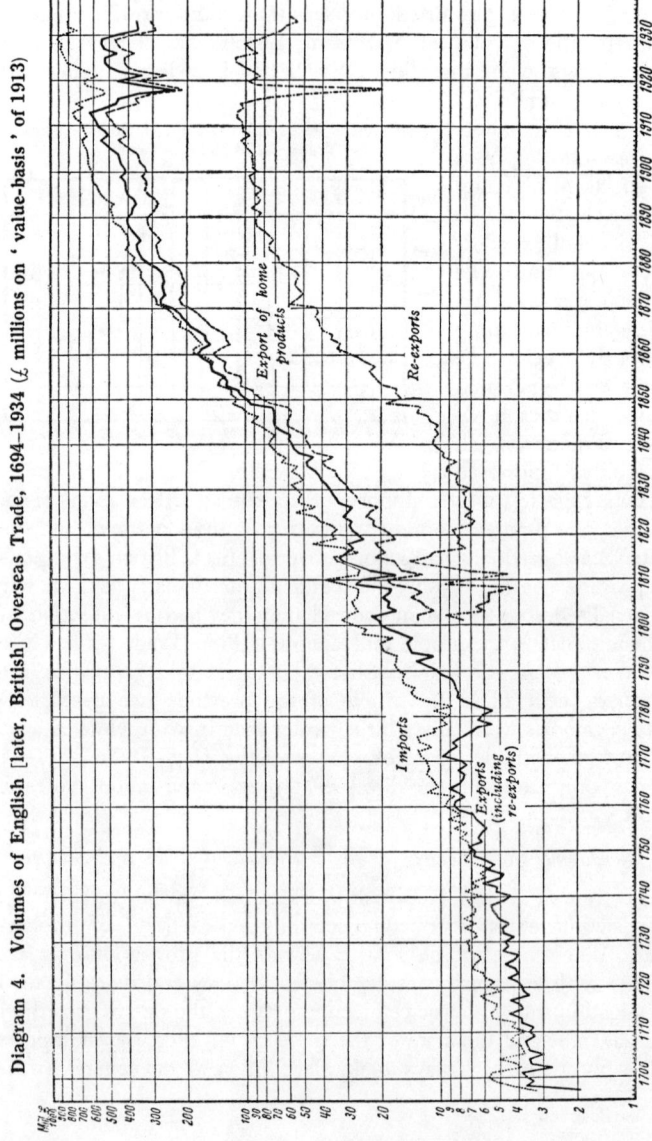

Diagram 4. Volumes of English [later, British] Overseas Trade, 1694–1934 (£ millions on 'value-basis' of 1913)

— 45 —

TABLE 9

GROWTH OF IMPORTS AND EXPORTS IN PERIODS OF BOOM AND SLUMP 1816–1913
(Millions of £)

S — Slump   B — Boom

Phase of Trade Cycle		Actual Values[3]				Volumes (1913 base-year)			
		Imports*		Exports[2]		Imports[3]		Exports[2]†	
		Boom	Slump	Boom	Slump	Boom	Slump	Boom	Slump
1816–17	S		+ 12.3		— 3.4		+ 4.6		— 0.6
1818	B	+ 32.6		+ 7.2		+ 13.2		+ 1.1	
1819–20	S		— 31.1		— 12.5		— 8.1		— 4.2
1821–25	B	+ 25.9		+ 0.1		+ 18.5		+ 2.2	
1826–27	S		— 24.5		— 7.8		— 10.9		— 1.4
1827–28	B	+ 5.5		+ 4.4		+ 9.3		+ 5.5	
1829–30	S		— 3.6		— 0.9		— 1.9		+ 1.5
1830–31	B	+ 10.4		+ 1.2		+ 7.1		+ 2.9	
1832	S		— 12.2		— 0.0		— 7.8		+ 2.2
1833–36	B	+ 23.4		+ 17.5		+ 14.5		+ 7.3	
1837–42	S		— 3.8		— 5.1		+ 6.2		+ 10.5
1843–46	B	+ 15.3		+ 11.4		+ 15.1		+ 11.7	
1847–48	S		+ 10.0		— 4.9		+ 17.3		+ 1.3
1849–54	B	+ 50.8		+ 52.5		+ 32.7		+53.8	
1855	S		— 8.9		+ 0.9		— 10.0		+ 2.0
1856–57	B	+ 44.3		+ 29.5		+ 24.4		+ 22.6	
1858	S		— 23.3		— 6.4		— 5.0		+ 1.2
1859–60	B	+ 45.9		+ 24.7		+ 38.1		+ 22.7	
1861–63‡	S		+ 38.4		+ 32.4		— 7.0		— 13.7
1864–66	B	+ 46.4		+ 42.0		+ 43.5		+ 31.1	
1867–68	S		— 0.6		— 11.1		+ 13.0		+ 19.0
1869–73	B	+ 76.6		+ 83.2		+ 67.3		+ 49.3	
1874–79	S		— 8.3		— 62.2		+ 53.3		+ 24.9
1880–83	B	+ 63.9		+ 56.6		+ 60.4		+ 73.7	
1884–86	S		— 77.0		— 36.8		— 10.7		+ 1.6
1887–90	B	+ 70.8		+ 59.6		+ 73.8		+ 44.9	
1891–94	S		— 12.4		— 54.4		+ 47.2		— 32.1
1895–1900	B	+114.7		+ 80.6		+ 91.8		+ 46.5	
1901–4	S		+ 27.9		+ 16.6		+ 29.8		+ 35.5
1905–7	B	+ 94.8		+146.9		+ 39.9		+103.3	
1908	S		— 52.8		— 61.2		— 31.9		— 38.6
1909–13	B	+175.7		+178.1		+113.5		+125.6	
Together 1816–1913		+897.0	—169.8 +727.2	+795.5	—216.8 +578.7	+663.1	+ 79.0 +742.1	+604.2	— 0.9 +603.3

* Before 1854 imports and re-exports were calculated according to the values given in Table 3 of the Appendix.
† Exports, including re-exports.   ‡ Cotton Famine.

perity.[1] Between 1816 and 1913 imports rose by £727 millions, while exports (including re-exports) rose by £579 millions. But for the years of depression in this period (which amounted to 40) there was a total fall of £170 millions in imports and £217 millions in exports. In the boom-years (which amounted to 58) there was an increase of £897 millions in imports and £796 millions in exports. On the whole, therefore, the growth of the value of British overseas trade took place in periods of prosperity. This conclusion is not merely drawn from the movement of actual values, which tend to rise and fall with the periods of prosperity and slump and which in themselves could give the information we are seeking. The same result—though not in quite so definite a form—is obtained if we calculate the growth of volumes of overseas trade for the same trade-cycle periods. It is in periods of prosperity that 80 per cent of the import volume-increases and rather over 100 per cent of the export volume-increases occur. The argument we have advanced is therefore confirmed. The argument we have advanced holds good if we consider the years 1816–1913 as a whole, but it does not apply to the periods of depression within that century.[2] In these periods of depression, on the contrary, the volumes of imports increased on seven occasions and the volumes of exports on as many as ten occasions. These increases, however, were nearly always much lower than those in the years of prosperity that preceded or followed the slumps. The fact that there have been numerous increases in exports in periods of slump or of recession is undoubtedly of special significance for an understanding of the problem of so-called ' crisis exports '.[3]

3. *Prices of Exports and Imports in Relation to the Growth of Overseas Trade*

It is characteristic of the development of British overseas trade since the beginning of the nineteenth century that imports and exports did not increase at even approximately equal rates.[4] On the contrary while the volumes of exports rose between 1820 and 1860 more sharply than the volumes of imports the reverse is true for the

---

[1] See Table 9, p. 45. The periods of trade-cycles were arrived at from the data given by W. L. Thorp, *Business Annals* (Publications of the National Bureau of Economic Research No. 8), New York, 1926, p. 146 ff. The first and last years [of the cycles] were established with reference to the movement of the production index. For example, the crisis year 1857 was included amongst the prosperous years because the production index was still increasing (see W. Hoffmann, *loc. cit.*)
[2] See Table 9, p. 45.
[3] See below, p. 77 ff.
[4] See Diagram 4.

period between 1860 and 1900. Between 1900 and 1914 export volumes again increased more rapidly and after the first World War only imports rose while exports actually declined.

The relationship of prices of exports and imports developed in a similar manner. The terms of trade turned against Britain when exports were increasing but went in her favour when imports were growing more quickly than exports.[1] This is particularly clear in

Diagram 5. Relation between Exports, including Re-Exports, and Imports (by Volume and Price), 1914–1933*

1913 = 100

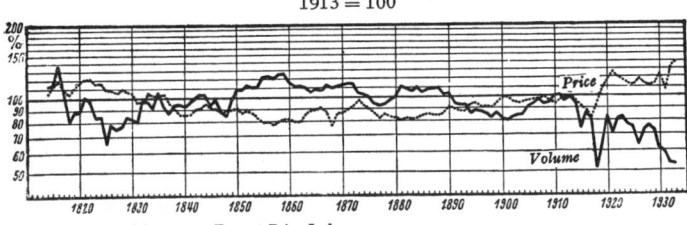

* i.e. Export Volume / Import Volume and Export Price Index / Import Price Index

the two periods between 1820 and 1860 and between 1913 and 1929. In the first period (1820–60) the terms of trade turned against Britain. The price-index for exports in 1820 was 19 per cent *above* the price-index for imports whereas by 1860 the price-index for exports was 19 per cent *below* the price-index for imports. In this period however the volume of exports increased much more than the volume of imports. The relationship of the indices of volumes changed from 91 to 118.[2] In the second period (1913–1929) on the contrary a favourable change in the terms of trade was accompanied by a relative falling off in the volume of exports. If we examine the whole period between 1814 and 1933 we find that British export activity was encouraged at times when export prices were declining in comparison with import prices. On the other hand, when import prices were declining in comparison with export prices there was always a more rapid increase in imports than in exports.

This statistical enquiry confirms the fact that when Britain's imports cost her more she had to pay for them by increasing her exports.

4. *Overseas Trade and National Income.*

In the course of this development the sum total of British overseas trade grew to a size which demonstrated the significance of this branch of the British economy. In 1929 total overseas trade

[1] See Diagram 5. [2] See Diagram 5.

amounted to about £2,100 millions and in 1913 it had been £1,400 millions. In comparison with this the corresponding turnover in the past was quite small. In 1870 it had still not reached £600 millions. In 1854, when for the first time actual current values were given in the statistics for all sections of overseas trade, the turnover amounted to £268 millions, while in the first quarter of the nineteenth century it was only about £100 millions. The contemporary significance of these figures as an indication of the extent of economic progress can be judged by comparing them with other figures of economic development which can be regarded as typical of the economy of that time. Statistics of the national income are best suited for this purpose for they embrace the whole economic activity of the country. The development of the national income reflects therefore both the speed and the extent of the nation's economic growth. A comparison of overseas trade and national income enables us to see the purely statistical significance of overseas trade in the past. It shows more than this. It indicates whether—and to what extent—overseas trade has changed its importance within the framework of the total economy. Such a comparison has been made, and has been carried back to the beginning of the nineteenth century on the basis of information about national income and overseas trade, of which new calculations have only recently been made.[1] By establishing a quotient of total overseas trade and national income, a measuring rod can be devised and changes in this figure indicate fluctuations in the relative importance of overseas trade in the economy as a whole. For the year 1913 this figure is taken to be 100 and changes in the quotient—calculated on this base-year—are shown in Table 10.

This table shows that the turnover of overseas trade expressed solely in terms of value was $4\frac{1}{2}$ times as important immediately before the first World War as it had been in the period of the Napoleonic Wars and even in the 1820s. In the 1930s it was quantitatively. of much smaller dimensions. It bore the same relation to the national income between 1927 and 1929 as it had done at the end of the 1850s. By 1930–33, however, it had declined to something like what it had been in 1840.[2]

[1] See Table 10.
[2] This also shows the limitations of such a purely statistical investigation. On the other hand British overseas trade is now [1937-8] much more important than it was eighty years ago, from the point of view of the *quality* of the goods involved and also from the point of view of its indispensability for the maintenance of the British economy. But at the moment we are concerned only with the significance of British overseas trade in purely quantitative terms.

The relationship of the volumes is similar. The quantitative significance of overseas trade, when related to national income, increased about 4½ times from the 1820s and 1830s until just before the first World War. It therefore developed substantially more quickly than the economic system as a whole. This growth of overseas trade relative to national income can already be seen to a considerable extent in the period before 1870. It was apparent in the most striking manner in the 1850s, which was the period when—as we have already shown—there were the most substantial developments in the rates of growth and 'expansion' of overseas trade.[1] Between 1870 and 1904 overseas trade and national income

TABLE 10
TOTAL OVERSEAS TRADE AND NATIONAL INCOME 1805—1933

Years	Total overseas Trade	National Income*	Index of Relation	Total overseas Trade (Volumes on basis of 1913 Values)	National Income† (1913 purchasing power)	Index of Relation
	(in £1,000,000s‡)		1913=100	(in £1,000,000s)		1913=100
1805–19	117.0	703.7	24.3	55.7	379	21.5
1820–29	102.8	607.1	24.8	75.3	460	24.0
1830–39	123.3	594.8	30.3	105.1	464	32.2
1840–49	159.5	634.2	36.8	157.7	534	43.2
1850–59	266.3	697.1	55.9	266.3	650	60.0
1860–69	463.1	862.5	78.6	382.8	780	71.9
1870–79	634.0	1123.6	82.5	580.8	1022	83.1
1880–89	686.3	1239.3	81.1	777.7	1318	86.3
1890–99	733.8	1431.3	75.1	942.4	1684	82.0
1900–04	890.2	1674.7	77.9	1073.9	1903	82.5
1905–09	1069.8	1753.9	89.3	1194.0	1916	91.2
1910–13	1299.1	1970.6	96.4	1330.4	2016	96.6
1927–29	2049.9	4460.7	67.3	1446.1	2550	83.0
1930–33	1306.7	4433.7	43.2	1209.6	2893	61.2

* The figures for national income were calculated by Dr. E. Quittner-Bertolasi in connection with research into capital-formation in England. [See also Colin Clark : *National Income and Outlay*, London, 1937; A. R. Prest, 'National income of the United Kingdom, 1870–1946' *Economic Journal*, March 1948, pp. 31–62.]
† Before 1854 cf. Table 3 of the Appendix.
‡ See Appendix, Table 7.
§ In calculating the national income on 1913 prices, the cost-of-living index of Wood-Layton-Board of Trade (1913=100) was extended back beyond 1850 by means of N. J. Silberling's cost-of-living index. For the construction of these indices, see G. H. Wood, ' Real Wages and the standard of comfort since 1850 ' (in the *Journal of the Royal Statistical Society*, Vol. 72 (1909), p. 91 ff) ; Layton and Crowther : *An Introduction to the Study of Prices*, London, 1933, p. 264 ; and *The Review of Economic Statistics*, vol. 5, supplement 2, October 1923 (Cambridge, Mass.), p. 235 [N. J. Silberling's well-known price-index for 1779–1850 is included in pages 219–61 of the last-mentioned work].
[1] See Table 8.

increased at about the same rate and it was not until the last decade before the outbreak of the first World War that the development of overseas trade was again greater than that of the British economy as a whole. The decline during the period after 1919 as compared with the period before 1914 is not so great as it would be if we made the calculations without taking account of alterations in prices. The index showing the relationship between overseas trade and national income shows for the yearly average 1927-9 a return to the level of 1870-1904. In 1930-33 indeed there was a decline to the level of the 1850's.

5. *Overseas Trade and Industrial Production*

To obtain a clearer view of the development of foreign trade we propose to compare trade with an index for industrial production which has been calculated from 1700.[1] It cannot indeed be regarded as so satisfactory a measuring rod as the national income, because the significance of the index itself increased as the British economy as a whole developed. Thus the national income, in terms of the purchasing power of 1913, increased between 1805-7 and 1911-13 by a yearly average of 1.4 per cent, while production increased by almost twice as much (2.6 per cent) and in the eighteenth century the rate of development of industrial production had been 1.6 per cent. This may be regarded with considerable certainty as far more than the increase in the British economy as a whole. Nevertheless the comparison of the two indices is a profitable one.

The first point to be noted in this connection is that overseas trade for approximately 150 years from 1700 onwards hardly increased any more quickly than production. The index relating overseas trade to industrial production for this period is mostly between 50 and 60 per cent of 1913. Incidental fluctuations of a violent character are presumably due to inevitable uncertainties in calculating both overseas trade and industrial production in this period. On the other hand, overseas trade grew more quickly than industrial production from the middle of the nineteenth century onwards; there was a particularly high rate of increase in the 1850s. In the first World War, production maintained its position better than overseas trade. After 1919 however overseas trade again increased more rapidly. There was the same relation between the annual averages of overseas trade and industrial production in the period 1927-29 as there had been in the years 1910-13. During the world economic crisis

[1] See W. Hoffmann, *loc. cit.*

[of 1929–33] overseas trade shrank so much that the index of its relation to industrial production fell again to about the level of 1880.[1]

TABLE 11

TOTAL OVERSEAS TRADE AND INDUSTRIAL PRODUCTION 1700–1933
(1913=100)

Years	Total overseas Trade	Industrial Production	Index of Relationship
1700–9	0.5	1.3	38.5
1710–19	0.6	1.4	42.9
1720–29	0.8	1.6	50.0
1730–39	0.9	1.7	52.9
1740–49	0.9	1.7	52.9
1750–59	1.0	2.0	50.0
1760–69	1.3	2.0	65.0
1770–79	1.4	2.4	58.3
1780–89	1.5	3.1	48.4
1790–99	2.4	4.3	55.8
1800–9	3.4	5.9	57.6
1810–19	4.3	7.2	59.7
1820–29	5.3	10.0	53.0
1830–39	7.5	14.7	51.0
1840–49	11.2	20.2	55.4
1850–59	19.0	28.3	67.1
1860–69	27.3	36.1	75.6
1870–79	41.4	48.1	86.1
1880–89	55.3	58.1	92.2
1890–99	67.1	68.1	98.5
1900–9	80.8	80.3	100.6
1910–13	94.8	91.8	103.3
1914–18	74.3	88.4	84.0
1918–26	85.1	81.9	103.9
1927–29	103.1	100.8	102.3
1930–33	86.2	94.1	91.6

II. *Classification of British Overseas Trade by Commodities*

Preliminary Observations

In the previous section we were considering British overseas trade purely from the point of view of its development since 1700. Since statistics of value were influenced by price-changes in this period only volumes were used for this purpose as they are more suitable. In the following sections we continue to deal to some extent with problems of development and in doing so we shall continue to base our researches upon volumes. In so far as we shall be dealing with questions of the composition of overseas trade by commodities—and that will be our main task—it seems to us to be more suitable to base our calculations on actual values. We propose

[1] The particularly interesting problem of the relation between the development of overseas trade and industrial production is discussed below p. 75 ff.

to assign actual current prices to the commodities with which we are dealing. In this way we shall see the real significance of the commodities and commodity-groups within the framwork of British commerce regarded as a whole. If we were to use theoretical volumes we should only find out what significance commodities and commodity groups would have had if they had been included in British overseas trade at 1913 prices. In certain circumstances we might obtain a distorted picture in this way.[1] Actual values have therefore always been used as the basis of our presentation when we are primarily trying to find out something about the commodity-structure of imports and exports.

Such a procedure is possible only after 1854 as far as imports and re-exports are concerned since before that date the official statistics provide no information about actual values. So before 1854 we use volumes in order not to omit completely an account of the state of affairs in earlier periods.

I. IMPORTS

(a) Classification by Commodity Groups

British imports are composed mainly of foodstuffs and raw materials whilst finished products are now only of slight importance. In the period of 130 years which we are considering, the relative proportions of these three commodity-groups within Britain's total imports have varied considerably. Characteristic of this change has been the growth of foodstuffs and finished goods in contrast to a decline in the proportion of raw materials in total imports. These changes took place for the most part between 1845 and 1875 (see Diagram 6). Before and after that period there were, of course, small alterations in the proportions but they did not substantially alter the basic structure of British imports.

The relative stability of the proportions of raw materials, food-

---

[1] This may be illustrated by the following example. In the 1830s an expert on British overseas trade could have declared, with every justification, that by far the most important British foodstuff exported was sugar refined in Britain, which in 1827 accounted for 40 per cent of Britain's food exports. In the second place, he would have mentioned butter and cheese with 13 per cent. On the other hand, by 1913 prices, sugar would have accounted for only 15 per cent, but butter and cheese would have accounted for over 25 per cent. By using volumes, therefore, we should fail to indicate the great importance which sugar had at that time [in 1827], and we should be giving to butter and cheese a quite unwarranted significance. The reason for this, of course, is that the price of sugar declined sharply until 1913, whereas in that year the prices of butter and cheese were much higher [than in 1827].

stuffs and finished goods in British imports before 1845 and after 1875 comes most clearly into view when we consider net imports. It is the demand for home consumption that alone determines the nature and quantity of net imports. The changes in the proportions of total imports, which were by no means insignificant before 1820, were almost entirely due—as can be seen by comparing Diagram 6(a) with Diagram 6(b)—to increased imports of food for re-export. By far the most important of these re-exports were tropical and semi-tropical products for which there was a particularly strong demand on the Continent [after 1812–14] owing to shortages caused by the blockade during the Napoleonic wars. The consequent changes in the proportions of the imports no longer appear in the net imports statistics.

TABLE 12

ANALYSIS OF IMPORTS BY COMMODITY-GROUPS 1814–1933

(per cent)

Commodity Group	Imports			Net Imports[1]		
	1814–45	1854–60	1875–1933	1814–45	1854–60	1875–1933
	Proportions of total volume (1913 values being the basis)					
Foodstuffs[2]	27.9	31.5	41.2	24.4	32.1	44.7
Raw Materials	64.4	61.2	41.6	70.4	61.1	38.3
Finished Goods	7.7	7.3	17.2	5.2	6.8	17.0
	Proportions by actual value					
Foodstuffs[2]	—	37.2	42.9	—	38.8	45.8
Raw Materials	—	55.9	39.1	—	54.8	36.0
Finished Goods	—	6.9	18.0	—	6.4	18.2

After 1875 the proportions of the three commodity-groups in the total imports were again remarkably stable and did not even change substantially during the first World War. There was merely a slight drop in the proportion of raw materials balanced by a modest increase in imports of finished products. The proportion of raw materials [to total imports] fluctuated between 40 and 45

[1] By 'Net Imports' we mean the difference between total imports and re-exports. This implies that the prices—upon which our calculation of values is based—are different for a re-exported commodity than they were for the same commodity when it was (presumably) imported. If we were to define the value at base-prices (volume) of net imports as the product of the quantity difference (i.e. the difference between the quantity imported and the quantity re-exported) and import price, which for many aspects of our research would be more useful, we should, of course, not obtain the same result.

[2] Including livestock.

per cent from 1875 to 1891 and between 35 and 40 per cent from 1891 to 1937-8. The proportions of these groups of commodities when calculated by actual values also showed no significant changes between 1875 and 1914. During the first World War, however, —and also after 1929—changes do occur. A comparison of Diagrams 6 and 7 shows that these changes are due chiefly to the fact that the average prices of the three groups of commodities do not all move in the same way.

Diagram 6. Analysis of Imports in Commodity-groups 1814–1933*

(Proportions of total Volume in percentages)

(a) Total Imports.

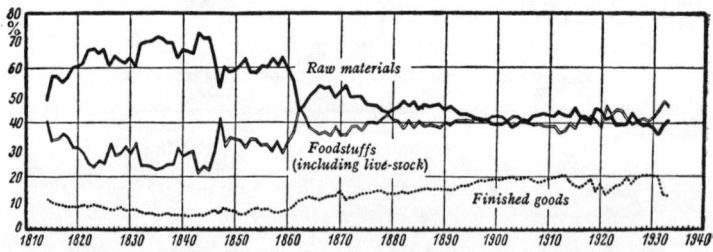

(b) Net Imports

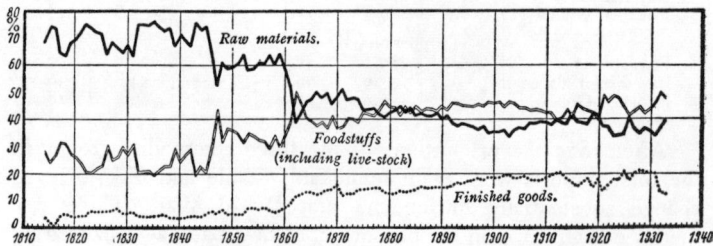

* From 1923 new area of trade statistics (United Kingdom without the Irish Free State [now Eire]).

The decisive change in the proportions of the three groups of imports therefore took place in the three decades after 1845.[1]

[1] The remarkable suddenness of the decline in the proportions of imported raw materials after 1860 is intimately connected with the Cotton Famine resulting from the American Civil War. As early as 1864—owing to the great rise in its cost —cotton accounted again for as great a proportion of Britain's total imports of raw materials as it had done in 1859.

— 55 —

It is this period that is of greatest significance in the following sections.

Diagram 7. Analysis of Imports in Commodity-groups 1854–1934*

(Proportions of actual value in percentages)

(a) Total Imports.

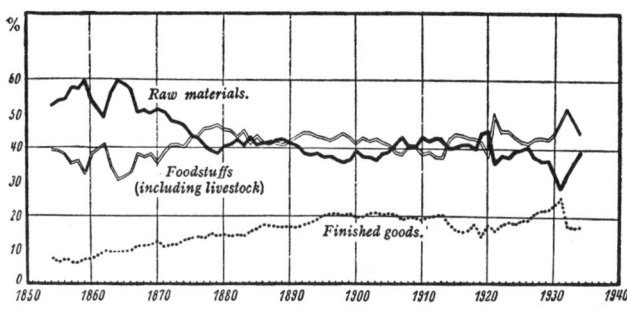

(b) Net Imports.

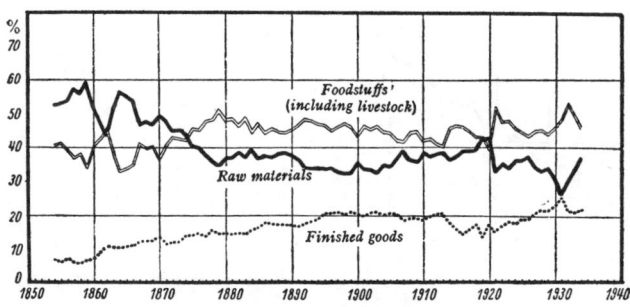

* From 1923 new area of trade statistics.

(b) *Imports of Raw Materials.*

The net imports of raw materials are determined mainly by the demands of Britain's manufacturing industries which depend almost entirely on overseas countries for their raw materials—coal being the most important exception. It has been shown that overseas trade developed more rapidly than industrial production during the nineteenth century. This alone explains the decline in the significance of imports of raw materials. It remains only to enquire whether this dependence [of the import raw materials] upon industrial production continues to be of significance in 1845–75 when the main decline in the imports of raw materials [as a proportion of total imports] took place.

If we compare the net imports of raw materials with industrial production between 1814 and 1913 we do in fact find that, even during the critical three decades, there was such a close correspondence between both curves in Diagram 8 that their dependence one upon the other is hardly open to doubt. It was only after the first World War that a change occurred and imports of raw materials outstripped industrial production. This discrepancy vanishes, however, if we limit our comparison to those raw materials which

Diagram 8. Net Import Volume of Raw Materials (Volume with 1913 as base-year) and of Industrial Production 1814–1933
1913 = 100

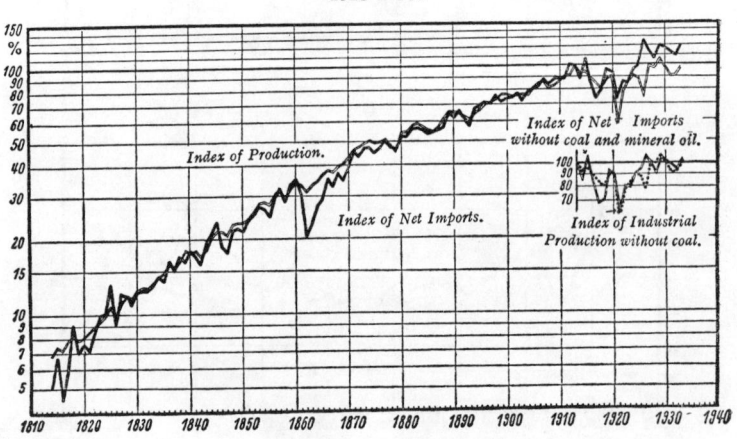

become part of the finished product without substantial change. If we exclude the two fuels—coal and mineral-oil—from figures of production and net imports[1] we then find that even for the period after the first World War there is again a close correspondence of both curves in Diagram 8.

[1] It is true that the index of production includes coal but it does not include mineral oil (see W. Hoffmann, *loc. cit.*). On the other hand coal appears in significant quantities only in the imports for 1926 and 1927 so that in the remaining years the exclusion of fuels from the index in fact virtually eliminates only the high mineral-oil imports.

TABLE 13

NET IMPORTS OF RAW MATERIALS AND INDUSTRIAL PRODUCTION 1818–1933
(VOLUME INDICES 1913—100)

	Annual Averages					
	1818–20	1840–45	1875–80	1911–13	1927–29	1932–33
Industrial Production	8.1	18.9	49.9	93.5	100.8	93.8
Net Imports of Raw Materials	7.7	19.2	48.1	96.6	113.3	114.3
Industrial Production (excluding coal)	8.4	19.6	50.3	93.3	102.7	96.7
Net Imports of Raw Materials (excluding coal and minl. oils)	8.0	20.1	49.9	97.1	99.7	98.1

The changes which have taken place in imports of materials—that is to say, the composition of such imports according to individual commodities and groups of commodities—are also intimately associated with the peculiarities of Britain's industrial development. Hoffmann's index shows that the output of the capital-goods industries grew much more quickly during the nineteenth century than that of the consumption-goods industries.

Consequently the proportion of imported raw materials to be used in the manufacture of capital goods increased in comparison with those destined for the consumption-goods industries.[1] This tendency appears most clearly if we compare the periods immediately before and immediately after the first World War.

In particular, imports of mineral oils greatly increased. This was a relatively new demand. With certain limitations we can also regard the imports of rubber, copper and the raw materials for making paper as new demands since these products were used mainly in the motor industry, electrical engineering and the paper-making industry, all of which have expanded to an extraordinary extent in Great Britain since 1913. There was obviously a powerful tendency for these industries to add to Britain's imports of raw materials since the raw materials they required were not produced at home or were produced only in quite inadequate amounts. Between 1909–13 and 1927–29 net imports of this 'new demand' increased by £56 millions at the same time as the total volume of raw material imports increased by barely £52 millions. Imports of textile raw materials on the other hand dropped considerably (by £20 millions). Before the first World War textile raw material imports accounted for

[1] See Table 14.

over 40 per cent of net imports, as opposed to only 25 to 30 per cent in the 1930s.

TABLE 14

SHARE OF DIFFERENT KINDS OF RAW MATERIALS IN TOTAL NET IMPORTS OF RAW MATERIALS 1827–1933 (PER CENT)

Commodities	Proportion by Volume							
	1827–28	1844–46	1859–61	1880–83	1896–99	1909–13	1927–29	1930–33
1 Consumption-g'ds* Raw Materials	63.5	67.7	69.0	61.4	53.7	53.9	39.9	39.9
Of these: Textile Materials	47.9	54.3	59.3	51.6	44.3	42.3	28.1	26.4
2 Capital-goods Raw Materials	8.0	12.9	16.7	27.4	34.3	36.3	50.3	49.9
Of these: Mineral Oils	—	—	—	0.9	2.5	3.6	15.5	16.8
Total Raw Materials for New Demands	0.2	0.2	1.6	4.3	7.3	10.3	27.8	31.6
3 Other Raw Materials	28.5	19.4	14.3	11.2	12.0	9.8	9.8	10.2
	Proportion by Value							
1 Consumption-g'ds Raw Materials*	—	—	68.0	59.6	52.8	53.9	46.6	42.4
Of these: Textile Raw Materials	—	—	55.2	47.8	38.7	42.3	33.3	28.8
2 Capital-goods Raw Materials †	—	—	18.3	27.4	38.7	36.4	43.0	47.0
Of these: Mineral Oils	—	—	Nil	1.3	2.8	3.1	10.8	14.3
Total Raw Materials for New Demands	—	—	1.8	3.5	8.8	10.8	19.0	23.3
3 Other Raw Materials	—	—	13.7	13.0	8.5	9.7	10.4	10.6

* Textile Raw Materials; Raw Skins and Hides; Fruits and Seeds producing oils and fats; Tobacco-leaf; Animal Oils and Fats.

† Raw Materials for new demands: Mineral Oils; Rubber; Raw Copper; Raw Materials for paper-making. Other raw materials for capital goods: ores and scrap; metals; timber.

The total imports of raw materials—including those intended for re-export—increased during the first half of the nineteenth century even more quickly than net imports. This was mainly due to the growing share which raw materials had in Britain's re-exports.[1]

The growth and composition of Britain's imports of raw materials have therefore been determined primarily by the country's industrial

[1] See Diagram 9.

development. This applies to the whole period under discussion but it is particularly true of the years 1845–75. The decline in this period of the share of raw materials in Britains' total imports was

Diagram 9. Analysis of Re-exports in Commodity-groups 1814–1933*

(percentage proportions by Volume)

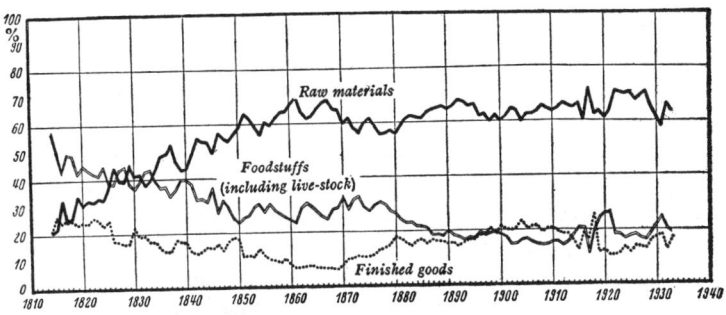

* From 1923 new area of trade statistics.

not due to any specific change in industrial demand but was primarily due to a particularly striking growth in imports of foodstuffs. We examine this phenomenon in the following section.

(c) *Imports of Foodstuffs*

The relative increase in Britain's imports of foodstuffs took place between 1845 and 1880.[1] It began with Britain's first fundamental tariff reforms and it can be shown that the steady completion of the Free Trade edifice between 1842 and 1860 was the most important factor influencing the change in the composition of the structure of Britain's imports.

No light is thrown on this matter by considering the development of the home production of foodstuffs. In so far as satisfactory data are available it appears that home production of foodstuffs reached a level in the 1850s which was subsequently seldom surpassed [up to 1937–8]. Indeed crop-production[2] actually declined so that the total net increase was due entirely to the greater production of food-

---

[1] See Diagrams 6 and 7.
[2] [Dr. Schlote's phrase 'pflanzliche Produktion' means what is grown on the farm (i.e. cereals, potatoes, turnips, etc.) as opposed to what is produced from livestock, poultry, etc.]

stuffs from animals.[1] On the other hand if we examine the development of imports of food,[2] we find that their growth consisted mainly of meat and other animal products, and these were the very products in which home-production was on the increase.

In view of the state of home production it is clear that the increase in imports of food was due entirely to the growth in population and purchasing power. These factors do not, however, explain either the relatively rapid developments between 1845 and 1880, or (more specifically) the accelerated rate of growth after 1845 and again after 1860.[3] We hope to be able to show that there was a connection between this growth and certain changes in British commercial policy. We propose in the following paragraphs to discuss this with special reference to a few important commodities.

Wheat

From 1828 a sliding scale of duties[4] was in force for wheat imports with preferential rates for colonial wheat. The duties in the sliding scale were considerably reduced in 1842 and again in 1846. In 1849 a fixed duty of 1s. per quarter came into effect and on June 1, 1869, this duty was repealed. The significance of the rates of duty is not evident until they are compared with contemporary prices. The following survey shows that the preferential duties for colonial wheat gave the colonies a very definite economic privilege on political grounds. From a practical point of view the preference was of slight importance since the annual average import of colonial wheat was not even 3 per cent of wheat imports between 1828 and 1859. It was in 1839 that the annual average home price of wheat was at its maximum for the period 1825-46 and the amount of duty levied in 1839 meant that the price was raised by 15 per cent. Even in these circumstances 550,000 tons of wheat were imported. When, in 1835, the home price fell to the lowest annual average figure in this period the import duty amounted to 121 per cent of the price and this was in fact a prohibitive duty. Table 15 also shows that it was only after the substantial tariff reform of 1846 that there was a decisive drop in duties on wheat—when related to contemporary prices.

[1] See L. Drescher, Die Entwicklung der Agrarproduktion Grossbritanniens und Irlands seit Beginn des neunzehnten Jahrhunderts. Bemerkungen zum Index der Agrarproduktion (*Weltwirtschaftliches Archiv*, Jena 1935) Vol. 41, p. 270 ff.
[2] See Table 21.
[3] See Diagram 6.
[4] A more detailed study of the customs duties on wheat and the other commodities discussed here is given in the Appendix, which should be consulted for more detailed information (see pp. 111-3) below.

TABLE 15

HOME PRICES OF WHEAT, RATES OF DUTY RULING AND IMPORTS OF WHEAT FOR CONSUMPTION 1829–1868

Year	Rate of Duty on Wheat			Duty on Wheat		Imports for Consumption
	Prices	shillings per quarter Foreign	Colonial	as per cent of price Foreign	Colonial	metric tons
1829	66¼	20⅔	5	31.2	7.5	59,748
1835	39¼	47⅔	5	121.2	12.7	3,379
1839	70⅔	10⅔	0.5	15.1	0.7	550,350
1841	64⅜	22⅔	5	35.2	7.8	501,269
1843	50 1/12	20	5	39.9	10.0	176,361
1845	50⅝	20	5	39.3	9.8	29,648
1847	69¾	4	1	5.7	1.4	599,954
1848	50½	7	1	13.9	2.0	407,000
1849–68*	52 3/10	1	1	1.9	1.9	1,087,770

* [Annual average].

In Table 16 the effect of the duty does not appear so clearly because in the first half of the nineteenth century the yield of the harvest in Britain was the sole factor which determined the amount of wheat imported. It is true that imports rose after 1828 when the prohibitions of wheat imports provided for under previous Acts were replaced by the sliding scale. This increase, however, was due mainly

TABLE 16

POPULATION, PRICES, IMPORTS AND WHEAT HARVESTS FOR THE PERIOD WHEN DUTIES WERE BEING CHANGED, 1825–1875*

Year	Population of U.K.	Home prices	Wheat Imports for Consumption †	Wheat Harvests	
				in Gt. Britain	in the U.K.
	Millions	Shillings per quarter	(annual average) Metric tons	(annual average) Millions of metric tons	
1825–28	22.9	61.5	10,864	2.85	
1829–36	24.7	55.3	57,537	3.03	
1837–41	26.4	64.3	385,423	3.07	
1842–45	27.1	52.8	284,423	3.14	
1846–48	27.2	58.3	481,150	2.92	3.4
1849–54	27.4	48.2	861,790	3.62	3.9
1862–68	30.2	51.5	1,430,836	2.96	3.1
1869–75	32.2	52.6	2,057,722	2.55	2.7

* Years in which import duties were changed are printed in heavy type.
† After the abolition of the duty, net imports.

to the bad harvests between 1828 to 1830 and also to the Irish potato famine of 1830.[1]

After 1838 the home price of wheat was high, and this was probably due mainly to a failure of home production to meet demand. At the same time imports rose considerably because—especially at the prevailing price-level—the burden of import duty was relatively slight.[2] After 1846 the considerable drop in the duty permitted a rapid increase in imports. By the beginning of the 1850s imports were already over 20 per cent of Britain's own output. In the 1870s wheat imports reached the level of (and eventually surpassed) British production.

Livestock

After 1770 imports of livestock were prohibited. This prohibition was replaced in 1842 by duties, but they were abolished at the beginning of 1846. The effect of these measures can be seen very clearly from Table 17. When the prohibition was removed, imports, particularly of sheep, were still small, but when the duties were abolished, imports greatly increased. In comparison with Britain's own flocks and herds, however, imports were still insignificant.[3]

TABLE 17

CATTLE AND SHEEP IMPORTED BEFORE AND AFTER EXEMPTION FROM DUTY 1841–1850

Year	Cattle	Sheep	Year	Cattle	Sheep
1841	Imports prohibited		1846	45,043	94,624
1842	4,264	644	1847	75,717	142,720
1843	1,521	217	1848	62,738	130,583
1844	4,889	2,817	1849	53,449	129,266
1845	16,833	15,957	1850	66,462	143,498

The consequences of reducing and abolishing import duties on meat were obvious. Import duties for ham and bacon were reduced in 1825, 1842 and 1846. In 1846 the duty on ham was abolished but bacon continued to pay duty until the middle of 1853.

[1] Throughout the decade 1828–1837 the wheat imported for consumption amounted in all to 1,215,000 tons, of which no less than 1,060,000 tons entered Britain during the years 1828–1831. Between 1832 and 1837 there was an annual import for consumption of 25,800 tons in comparison with a home output of approximately 3 million tons from the British harvest.
[2] See Tables 15 and 16.
[3] Re-exports are so slight, that imports can in practice be regarded as imports for consumption.

TABLE 18
IMPORTS OF HAM AND BACON FOR CONSUMPTION 1820–1860 (CWT.)

Years	Ham and Bacon	Years	Ham and Bacon	Years	Ham	Bacon
1820–24	376	1837–41	1649	1846–52	182,663	8,351
1825–33	1985	1842–45	3978	1853–60	258,322	15,661

The import of other kinds of meat was at first forbidden. The prohibition on salt meat was removed in July 1827, and that on fresh and slightly salted meat was removed in 1842. Since these commodities are perishable, imports were at first only small. In 1842 the duty on salt meat was reduced and in 1846 it was abolished. The effect of these measures was again obvious. In 1845 imports of salt beef and pork for consumption still amounted to only 4,900 cwt. In 1846 these imports amounted to 241,300 cwt., although the disappearance of the duty came into effect only in the second half of the year.

TABLE 19
IMPORTS FOR CONSUMPTION OF SALT BEEF AND PORK UP TO 1849

Year	cwt.	Year	cwt.
1827	Imports prohibited	1842–45	11,055
1827–33	2,986	1846–49	358,458
1834–41	4,621		

Butter, Cheese, Eggs.

Meat was not imported to any great extent until the 1870s and after. Butter, cheese and eggs, however, were already playing an important part [in British imports] in the first half of the century. The big reductions in customs duties on butter and cheese occurred in 1846, 1853 and 1860, and on eggs in 1853 and 1860. The sweeping away of the duties in 1860 led to a sudden and sharp increase in imports. If we compare imports for 1859 (the last year of Protection) with those of 1861 (the first complete year of Free Trade) the following increases in imports took place:

Butter, 565,000 cwt. or 138 per cent.
Cheese, 301,000 cwt. or 76 per cent.
Eggs, 455,000 great hundreds[1] or 37 per cent.

The rise in imports of cheese within this short period of time is

[1] [A 'great hundred' is 120.]

approximately equal to that between 1823 and 1859. Egg imports increased between 1859 and 1861 as much as between 1848 and 1859.

TABLE 20

IMPORTS FOR CONSUMPTION [1] OF BUTTER, CHEESE AND EGGS, 1843–1865

Years	Butter	Cheese	Eggs
	1000 cwts.		1000 great hundreds
1843–45	189	210	593
1846–52	298	351	792
1853–59	439	384	1040
1860–65	986	730	2180

It can be shown that changes in import duties had similar effects on most other foodstuffs. The significant effects of Free Trade upon imports of food have already been clearly indicated by the examples we have given. The suddenness and extent of the increase in imports after each important reduction in duties lead almost inevitably to the conclusion that it was the policy of Free Trade which first made possible the striking growth of food imports within the framework of total imports in the period following the tariff changes of 1846.

Even within the group of foodstuffs characteristic changes occur. At the beginning of the nineteenth century these imports consisted mainly of commodities which we usually call 'luxuries'. In view of the standard of life of the vast majority of the population at that time, the term 'luxuries' is a reasonable one. Even in the 1830s more than two-thirds of net imports of foodstuffs[2] consisted of tropical and semi-tropical products and alcoholic drinks. Between one-seventh and one-eighth of the imports of foodstuffs consisted of butter, cheese and eggs, which at that time were not regarded as staple foodstuffs for the bulk of the population. Indeed in the first half of the nineteenth century only grain and flour should really be regarded as necessities from the point of view of food imports. These imports, however, represented statistically only a small fraction of food imports. They came only in years of bad harvest, but were an urgent necessity at such times.

Subsequently a change occurred from pure luxuries to such foodstuffs as played an important rôle in the household economy of the vast mass of the population. The consumption of meat has

---

[1] Total imports of eggs. Re-exports were insignificant.
[2] This proportion would be still higher by real values (see also the development of the proportions by value and volume after 1854–8 in Table 21).

become of ever-increasing importance with improvements in the standard of living. In spite of the rising output of Britain's own meat products, imports of meat rose very considerably—particularly after the mid-1870s. This development was encouraged and,

TABLE 21

PROPORTION OF NET IMPORTS OF FOODSTUFFS REPRESENTED BY ESSENTIAL PROVISIONS AND LUXURY FOODS AND DRINKS (PER CENT) 1820–1933

Commodity	1820/25	1833/34	1842/34	1854/58	1868/70	1881/82	1898/99	1909/13	1927/29	1932/33
Proportion by volume										
Tropical and sub-tropical foodstuffs and sugar	39.6	39.6	31.6	22.9	17.2	14.9	13.6	14.4	13.0	13.1
Alcoholic beverages	26.6	28.4	14.3	7.9	9.7	4.7	3.3	2.1	3.0	2.4
'Luxury' foodstuffs together	66.2	68.0	45.9	30.8	26.9	19.6	16.9	16.5	16.0	15.5
Butter, cheese, eggs	14.4	13.1	11.2	11.0	14.9	14.7	14.6	15.6	17.3	19.3
Meat, fish, animal and vegetable fats, condensed milk	Nil	Nil	1.0	7.3	7.3	17.2	24.4	24.5	28.0	27.4
Rice, vegetables, fruit	7.0	6.5	7.8	10.2	9.7	8.2	8.7	9.1	11.1	11.7
Vegetable oils	2.8	6.5	6.9	6.5	3.8	1.8	1.5	2.6	2.5	1.7
Grain and milled products	9.0	5.1	25.7	33.9	36.7	36.4	31.0	29.8	21.2	20.6
Other foodstuffs	0.6	0.8	1.5	0.3	0.7	2.1	2.9	1.9	3.9	2.8
Proportion by value										
Tropical and sub-tropical foodstuffs and sugar	—	—	—	33.4	27.5	22.8	16.3	15.3	13.7	13.4
Alcoholic beverages	—	—	—	7.0	7.1	4.2	4.0	2.1	2.5	2.9
'Luxury' foodstuffs together	—	—	—	40.4	34.6	27.0	20.3	17.4	16.2	16.3
Butter, etc.	—	—	—	6.2	11.3	11.8	14.2	15.4	17.2	16.7
Meat, etc.	—	—	—	4.0	4.8	11.3	20.7	23.1	27.4	28.8
Rice, vegetables, fruit	—	—	—	7.5	7.5	7.4	9.1	9.0	13.4	16.8
Vegetable oils	—	—	—	5.7	3.4	1.5	1.1	2.5	1.8	1.1
Grain and milled products	—	—	—	35.7	37.4	39.5	32.6	30.6	19.6	16.5
Other foodstuffs	—	—	—	0.5	1.0	1.5	2.0	2.0	4.4	3.8

indeed, first made possible on a large scale, by numerous technical improvements—the gradual development of steamships, and of the technique of refrigeration. The real reason for the great increase in meat imports was the improved standard of living of large sections of the population, which was a result of rising real wages. According to Layton's[1] calculations the real wages [of those fully employed]

[1] W. T. Layton: *An Introduction to the Study of Prices* (London, 1920), p. 184. [See also appendix E, Table 1, on pp. 273-4 of the 1938 edition of this work by Sir Walter T. Layton and Geoffrey Crowther.]

were between 70 and 80 per cent higher in 1900–1910 than they had been in 1850.

Britain's dependence upon imported foodstuffs—which was insignificant a hundred years ago—was, as this table shows, quite considerable by the 1930s. These imports include the necessities of life. We should, however, note in this connection that food imports (as we shall show later on) are to an increasing extent drawn from the Empire. Since 1932 the Empire's share in Britain's food imports has amounted to more than 40 per cent of her total food imports.[1]

The re-export of food was at one time considerable but has lost much of its former significance.[2] Originally it was mainly tropical and sub-tropical products which were re-exported. The most important items were coffee, tea, and alcoholic beverages, and—before 1914—rice as well. At present [1937–8] such exports also include fruit, maize, butter and tinned meat and fish. If we consider the structure of Britain's total food imports we find that the commodities we have just mentioned represent a higher proportion of the total than was the case with net imports. In the 1820s and 1830s almost 75 per cent of the total imports of foodstuffs was represented by 'luxury foodstuffs' such as tropical and sub-tropical products, sugar and alcoholic drinks, in comparison with only 16 to 18 per cent in the 1930s. The change in the structure of Britain's total net food imports (i.e. gross imports less re-exports) is therefore similar to that of the change in gross food imports.

(d) *Imports of Finished Manufactured Goods*

The relative increase in the quantity of finished goods imported dates from 1860.[3] Before that date manufactured goods had been only an insignificant part of Britain's total imports and had indeed been re-exported to an increasing extent.[4] Between 1820 and 1859 the net imports of finished goods—as a proportion of total imports—was 6 per cent. Between 1860 and 1892 the proportion varied between 10 and 15 per cent. In the following period it varied from 15 to 20 per cent, and after 1931 it fell again to 12 per cent. The most important were textiles and leather goods. Before 1860 imports of clocks,

---

[1] See Table 40 below, p.
[2] See Tables 5 and 10 of Appendix, also Diagram 9.
[3] See Diagram 6.
[4] Before 1842 re-exports of finished goods amounted to one-third (in 1842–50 a quarter on the average) of the imports of finished commodities. Subsequently the proportion of re-exports was substantially lower—nearly 12 per cent in 1861–70, about 15 per cent in 1909–13 and about 8 per cent in 1927–9.

watches and tobacco products were significant, as were imports of semi-manufactured products such as leather, dressed furs, rolled iron and zinc products. Certain chemicals—potash, saltpetre and boracic acid being the most important—were also imports of some significance.

Until the end of the nineteenth century it was mainly finished consumption goods that were imported.[1] After the 1890s, however, production goods—chemicals, machinery, iron and steel, and paper —gained in importance and this tendency continued after the first World War. By the 1930s such goods formed the main part of Britain's imports of finished manufactured goods.

TABLE 22

NET IMPORT OF FINISHED MANUFACTURED GOODS 1858–1933 (PERCENTAGE BY VALUE)

Commodity	1858–60	1868–70	1889–92	1900–02	1911–13	1927–29	1932–33
Textiles	48.1	63.8	45.2	37.8	33.9	29.1	19.5
Leather, Furs and Skins	12.2	7.6	12.7	11.4	11.3	10.7	10.0
Other Consumption Goods*	10.3	6.2	8.8	9.6	5.6	5.6	7.0
Total of Consumption Goods	70.6	77.6	66.7	58.8	50.8	45.4	36.5
Iron and Steel	4.3	2.6	5.2	7.0	7.7	9.3	5.9
Machinery	—	—	—	3.6	3.9	6.4	8.0
Motor Vehicles and Parts	—	—	—	0.6	2.4	2.1	0.7
Electrical engineering products	—	—	—	1.0	1.0	2.1	2.4
Chemicals	13.9	4.8	7.4	7.1	8.5	7.9	11.3
Paper Goods	0.6	2.1	3.3	4.6	5.5	7.3	12.0
Other Production Goods†	4.2	4.1	4.5	5.4	4.1	4.3	4.5
Total of Production Goods	23.0	13.6	20.4	29.3	33.1	39.4	44.8
Unclassified	6.4	8.8	12.9	11.9	13.1	15.2	18.7

* Watches, musical instruments, toys, books and other printed material, pictures, drawings, pottery and porcelain, goloshes, tobacco products, candles, perfumes, soaps, cutlery.
† Goods made from non-ferrous metals; glass and glass wares.

The effect of the change to Free Trade on imports of finished goods is also unmistakeable. Peel's tariff reform of 1842 reduced all import duties on finished goods, and 20 per cent *ad valorem* became the maximum import duty. In 1846 import duties were abolished on the most important classes of cotton, woollen and silk goods. Gladstone's reform of 1853 removed almost entirely all import duties on finished goods. Import duties were retained only on completely finished manufactured goods involving highly specialized

[1] See Table 22.

skill. Such goods, however, paid no more than 10 per cent *ad valorem*. In 1860 the Free Trade edifice was finally completed.

TABLE 23
NET IMPORTS OF FINISHED MANUFACTURED GOODS 1833–1933

Years	Millions of £	per cent*	Years	Millions of £	per cent*
1833–37	2.23	4.5	1870–74	31.43	13.4
1837–41	2.44	4.1	1875–79	40.49	14.3
1842–45	3.19	4.5	1880–89	46.98	14.0
1846–52	5.07	5.5	1890–99	76.16	16.7
1853–59	8.15	6.9	1900–13	108.14	18.7
1860–64	15.34	10.6	1925–31	132.10	19.1
1865–69	23.71	13.2	1932–33	90.81	12.0

* Share of total net imports.

The trend of net imports within the periods illustrated by Table 23 shows that the reductions in duty led to substantial increases in imports. This is particularly true after the complete establishment of Free Trade in 1860. In later years an impetus of this kind was lacking, yet there continued to be an increase in the imports of finished manufactured goods. The rate of increase in these imports was, however, slower than during the period of tariff reductions. The increasing industrialisation of the Continent and the U.S.A. influenced this development. These newly-industrialised regions competed more and more keenly with Britain [not only in their own protected markets but] in Britain's unprotected home market. It will be recalled that this led to violent newspaper articles and to vigorous political propaganda[1] in favour of a return to Protection. This propaganda did not however induce the Government to take any effective counter-measures.

2. Exports

(a) Classification according to Commodity-Groups

In considering British exports we have to differentiate between re-exports and exports of goods made at home. Before 1914 over 65 per cent of Britain's total exports (i.e. exports of both home-

---

[1] See R. J. S. Hoffman, *Great Britain and the German Trade Rivalry, 1875–1914* (Philadelphia 1933), and A. Banze, *Ein Beitrag zur Geschichte der deutsch-englischen Beziehungen 1897–1907*, Historische Studien, Vol. 274 (Berlin 1935). Banze's work contains many references to other sources of information on this subject. [See also B. H. Brown, *The Tariff Reform Movement in Great Britain, 1881–1895* (New York, 1943).]

produced and overseas goods) consisted of manufactured articles. No less than 75 per cent—and more—of Britain's home-produced exports were manufactured articles. The composition of Britain's

Diagram 10. Analysis of Exports in Commodity-Groups, 1814–1933*
(percentage of ' Volume')

(a) Home Products.

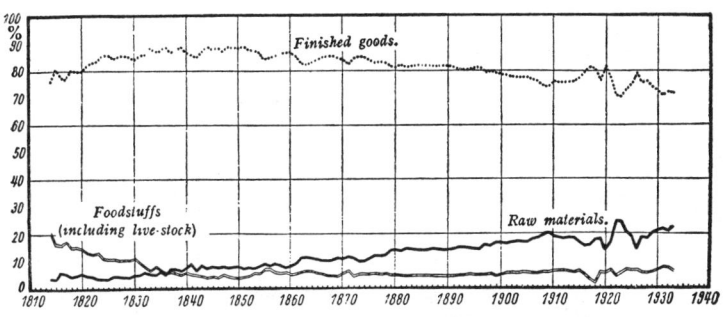

(b) Exports including re-exports

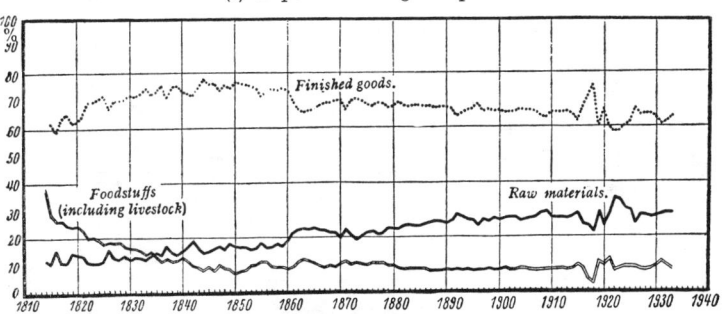

* From 1923 new area of trade rtatistics.

total exports by commodity-groups was similar to that of Germany. Britain's exports of raw materials, however, as opposed to foodstuffs, had a somewhat greater significance than Germany's exports of raw materials.[1] This structure of exports is typical for a manufacturing

[1] Germany's exports for 1911–13 (annual average) were : foodstuffs 11.3 per cent, raw materials 21.7 per cent, and manufactured goods 67 per cent. In 1927–29 the corresponding figures were 6 per cent, 21.8 per cent and 72.2 per cent and so are very similar to the composition of the British export trade. German exports include re-exports.

country, and it already existed at the beginning of the nineteenth century. At first, indeed, foodstuffs played a more important part [in exports],[1] but their significance rapidly declined. Characteristic

Diagram 11. Analysis of Exports in Commodity-Groups, 1814–1933*

(percentage of actual value)

(a) Home Products

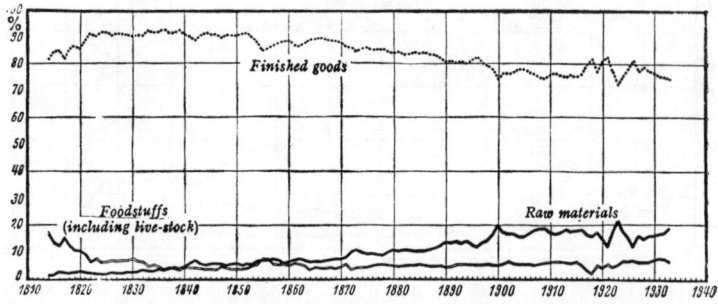

(b) Exports including re-exports

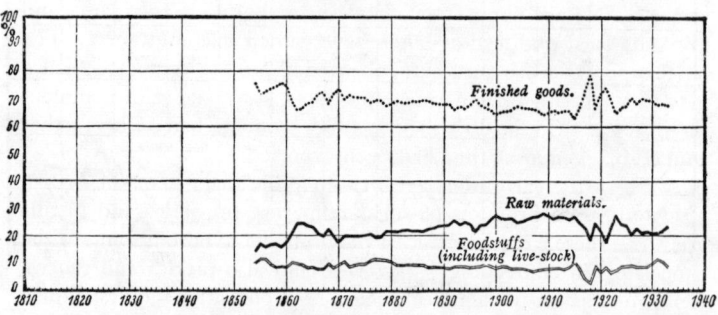

* From 1923 new area of trade statistics.

of this development was the relative growth of exports of raw materials which was a feature of the entire period under discussion and which actually continued after the first World War. The proportion of finished goods, on the other hand, declined slowly after about 1840.

[1] Mainly refined sugar, but also meat, butter, cheese, corn and meal.

TABLE 24
ANALYSIS OF EXPORTS IN COMMODITY-GROUPS 1814–1933 (PER CENT)

Commodity Group	Proportions by Volume						Proportions by Value					
	1814/17	1838/40	1854/57	1911/13	1927/29	1932/33	1814/17	1838/40	1854/57	1911/13	1927/29	1932/33
Home Products												
Foodstuffs*	17.5	5.4	6.4	6.3	5.8	6.6	14.8	4.0	6.6	6.3	6.5	7.1
Raw materials	4.5	7.2	8.5	18.3	19.0	21.5	2.1	4.5	7.2	17.6	15.4	17.9
Finished goods	78.0	87.4	85.1	75.4	75.2	71.9	83.1	91.5	86.2	76.1	78.1	75.0
Total Exports												
Foodstuffs*	29.6	11.5	10.1	7.9	7.9	8.8	—	—	10.6	7.9	8.7	9.4
Raw materials	11.9	14.0	16.6	26.6	27.4	28.5	—	—	16.0	26.5	21.7	22.5
Finished goods	58.5	74.5	73.3	65.5	64.7	62.7	—	—	73.4	65.6	69.6	68.1

* including livestock.

(b) *Exports of Foodstuffs and Raw Materials*

Britain's exports of foodstuffs and raw materials during the nineteenth century were largely a transit trade. Exports of these commodities consisted mainly of goods which had previously been imported.[1] Since about 1900, however, exports of foodstuffs and raw materials produced at home have gained in importance. The latter exports for the most part consisted of processed foods, and also —to an increasing extent—waste products, scrap and semi-manufactured goods. These British industrial products had to be further worked up even after they had been exported.

Even in the early nineteenth century the main items of British re-exports were products of sugar-refineries, breweries and distilleries. To these were later added the products of oil mills and of the chocolate and confectionery factories, and also pickles and sauces. Flour, too, gained in significance as a re-export after the first World War.

Fish exports were also of some importance and in our table they have been included in the group of non-processed foods.[2]

In 1937–8 British re-exports consisted mainly of tropical and sub-tropical goods, and also meat, fish, butter, cheese and fruit.

[1] See Tables 25 and 26.
[2] In this group we have, however, included tinned and preserved fish (mainly salt fish) which should, strictly speaking, not be regarded as products of the foodstuffs industry as normally defined.

Re-exports of vegetable oils, previously considerable, became quite unimportant after the first World War.

Britain's most important exports of home-produced raw materials were coal,[1] metals and textile fibres. These accounted for between 70 and 80 per cent of Great Britain's total exports of raw materials. Coal was of absolutely fundamental importance as a raw material

TABLE 25
ANALYSIS OF EXPORTED FOODSTUFFS BY IMPORTANT COMMODITY-GROUPS 1827–1933
(PERCENTAGE BY VALUE)

Commodity	1827/29	1857/59	1867/69	1882/84	1890/92	1902/04	1911/13	1927/29	1932/33
Home Products									
Products of the foodstuffs industry	49.3	59.5	60.4	63.6	66.0	58.8	56.6	62.7	62.5
Fish and tinned fish..	6.3	8.2	10.7	16.7	15.1	21.4	23.6	16.8	16.3
Other foodstuffs	44.4	32.3	28.9	19.7	18.9	19.8	19.8	20.5	21.2
Foreign and Colonial Products									
Tropical and semi-tropical goods* and all beverages	—	73.1	79.5	67.2	59.5	48.5	42.2	52.1	52.9
Grain, milled products, fruit, vegetables	—	10.8	5.5	13.3	12.5	11.7	15.6	15.8	21.0
Animal foodstuffs*	—	2.2	2.4	10.4	16.6	20.5	26.6	26.9	21.8
Crude and refined Vegetable Oils	—	12.7	9.8	7.0	7.7	11.6	10.3	0.9	0.4
Other foodstuffs	—	1.2	2.8	2.1	3.7	7.7	5.3	4.3	3.9

* Including rice and sugar.   † Meat, corned meat, fish and tinned fish, butter, cheese and fats.

export. The metals exported were primarily tin, pig-iron and copper, the principal textile raw materials were wool, wool-clippings and wool-combings—and also raw and processed cotton waste.

Products that were mainly of a semi-manufactured character played an important part in Britain's exports—though not in her re-exports. The semi-manufactured goods which were exported in considerable quantities included woollen and cotton yarn (and silk, too, up to the 1870s) and also raw hides, pelts and rubber. The metals consisted chiefly of tin and copper. Sulphate of ammonia was the principal fertilizer exported. At one time there was a considerable re-export of chemical raw materials and drugs which included natural dyes, indigo, cochineal and madder as well as Peruvian bark.

(c) *Exports of Finished Manufactured Goods*

The products of the textile, metal and engineering industries were the most important home-produced manufactured goods to be

[1] Brown coal [lignite] is not included.

exported. In the past hundred years, the most important change has been that other commodities gradually gained a growing importance alongside these groups. Leather goods, furs, skins, chemicals, pottery and porcelain as well as non-ferrous metal goods were represented in Britain's list of exports even in the early days. To these goods were later added the products of the newer industries, the most important being electrical engineering, the manufacture of motor vehicles, and paper-making. These exports showed a very considerable increase, particularly after the first World War.

TABLE 26

CHANGES IN EXPORTS OF RAW MATERIALS CLASSIFIED BY COMMODITIES 1827–1933
(Percentage proportions by value)

Commodity	1827/29	1840/42	1857/59	1867/69	1882/84	1890/92	1902/04	1911/13	1927/29	1932/33
Home Products										
Coal, coke, etc.	17.3	22.2	38.3	40.8	40.3	52.5	56.3	52.2	43.5	52.1
Ores and scrap	Nil	0.2	1.4	2.7	1.5	1.1	1.1	0.7	1.8	0.6
Metals	64.6	52.6	31.9	28.7	23.8	18.9	12.7	12.7	13.4	11.3
Cement, clay	—	0.2	2.5	3.3	4.1	4.0	2.4	2.3	3.5	2.6
Wool, wool-clippings, wool-combings	6.3	15.6	12.2	7.2	6.0	7.0	9.5	9.1	13.5	11.6
Cotton waste	—	—	—	—	—	—	—	1.7	1.4	0.9
Hides and skins	—	—	3.4	3.4	3.2	1.9	2.8	2.1	2.4	0.8
Manures	—	—	0.6	1.9	8.2	6.1	5.9	6.4	4.3	4.0
Petroleum, refined	—	—	—	—	—	—	—	1.9	3.3	3.7
Bran, oil-cakes and other fodders	—	—	—	—	—	—	1.3	2.9	2.8	1.8
Other raw materials	10.8	9.2	9.7	12.0	12.9	8.9	8.0	8.0	10.1	10.6
Foreign and Colonial Products										
Textile raw materials	—	—	53.5	68.7	58.4	58.7	47.9	39.5	46.5	62.5
Hides, skins and furs (raw)	—	—	8.1	4.6	6.4	7.5	9.8	10.7	19.9	25.0
Rubber	—	—	0.6	0.9	3.6	4.4	10.6	20.8	15.7	4.2
Metals	—	—	3.8	5.0	6.2	7.4	9.9	11.6	4.7	3.5
Chemical raw materials and drugs	—	—	14.4	8.7	7.4	3.5	1.1	1.2	0.5	0.5
Other raw materials	—	—	19.6	12.1	18.0	18.5	20.7	16.2	12.7	14.2

Exports of finished goods consisted mainly of consumption-goods. That is still true to-day [1937–8], except that textile exports —once of fundamental importance—have declined sharply, both absolutely and relatively, since the war of 1914–18. In Table 27 an attempt has been made to classify British exports as consumption and capital goods. Such a classification can only be approximate as precise division of exports on this basis is hardly possible. The classi-

TABLE 27

CHANGES IN EXPORTS OF FINISHED MANUFACTURED GOODS CLASSIFIED BY COMMODITIES 1827–1933

(Percentage proportions by value)

Commodity	1827/29	1840/42	1857/59	1867/69	1882/84	1890/92	1902/04	1911/13	1927/29	1932/33
Home Products										
Textiles	78.2	78.7	67.9	71.6	61.2	58.7	53.7	51.2	44.4	39.7
Leather, furs and skins	1.1	0.9	2.0	1.5	2.4	2.4	2.3	2.5	2.6	2.1
Pottery and porcelain	1.4	1.3	1.3	1.1	1.2	1.2	1.0	1.0	1.1	1.1
Books, pictures, prints	0.3	0.3	0.6	0.6	1.0	1.1	1.3	·1.3	1.4	1.7
Drugs, perfumes, soaps, candles, etc.	0.8	0.8	0.6	0.8	1.2	1.3	1.5	1.6	1.8	2.6
Bedsteads, hardware, cutlery	4.2	3.2	3.4	2.1	1.8	1.3	0.9	1.1	0.7	0.6
Tobacco products	Nil	Nil	Nil	Nil	Nil	Nil	0.3	0.7	1.6	1.5
Other consumption goods*	1.5	1.5	1.2	1.3	1.6	1.3	2.3	2.4	2.8	2.7
Consumption goods	87.5	86.7	77.0	79.0	70.4	67.3	63.3	61.8	56.4	52.0
Ironmongery (including bicycles;	4.3	6.1	11.8	10.5	12.2	12.6	12.7	12.5	12.2	11.2
Machinery (including electric)	0.7	1.3	3.5	2.4	5.8	6.9	8.9	8.8	9.9	10.5
Locomotives, railway carriages	—	—	0.2	0.8	1.1	1.7	1.9	1.4	1.7	0.6
Ships' hulls	—	—	—	—	—	—	1.3	1.2	1.0	0.6
Motor vehicles, chassis, rubber tyres	—	—	—	—	—	—	0.1	0.8	2.5	3.7
Electrical engineering products	—	—	0.4	0.3	0.8	0.8	1.0	1.1	2.2	2.3
Goods made of non-ferrous metals	1.1	1.5	2.1	1.8	1.6	1.3	1.3	1.3	1.2	1.3
Chemicals	0.4	1.0	2.0	2.0	3.2	4.1	4.0	3.0	2.9	4.2
Paper and paper goods, office materials	0.6	0.6	0.9	0.7	1.2	1.3	1.4	1.4	2.0	2.7
Other capital goods ‡	1.6	0.8	0.9	1.1	1.4	1.5	1.4	2.2	1.9	1.9
Capital goods	8.7	11.3	21.8	19.6	27.3	30.2	34.0	33.7	37.5	39.0
Unclassified goods	3.8	2.0	1.2	1.4	2.3	2.5	2.7	4.5	6.1	9.0
Foreign and Colonial Products										
Textiles	—	—	54.4	33.6	21.6	31.8	45.7	44.2	38.3	28.9
Leather and leather goods	—	—	3.2	2.4	15.8	18.0	11.8	12.0	11.3	12.3
Iron wares and machinery	—	—	4.1	11.8	17.5	9.5	8.8	8.0	7.6	10.0
Other manufactured goods	—	—	38.3	52.2	45.1	40.7	33.7	35.8	41.8	48.8

* Jewellery, watches, musical instruments, furniture, toys, sports goods, goloshes, matches, cleaning materials—and also goods purchased by foreign governments, such as warships, arms and munitions.

‡ Instruments and apparatus, glass and glass wares, rubber goods, timber products (excluding furniture), driving belts.

fication adopted, however, may be sufficiently accurate to indicate certain very definite tendencies in the development of Britain's export trade. The share of capital goods [in Britain's total exports of finished goods] grew until about the end of the nineteenth century and again after the first World War. Consumption-goods, on the other hand, which amounted to nearly 90 per cent of exports in the 1820s constituted only 50 per cent to 60 per cent in the 1930s.

British export-industries which have expanded rapidly in recent decades are mainly the manufacture of motor-vehicles (and rubber tyres), electrical engineering (including the production of electrical machinery) and also paper-making. At the beginning of the twentieth century these goods accounted for only 2.1 per cent of Britain's exports of finished goods, and immediately before the outbreak of the first World War for only 3.4 per cent. The percentage rose to an annual average of 7.5 in 1927–29, and to 9.4 during the world economic depression of 1932–33. Attention has already been drawn to the relative increase of these goods in British exports (owing to ever-increasing demands in the twentieth century) and to the consequent increase in imports of raw materials necessary for manufacturing such goods.

(*d*) *Exports of Finished Manufactured Goods and Industrial Production*

The statistical relationship between industrial production and exports can be shown most clearly by using an index (*Exportquotenindex*) which shows the proportion of finished manufactured goods exported as a proportion of total industrial production.[1] This calculation can be made on the basis of the indices available for industrial production and for exports of manufactured goods produced at home. However these two indices cannot be compared without adjustments because the index of production includes what is produced by the foodstuffs and raw materials industries. The adjustment we have made has been to add to the volumes of exports of manufactured goods (base-year 1913) the appropriate volumes for processed foods, coal, coke, etc., and also metals. In this way we have obtained an index for 'total volumes' which can, without serious danger of error, be compared with the index of production. [In the years 1814–26 no adjustment of a production index to an index of 'total volumes' has been required]. Here we have simply compared the index of production with the index of exports of *all* native products—since at that time the index of exports of all native

[1] [*Exportquoten* has been translated as 'export proportions.']

products was made up, to an overwhelming extent, of the goods under consideration.

The result of this calculation is given in Diagram 12.[1] From this diagram it will be seen that—with 1913 as the base-year—between 1814 and 1840 the ' export proportion '—as compared with 1913— was about half but rose in the 1840s and 1850s to about 80 per cent of

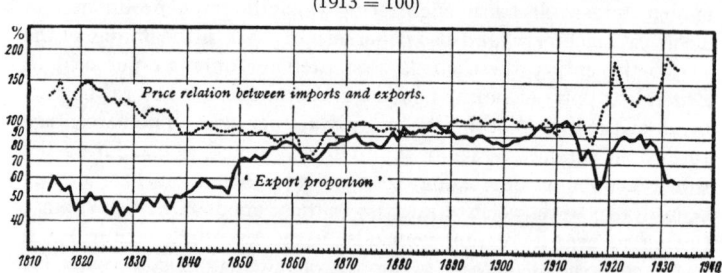

Diagram 12. Indexes of (a) Price Relation between finished goods and raw materials, and (b) ' Export proportions ' of British industry, 1814-1933
(1913 = 100)

Index of ' Export Proportion ': 1814–1826 Index of the export of home products.
                                            Index of industrial production.
                                 1827–1933 Index of the export of finished goods, metals, coal and processed foodstuffs.
                                            Index of industrial production.

Index showing price relation
between imports and exports: 1814–1853 Export-price-index of finished goods.
                                        Price index of total imports.
                             1854–1933 Export-price-index of finished goods.
                                        Import-price-index of raw materials.

what it became in 1913. Soon after 1870 it was 90 per cent and by the middle of the 1880s it reached the level not regained until 1913. Between about 1887 and 1900 there was a decline to 83 per cent of the figure for 1913, but this was made up again in the fourteen years before the outbreak of the first World War. During that war the ' export proportion ' fell sharply to 56 per cent in 1918 but subsequently increased again very quickly, though not quite to the level of 1913. During the world economic depression of 1930–33 the ' export proportion ' was about 60 per cent of the level of 1913, which was only a little higher than the figure for the forties of the previous century.[2]

[1] See also Appendix, Table 17.
[2] For the calculation of the absolute ' export proportions ' see A. W. Flux, ' The national income ' (*Journal of the Royal Statistical Society*, vol. 92 (1929), p. 1 et seq). He estimates the ' export proportion ' for the production census years 1907 and 1924 at 30.5 and 27 per cent respectively. See also in this connection Leak's

We propose to consider the development of the 'export proportion' in detail and to note how it changes in periods of good and bad trade as we have already done for Britain's total trade (indicated in Table 9). If we examine the 20 years as years of transition from prosperity to depression we find that the 'export proportion' was, on ten of those occasions, higher in the period of depression than it had been in the immediately preceding period of prosperity. Thus, on half the occasions examined, British industry (despite the unsatisfactory nature of the home market) was able to export abroad an increased proportion of its total production. In this calculation we have also included certain periods in which external events, such as the American Civil War (Cotton Famine, 1861-3) and the first World War, inevitably tended to reduce the 'export proportion'. If we exclude these exceptional occasions, there remain only fifteen periods of depression from 1827. In nine of these periods there was a higher 'export-proportion' than there had been in the immediately preceding years of prosperity. The results of the calculations so far discussed indicate therefore that the phenomenon of so-called 'crisis exports' appears to be capable of statistical proof.

criticisms in the *Journal of the Royal Statistical Society*, vol. 97 (1934), p. 545. For a detailed calculation of 'export proportions' see Daniels and Campion: *The relative importance of British export trade (London and Cambridge Economic Service*, Special Memorandum, London, 1935, no. 41). Daniels and Campion calculated not only 'export proportions' showing the relationship between total exports and national production, but also between the 'net output content', of exports and the net production (see particularly pp. 13 and 17). Only their first calculation—total exports and national production—could be compared with the 'export proportions index' that we have calculated. In the following tables we have taken the 'export proportions' of Daniels and Campion and have re-calculated them to check our own 'export proportions index' in order to see if there were agreement between our direct calculation and their indirect calculation. The agreement between the two was most satisfactory. Daniels and Campion give the following 'net production-export proportions': 1913 about 27 per cent; 1924-25, 21-24 per cent; 1930-31, 16.5-20 per cent; 1934, 13.5-16.5 per cent.

Year	Index of 'Export Proportion'	Flux 1907= 30.5 per cent	Daniels and Campion† 1924-25= 27.5-29.5 per cent	1930-31= 20.5-22.5 per cent
1907	100.2	30.5	31.1-33.4	30.7-33.7
1913	100.0	30.6	31.1-33.3	30.6-33.6
1924	88.2	26.8*	27.4-29.4	27.0-29.7
1924-25	88.5	26.9	27.5-29.5	27.1-29.8
1930-31	66.9	20.4	20.8-22.3	20.5-22.5

* According to Flux 1924: 27 per cent.
† Provisional estimate for 1934: 17.5-19.5 per cent.

The decline in the 'export-proportion' in the 1890s was particularly striking. The decline was a considerable one and was of relatively long duration. The [index of the] 'export proportion' (1913 = 100) sank from 97 in 1884–1890 to 89 in 1891–4 and to 87 in 1895–1900. It was only in 1905–7 that it recovered to 95. This development was clearly associated with changes in the terms of trade. To illustrate this we have included the terms of trade in Diagram 12

TABLE 28

CHANGES IN 'EXPORT PROPORTION' OF THE CONSUMPTION-GOODS INDUSTRY
1815–1933
(1913 = 100)

Period	Years of Prosperity	Years of Depression	Period	Years of Prosperity	Years of Depression
1815	61		1867–68		83
1816–17		53	1869–73	88	
1818	53		1874–79		85
1819–20		45	1880–83	93	
1821–25	49		1884–86		97
1826		43	1887–90	97	
1827–28	45		1891–94		89
1829		45	1895–1900	87	
1830–31	44		1901–04		87
1832		49	1905–07	95	
1833–36	49		1908		96
1837–42		51	1909–13	101	
1843–46	56		1914–18		74
1847–48		53	1919–20	69	
1849–54	71		1921		82
1855		74	1922–24	90	
1856–57	80		1925–26		91
1858		84	1927–29	85	
1859–60	85		1930–31		67
1861–63		76	1932–33	60	
1864–66	74				

in addition to the 'export proportion'. The terms of trade were calculated by dividing the price-index of exported finished goods by that of imported raw materials. For the period before 1854 we have—in the absence of statistics of real values for imported raw materials—used the index of total imports in place of an index of imports of raw materials. The indices were compiled from the actual values already calculated and shown in Table 3 of the appendix.[1]

There is a striking correlation between the two curves which is particularly marked after the 1870s when the rate of increase of

[1] See Appendix, Table 17.

Britain's foreign trade declined. The terms of trade and the index of 'export proportion' show closely parallel tendencies. The striking decline of the 'export proportion' between 1890 and 1905—to which we have already drawn attention—coincided with a favourable change in the terms of trade. As the terms of trade turned in Britain's favour again after the first World War there was once more a parallel drop in the 'export proportion'. When we reflect upon the importance of the effect of changes in the terms of trade upon the amount of British exports of industrial products over a long period we are inclined—when considering the crisis in Britain's overseas trade in the 1930s—to attribute to this factor a greater significance than has usually been accorded to it.

III. THE GEOGRAPHICAL DISTRIBUTION OF BRITISH OVERSEAS TRADE

1. *Distribution of British Overseas Trade by Continents*

If we consider the extent of British overseas trade from the geographical standpoint in broad outline it is clear that during the whole period of more than 200 years under review there has been a considerable predominance of the trade with Europe and America.

It is true that as early as the eighteenth century the other continents had become of some importance but even in the 1930s two-thirds of British overseas trade was with Europe and America. As between these two continents, however, significant changes have occurred. In the eighteenth century a characteristic feature of Britain's overseas trade was its pronounced tendency to move away from Europe. This was even more true of imports than of exports. On the other hand America's share in Britain's overseas trade was increasing rapidly so that the tendency we have noted might be called the 'Americanisation' of British overseas trade.

The changes occurring during the first half of the nineteenth century could not be clearly identified owing to the lack of uniformity in recording the statistics. In 1854 imports could be classified geographically both by official and real values.[1] The proportion of overseas trade falling to various areas—calculated on official values for 1854—differ little from the proportion of 1801–2. No comparison is possible for exports—even by official values—since a geographical distribution is available only for re-exports. In the second half of the

[1] See Table 29.

TABLE 29

PERCENTAGE OF BRITISH OVERSEAS TRADE WITH EUROPE AND AMERICA 1698–1929

	England and Wales*	Great Brit'n.*	Great Britain and Ireland †					Great Britain and Northern Ireland†
	1698–1701	1801–02	1854‡	1854	1857–61	1909–13	1927–29	1927–29
Imports								
Europe	64.8	32.7	31.4	42.3	37.6	40.8	37.0	39.4
America	19.6	45.4	42.1	36.6	35.4	32.3	34.1	32.5
Total ..	84.4	78.1	73.5	78.9	73.0	73.1	71.1	71.9
Exports ‖								
Europe	80.8	55.2	—	39.4	45.1	38.5	35.6	39.1
America	11.9	33.5	—	35.6	25.9	24.2	23.1	21.8
Total ..	92.7	88.7	—	75.0	71.0	63.3	58.7	60.9

* Official values. † Actual values.
‡ The share of Europe and America in overseas trade could not be calculated by official values.
‖ Including re-exports.

TABLE 30

OVERSEAS TRADE OF UNITED KINGDOM WITH AFRICA, ASIA AND AUSTRALIA
1854–1929
(percentage by value)

	1854–57	1909–13	1927–29	
			Great Britain and Ireland	Great Britain and Northern Ireland
Imports				
Africa	6.8	6.4	7.4	7.2
Asia	17.0	12.4	12.7	12.4
Australia	3.1	8.1	8.7	8.4
Exports				
Africa	4.5	10.1	11.8	11.3
Asia	14.0	22.3	23.2	22.1
Australia	9.3	8.8	11.3	10.8
Exports including Re-exports				
Africa	4.2	8.8	10.7	10.2
Asia	12.1	18.8	20.3	19.3
Australia	8.8	7.9	10.1	9.2

nineteenth century Europe's share of Britain's imports fell only slightly while America's share showed a more pronounced fall. On the other hand the capacity of both continents to absorb Britain's exports showed a marked decline. This was particularly true of America—and within the American continent the drop was most significant in the United States. The joint share of Europe and America in Britain's exports dropped from 71 per cent of Britain's total exports in 1860 to 63 per cent before the first World War and to 59 per cent in 1927–29 (annual average).

On the other hand the other continents become steadily more important as purchasers of British exports. Since the middle of the previous century Africa's share has doubled although—like that of Australia—it has remained small [one tenth of the total (1927–29)]. Asia's share has grown from an eighth (1854–7) to nearly one-fifth of Britain's total exports (1927–29).

2. *British Overseas Trade with Industrial and Agrarian Regions*

It is of greater economic significance if we analyse the territories to which Britain has exported goods and from which she has imported goods on an economic [rather than on a geographical] basis—that is to say by industrial and agrarian regions [rather than by continents].

We include the following countries in the industrial group; Germany, the Netherlands, Belgium, Luxembourg, Switzerland, and Austria-Hungary (or after 1918 the Succession States).[1] The area covered by these countries—from the point of view of their commercial statistics[2]—we shall call 'Central Europe'. This area, added to France and Italy, we shall call 'Industrial Europe'. The U.S.A. is also regarded as an industrial state.[3]

These territories developed as industrial countries only after the middle of the last century. In considering British commercial relations with these territories, we are examining one aspect of the problem of the way in which the progressive industrialisation of agricultural countries affects their trade with other countries which are already centres of manufacture. Special factors have sometimes operated which do not permit us to generalise unduly from statistical calculations.

[1] By our criterion Hungary has not been an industrial country since 1919. It has only been included to improve the comparison.
[2] See above p. 35 ff., particularly Table 7.
[3] Japan, whose industrial exports became important only after the first World War, has been excluded, since we are concerned with such a long period of time. If Japan were included, the situation as a whole would be little changed.

The example, which we are considering is, however, exceptional from one important point of view. Britain, the leading industrial power, admitted the manufactured goods of her rising competitors duty-free, whilst these competitors themselves erected more or less

TABLE 31

OVERSEAS TRADE OF UNITED KINGDOM WITH INDUSTRIAL AND AGRICULTURAL COUNTRIES
1827–1929
(Percentage by value)

Countries	1827/30	1837/40	1854/57	1867/69	1877/79	1887/89	1801/01	1909/13	1927/29 Great Britain and Ireland	1927/29 Great Britain and Northern Ireland
Imports										
Central Europe	—	—	15.3	14.1	15.6	17.9	17.1	17.9	14.6	15.3
Industrial Europe	—	—	23.2	27.1	27.7	29.0	28.3	25.3	21.0	21.8
United States	—	—	34.5	14.6	21.6	20.0	17.1	29.7	16.1	16.9
All industrial countries	—	—	57.7	41.7	49.3	49.0	45.4	55.0	37.1	38.7
Agricultural countries	—	—	42.3	58.3	50.7	51.0	54.6	45.0	62.9	61.3
Export of home products										
Central Europe	17.4	19.5	17.4	20.0	17.9	14.1	17.2	15.6	12.8	13.5
Industrial Europe	25.2	29.1	25.2	29.1	28.3	23.2	26.1	23.9	18.5	19.5
United States	16.0	13.4	18.5	12.4	8.8	12.5	6.6	6.5	6.4	6.5
All industrial countries	41.2	42.5	43.7	41.5	37.1	35.7	32.7	30.4	24.9	26.0
Agricultural countries	58.8	57.5	56.3	38.5	62.9	64.3	67.3	69.6	75.1	7.40
Exports including re-exports										
Central Europe	—	—	22.0	24.9	23.1	19.6	20.1	18.3	16.0	17.0
Industrial Europe	—	—	32.1	37.2	36.3	29.6	29.5	27.3	23.4	24.4
United States	—	—	15.9	10.8	8.4	14.0	10.4	10.7	7.8	8.4
All industrial countries	—	—	48.0	48.6	44.7	43.6	39.9	38.0	21.3	32.8
Agricultural countries	—	—	52.0	51.4	55.3	56.4	60.1	62.0	68.8	67.2

high tariff barriers against British imports. This was particularly true of the United States whose policy of high protective tariffs was only occasionally and slightly modified. But the industrial states of the Continent also erected tariff barriers which were, at any rate to some extent, an essential preliminary condition for the success of their policies of industrialisation.[1]

[1] We have mentioned here only one obvious factor which directly influences the situation. The preliminary conditions for industrialisation were peculiarly favourable in the territories of 'Industrial Europe'. Ethnical, climatic, demographic, cultural and historical factors were all conducive to industrialisation. This no longer applies to the territories which are still regarded as capable of industrialisation to-day [1937–8]. Hence the problem of the influence of industrialisation of agrarian countries upon their commercial relations with manufacturing countries engaged in the export trade is possibly not so important to-day as it was in the example discussed above. [For a more recent study of this problem, see *Industrialisation and Foreign Trade* (League of Nations Publications, II, Economic and Financial, 1945, II A 10), 167 pp. The preface states that this volume is 'mainly the work of Mr. Folke Hilgerdt'.]

If we examine long-term trends in British overseas trade—regarded in the light of history—we see that her commerce with territories that were becoming industrialised was characterised, to a striking extent, by a relative decline in her exports to those countries.[1] About 1870 all the industrial territories absorbed 41 per cent of Britain's exports of home products, this figure being made up as follows: Central Europe 20 per cent, France and Italy together 9 per cent, and the U.S.A. 12 per cent. Just before the first World War these proportions were: Central Europe barely 16 per cent, France and Italy 8 per cent, the U.S.A. 6.5 per cent—the total, therefore, then being only 30 per cent. As far as imports are concerned no similar general trend can be observed. The proportions of Britain's imports provided by Central and Industrial Europe rose until 1890. After that, however, the proportion of British imports from France and Italy showed a relative decline, whilst that from Central Europe remained about the same. The share of Britain's imports provided by the United States was subject to very considerable variations over the whole period. If we consider the entire period between 1854 and 1913 we see that the share of all the industrial countries taken together in the provision of Britain's imports changed little between 1854–7 (57.7 per cent) and 1909–13 (55 per cent). The sharp drop in the 1860s (1867–9 = 41.7 per cent) should, however, be noted. During and immediately after the first World War the long-standing commercial links between Britain and the industrial countries were appreciably weakened—with regard to both exports and imports.

These results are confirmed if we compare the development of the volume of British exports to industrial regions with that agrarian regions. Such a comparison is indeed only a somewhat superficial one since practical difficulties prevent an accurate calculation of export volumes classified by countries. A rough calculation of such volumes has been attempted in the following manner. We have divided British exports to industrial countries into foodstuffs, raw materials and finished goods.[2] Each of these three groups was reduced by the same price-index (base-year 1913) as has been obtained for Britain's total trade in these groups of commodities. The imports of foodstuffs from industrial countries, for example, were reduced by the price-index for all British imports of foodstuffs. The separate volumes obtained for each group of goods in this way, when added together

[1] See Table 31.
[2] See also Tables 33 [imports] and 34 [exports].

TABLE 32
OVERSEAS TRADE OF UNITED KINGDOM WITH INDUSTRIAL AND AGRARIAN COUNTRIES 1854–1929 (VOLUMES)

Area	in £1,000,000's at base-year 1913						Index Number			
	1854–57	1877–79	1898–1901	1909–13	1927–29*		for 1898–1901 when 1854–57 =100	for 1909–13 when 1898–1901 =100	for 1909–13 when 1854–57 =100	for 1927–29* when 1909–13 =100
Imports										
Industrial Europe	30.6	91.8	166.6	180.4	190.4		544	108	590	106
United States	26.3	80.3	163.8	131.3	148.5		623	80	499	113
Total for industrial countries	56.9	172.1	330.4	311.7	338.9		581	94	548	19
Total for agrarian countries	83.2	176.6	290.0	407.3	558.6		349	140	490	137
Total Imports	140.1	349.7	620.4	719.0	897.5		443	116	513	125
Export of Home Products										
Industrial Europe	29.2	64.5	86.5	116.6	92.5		296	135	399	79
United States	21.4	20.1	22.5	31.4	31.2		195	140	147	99
Total for industrial countries	50.6	84.6	109.0	148.0	123.7		215	136	292	84
Total for agrarian countries	65.6	133.8	223.1	334.8	331.4		340	150	510	99
Total exports of home products	116.2	218.4	332.1	482.8	455.1		286	145	415	94
Exports including Re-exports										
Industrial Europe	43.9	100.5	126.4	161.6	144.4		288	128	368	89
United States	22.4	24.1	47.0	62.7	38.0		210	133	280	77
Total for industrial countries	66.3	124.6	173.4	224.3	192.4		262	129	338	86
Total for agrarian countries	71.9	150.8	251.6	365.2	356.6		350	145	508	98
Total exports	138.2	275.4	425.0	589.5	549.0		308	139	427	93

* Excluding Eire.

gave the approximate total volume for each period under consideration. Export volumes for agrarian countries were calculated by deducting Britain's trade with industrial regions from the total overseas trade.[1]

TABLE 33

BRITAIN'S IMPORTS FROM INDUSTRIAL COUNTRIES, IN COMMODITY GROUPS 1854-1929

Commodity group	in £1,000,000s					Per cent				
	1854/57	1877/79	1898/01	1909/13	1854/29*	1854/57	1877/79	1898/01	1909/13	1927/29*
Industrial Europe										
Foodstuffs	13.5	40.2	42.0	44.0	56.3	35.0	38.7	29.7	24.9	22.1
Raw materials	11.2	14.0	13.0	18.7	34.4	29.4	13.4	9.2	10.6	13.5
Finished manufactured goods	8.5	42.4	71.9	98.9	163.8	22.4	40.8	50.9	55.9	64.4
Unclassified	4.8	7.4	14.6	15.3	—	12.6	7.1	10.2	8.6	—
Total	38.0	104.0	141.5	176.9	254.5	100	100	100	100	100
United States										
Foodstuffs	7.5	44.3	60.8	32.9	54.3	24.0	51.3	46.2	25.9	27.9
Raw materials	21.1	32.1	51.5	70.8	100.2	67.4	37.2	39.2	55.7	51.4
Finished manufactured goods	0.4	2.9	14.9	17.0	40.4	1.3	3.4	11.3	13.4	20.7
Unclassified	2.3	7.0	4.3	6.3	—	7.3	8.1	3.3	5.0	—
Total	31.3	86.3	131.5	127.0	194.9	100	100	100	100	100
All Industrial Countries										
Finished manufactured goods	8.9	45.3	86.8	115.9	204.2	12.8	23.8	31.8	38.1	45.4
All Agrarian Countries										
Finished manufactured goods	2.4	7.3	13.2	20.6	50.0	2.5	3.9	5.8	5.2	6.6
Total Imports	164.1	375.4	500.2	699.3	1211.6	—	—	—	—	—

* Excluding Eire.

If we examine the results of these calculations we see once more the characteristic developments already noted. From the middle of the nineteenth century to the outbreak of the first World War the exports of the United Kingdom to agrarian countries increased five-fold but her exports to industrial countries showed hardly a three-fold increase. The same trends continued after the first World War. On the other hand up to 1914—particularly in the second half of the nineteenth century—British imports from indus-

[1] See Table 32.

trial regions increased with considerably greater rapidity than imports from agrarian countries. Only in the present century has

TABLE 34

EXPORTS OF HOME PRODUCTS TO INDUSTRIAL COUNTRIES BY COMMODITY GROUPS, 1827-1929

Commodity Group	In £1,000,000's						Per cent					
	1827/30	1854/57	1877/79	1898/1901	1909/13	1927/29*	1827/30	1854/57	1877/79	1898/1901	1909/13	1927/29*
Industrial Europe												
Foodstuffs	1.0	1.6	2.8	3.0	5.3	6.9	10.6	5.8	5.1	4.2	4.9	5.2
Raw materials	0.2	3.9	7.3	19.3	27.8	46.3	2.3	14.2	13.3	27.7	25.5	34.7
Finished manufactured goods	7.8	20.3	41.2	42.4	65.8	80.3	83.4	74.7	74.8	60.9	60.5	60.1
Unclassified	0.3	1.3	3.7	4.9	10.0	—	3.7	5.3	6.8	7.2	9.1	—
Total	9.3	27.1	55.0	69.6	108.9	133.5	100	100	100	100	100	100
United States												
Foodstuffs		0.3	0.1	0.7	2.2	1.9	—	1.5	0.6	3.9	7.5	4.1
Raw materials		1.1	2.1	2.2	5.5	12.1	—	5.5	12.3	12.4	18.6	26.4
Finished manufactured goods	5.5	17.9	14.2	14.1	20.0	31.9	93.2	89.9	83.0	79.2	69.5	—
Unclassified	0.4	0.6	0.7	0.8	1.9	—	6.8	5.1	4.1	4.5	6.4	—
Total	5.9	19.9	17.1	17.8	29.6	45.9	100	100	100	100	100	100
All Industrial Countries												
Finished manufactured goods	13.3	38.2	55.4	56.5	85.8	112.2	86.9	81.1	76.9	64.6	61.9	62.5
Raw materials and foodstuffs*	1.9	8.8	16.7	30.9	52.7	67.2	13.1	18.9	23.1	35.4	38.1	37.5
Total							100	100	100	100	100	100
All Agrarian Countries												
Finished manufactured goods	20.3	54.6	111.3	149.7	259.8	450.8	93.3	90.0	91.0	83.2	82.1	83.3
Total Exports	37.0	107.7	194.4	267.3	455.0	720.7						

* Excluding Eire.
† The unclassified items are composed almost exclusively of goods in these categories.

there been a relative loosening of economic ties in imports—a tendency already noted in exports.

Obviously this development was closely associated with the increasing industrialisation of the countries under consideration.

This may be seen by examining the change in the composition of Britain's overseas trade with the industrial regions of the world.[1]

In the 1850s British imports from the industrial regions consisted of between 85 and 90 per cent foodstuffs and raw materials and only 10 or 15 per cent manufactured goods. The proportion of manufactures [imported from industrial regions] had however already increased to about 25 per cent by 1880. Then it rose to about 38 per cent at the outbreak of the first World War and actually amounted to 45 per cent in 1927-9. In this connection it should be noted that by far the greater part of Britain's imports from the United States consist of foodstuffs and raw materials. If we examine only the development of Britain's imports from 'Industrial Europe' we shall see that the proportion of manufactured goods rose from less than a quarter in the middle of the nineteenth century to 56 per cent before the first World War and to almost two-thirds in 1927-29 (annual average).

Moreover while Britain's imports of finished manufactured goods from industrial regions have increased considerably there has been a corresponding relative fall in the export of British manufactured goods to those territories. Between the 1850s and the outbreak of the first World War the proportion of Britain's total exports absorbed by the industrial regions dropped from 81 to 62 per cent. At the same time the proportion of Britain's exports of raw materials absorbed by the industrial regions rose considerably. Thus Britain's coal played the most important rôle in her trade with 'Industrial Europe' while her wool and metals (particularly tin) played a similar part in her trade with the United States.

Our calculations have shown that the long-term trend in the volume of British overseas trade with countries in process of industrialisation was indeed one of considerable expansion—though by no means to anything like the same extent as the increase of her trade with agrarian countries. There have moreover been striking changes in the composition of British overseas trade with the regions that we have mentioned as having gone through the process of industrialisation. British manufactures showed a considerable decline as a proportion of total exports. But, as a proportion of imports, manufactures increased considerably. The absolute increase in the value of Britain's commerce with the Continent suggests that the progressive industrialisation of this part of the world has been of advantage to Britain's overseas trade. This advantage has been due

[1] See Tables 33 and 34.

mainly to the very industrialisation we have discussed—an economic process which has above all enabled the agrarian regions of the Continent to develop their production of raw materials and foodstuffs and to increase considerably their capacity both to absorb British imports and to export commodities to Britain.

3. *British Trade with the Empire*

As early as the middle of the nineteenth century, nearly half of Britain's overseas commerce with predominantly agrarian regions was Empire trade.[1] The Empire's share of Britain's total trade[2] was 23 per cent for imports, 30 per cent for exports and 14 per cent for re-exports. Hence the Empire was already playing an important part as a buyer of British products. Even at an earlier period—throughout the first half of the nineteenth century—the Empire had absorbed between 25 and 30 per cent of Britain's exports.[3]

The Empire's share of Britain's overseas commerce changed little up to the outbreak of the first World War. In the last five years of peace before 1914 the Empire's share of Britain's imports amounted (on the average) to 25 per cent, and the figures for exports and re-exports were 35 per cent and 12 per cent respectively.

As diagram 13 shows, all that is of more than accidental significance in this connection is the increase by one-sixth of the Empire's share of total exports in comparison with the 1850s. On the other hand the curves representing proportions of imports and re-exports do not show any general trend, either upward or downward.

In the following twenty years (1914-34) there was a definite change. The proportion of exports to the Empire—with interruptions due to the first World War and the world economic depression—continued to increase and in 1936 amounted to 94 per cent [of exports to agrarian countries]. Thus in that year almost half of Britain's exports produced at home went to Empire territories. The Empire's share in supplying Britain's imports also expanded considerably. Before the first World War—apart from a short period in the early 1860s—25 per cent was the maximum proportion of Britain's imports drawn from the Empire. After 1913, however, the proportion of Britain's imports from the Empire was always over 25 per cent, even in years of war and depression. In 1936 the proportion of imports from the Empire reached a

---
[1] Up to the first World War 46-48 per cent of the total ; 1927-29—referring to the same area of trade statistics—49.7 per cent; 1933-35; 51.4 per cent.

[2] See Appendix, Table 20B and also Diagram 13.

[3] It should be remembered that no calculation of the Empire's share in Britain's imports and re-exports (by value) can be made before 1854.

level of 39.1 per cent.[1] This was the highest percentage attained in the whole period we have examined. The Empire's proportion of re-exports is small (about an eighth of Britain's total re-exports) and has scarcely changed over many years.

Thus in general the following changes have taken place. The Empire's share in the exports of the Mother Country has risen, albeit very slowly. The Empire's share in supplying Britain's imports and re-exports, has been substantially smaller [than her share of Britain's exports] and there has been no tendency towards an improvement in this respect. Britain's economic links with the Empire have moreover been drawing closer up to the end of the period under consideration. This trend can be discerned before the outbreak of the world economic depression but it became of real significance after 1931-2. When Britain embarked on her new economic and commercial policy [i.e. the return to Protection] and signed the Ottawa Agreements,[2] her trade with the Empire increased by leaps and bounds.

TABLE 35

EMPIRE'S PROPORTION OF BRITAIN'S OVERSEAS TRADE 1909-1935 (PERCENTAGE OF TOTAL TRADE)

Overseas Trade	United Kingdom of Great Britain and Ireland i.e. [area of 1801-1923]					
	1909-13	1914-18	1919-26	1927-29	1930-32	1933-35
Imports	24.7	28.8	28.1	27.1	27.6	35.4
Exports	35.4	34.1	38.4	42.3	39.9	43.6
Re-exports	12.3	12.8	10.2	11.9	13.3	12.6
Total trade	27.5	29.6	30.7	31.6	30.8	37.2

The increase in the share of the Empire in Britain's overseas trade in the 1930s is also of significance when compared with Empire trade a century ago. The only similar sudden increase in Empire trade in the nineteenth century was in the early 1860s. This increase, however, soon disappeared and there was an equally rapid decline in 1864-66. The reasons for this are obvious. Owing to the American Civil War Britain's imports of raw cotton from the U.S.A. fell sharply. To secure a substitute—however inadequate—for this vital raw material of British industry cotton had to be imported to a greater extent from India. Some American cotton was imported

[1] See Table 20B of Appendix.
[2] See G. Mackenroth and F. Krebs : *Die Wirtschaftsverflechtung des britischen Weltreichs* (Zwischenstaatliche Wirtschaft, vol. 12, Berlin, 1935).

by way of the Bermudas which [from the point of view of the statistics] also contributed to the increase in the Empire's proportion of Britain's cotton supplies. This therefore was a temporary change in Britain overseas trade brought about solely by non-economic factors. The change was of little permanent significance for the future development of Britain's imports from the Empire since even the substitute-imports of Indian cotton subsequently declined.[1] It was only in the early 1860s that Britain's imports from Empire territories increased as rapidly as they did between 1931 and 1938.

The proportion of Britain's exports absorbed by the Empire has shown a much less regular development. The Empire's share of Britain's export trade dropped steadily and considerably between 1863 and 1871. A rise between 1871 and 1877, however, completely recovered the lost ground. A careful examination of the statistics shows that these changes did not represent any absolute fall in Britain's exports to the Empire. They were due to a sharp increase in Britain's exports—particularly to the United States and Central Europe. This increase in Britain's exports had been encouraged by the inflation in the United States (which originated during the Civil War); the railway boom in many countries and finally the Franco-Prussian War (which mainly affected Central Europe). It proved to be the result of an unhealthy overproduction. After the crisis of 1873 the boom gave way to a lengthy depression during which Britain [like Germany] suffered from a general depression in foreign trade.

In the same way the decline in the proportion of Britain's exports absorbed by the Empire in the 1860s was not due to fundamental structural changes. The rise in the proportion of British exports absorbed by the Empire after 1931–32 may however, with considerable confidence, be ascribed to structural changes in the pattern of British overseas commerce. We may expect that Britain's commercial treaties with Empire countries—which preceded this increase in Empire trade—will achieve their purpose because many factors favourable to such an increase were exercising an influence even before the agreements were made. We consider, therefore, that for many years to come Empire trade (as a proportion of Britain's total overseas trade) will at least maintain the level of the 1930s.

Within the Empire the countries which possessed Dominion status[2] in the 1930s—Canada, Newfoundland, the Union of South

[1] See Table 39, p. 97.
[2] [Newfoundland's Dominion status was suspended in 1933 owing to insolvency.]

— 91 —

Diagram 13. Share of British Empire in United Kingdom Trade* 1814–1936

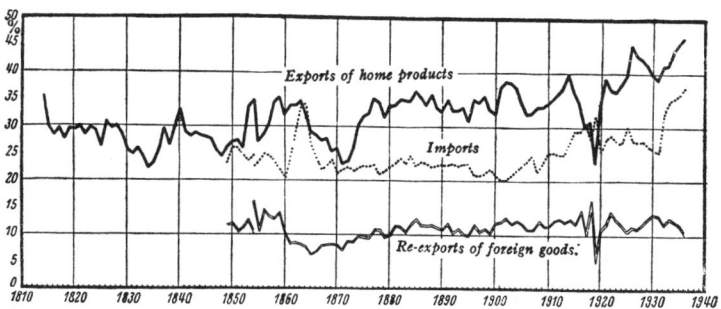

* Percentage of total trade based upon actual values. For the period 1849–54 the values of imports and of foreign goods [re-]exported have also been calculated on the basis of official values. The figures after 1923 refer to the old trade area [i.e. United Kingdom of Great Britain and Ireland.]

Diagram 14. Dominions' Share of Britain's Trade with the Empire,* 1814–1935

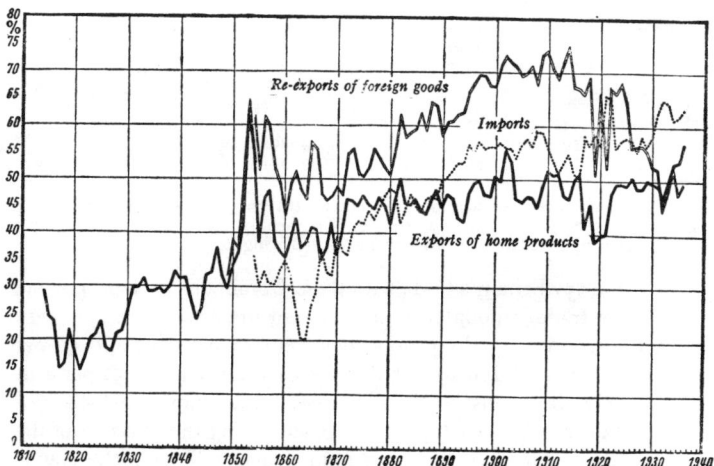

* Percentage of total trade based upon actual values. For the period 1849–54 the values of foreign goods [re-]exported have also been calculated on the basis of official values. The figures after 1923 refer to the old trade area [i.e. United Kingdom of Great Britain and Ireland].

Africa, Australia, and New Zealand—have been of greatest significance with regard to the development of Empire trade both during the nineteenth century and more recently [1933–8].[1]

TABLE 36
GEOGRAPHICAL DISTRIBUTION OF BRITISH EXPORTS 1861–1879

Area	in £1,000,000s			per cent		
	1861–63	1871–3	1877–9	1861–3	1871–3	1877–9
Central Europe	16.6	52.6	34.8	12.6	21.5	17.9
France and Italy	12.8	24.4	20.2	9.7	10.0	10.4
Industrial Europe	29.4	77.0	55.0	22.3	31.5	28.3
United States	12.9	36.3	17.1	9.8	14.8	8.8
Other foreign countries	44.6	—	56.6	33.8	29.5	29.1
Exports to all foreign countries	86.9	185.6	128.7	65.9	75.8	66.2
Exports to all Empire countries	45.0	59.3	65.7	34.1	24.2	33.8
Total Exports	131.9	244.9	194.4	100	100	100

TABLE 37
DOMINIONS' SHARE IN BRITISH TRADE WITH THE EMPIRE 1814–1935*
(PER CENT)

Years	Imports	Exports	Re-exports	Years	Imports	Exports	Re-exports
1814–20	—	20.9	—	1927–9	56.6	49.1	56.1
1827–30	—	21.5	—	1930–32	62.0	48.4	49.2
1837–40	—	30.6	—	1933–5	62.7	52.3	49.4
1854–57	32.2	47.1	58.7				
1877–79	44.7	45.4	53.9				
1898–1901	56.4	48.8	—	1927–29†	49.5	44.7	32.0
1909–13	54.6	50.1	71.9	1933–35†	58.2	48.6	26.8

* To make the comparison more exact Eire has not been included (as a Dominion). See also Tables 20A and 20B of Appendix.
† Excluding Eire from the area of the United Kingdom.

In 1854–57 Britain's trade with these Dominions (as a proportion of Empire trade) amounted to 32 per cent imports and 47 per cent exports. In 1909–13 the proportions were 55 per cent and 50 per cent respectively and in 1933–5 they were 63 per cent and 52 per cent respectively. The most marked increase in the Dominions' share of Britain's exports to the Empire took place during the first half of the nineteenth century. In the years immediately following the Napoleonic Wars (1814–19) the [future] Dominions took only 21 per cent

[1] See Appendix, Tables 20 to 25.

of Britain's exports to the Empire. It was only after the 1830s that this proportion began to increase and it reached from 47 to 48 per cent in the middle of the nineteenth century. The subsequent rise in the Dominions' share of Britain's exports to the Empire was only a gradual one—as the figures we provide indicate—so that the Dominions as a whole were in the nineteen thirties of little more significance than they were in the 1830s from the point of view of the share of Britain's exports to the Empire which they absorb.

If we examine British exports to the Dominions in detail, however, we find that considerable changes have taken place. Particular emphasis should be laid on the growing significance of the commercial bonds linking Britain with Australia and New Zealand, and also—especially from the point of view of absorbing British exports—with the Union of South Africa. On the other hand the significance of Canada for the United Kingdom's Empire trade has declined somewhat.

Before the first World War India held the first place in Britain's trade with the Empire. Subsequently, however, it fell to second place behind Australia and New Zealand. Britain's trade with India, however, has undergone a relative decline during the whole period under review. This was particularly true of British imports from India. In the middle of the nineteenth century, moreover, Britain's trade with her possessions in the West Indies took second place in imports from the Empire and exports to the Empire. But the share of the West Indies in Empire trade soon fell sharply—both relatively and absolutely. Up to the outbreak of the first World War British trade with British possessions in Asia [other than India], was becoming important. Later this applies also to the trade with the British colonies in Africa (excluding the Union of South Africa).

Hitherto in our calculations we have ignored the fact that not only the United Kingdom, but also the Empire has undergone territorial changes since 1914. Since the first World War the Empire has been expanded to include the greater part of the former German colonies as well as the mandated territory of Palestine (formerly a part of Turkey) and also the Anglo-Egyptian Sudan, which before 1921 was combined with Egypt in the commercial statistics and was therefore regarded as a ' foreign country '. When comparing Britain's Empire trade in 1919-38 with that in 1909-13, it is possible to make allowance for territorial changes by regarding the new territories and mandates as still being ' foreign countries ' as they were before 1920. The former German colonies concerned are Tanganyika,

S.W. Africa, Nauru and Western Samoa. Moreover large parts of the Cameroons and Togoland became British mandates and so are now part of the Empire. British overseas trade with these territories is not recorded separately but is included in the statistics for Nigeria (the Cameroons) or the Gold Coast (Togoland). Allowance cannot be made for these territorial changes in the commercial statistics, but this does not seriously affect the comparison with the period before 1914.

The necessary corrections have been made in Table 38. This table naturally shows somewhat lower Empire proportions in the total trade of the Mother Country but the upward tendency which we have discussed above can still be seen. The Dominions' share in British trade with the Empire now has a more prominent place while India's significance declines in an even more pronounced fashion. The greatest change naturally occurred with regard to the British colonies in Africa (excluding the Union of South Africa). It is true that there is still a not inconsiderable rise in the proportion of imports and exports but the proportion is substantially below the uncorrected figures.

Owing to these territorial changes there have been some alterations in the composition of Empire trade from the point of view of commodities. These alterations follow naturally from the territorial changes, though doubtless other factors have played their part. In Tables 23 to 25 of the Appendix we have classified by commodities Britain's trade with the Dominions and some of the more important colonies. We have taken six key-years for imports (Table 24) and seven key-years for exports (Table 25) and then we have arranged the commodities listed under each Dominion or colony in descending order of value for the first years chosen (1854 for imports and 1827 for exports). Commodities which either did not enter into Empire trade or which (because of their insignificance) were not included in the statistics were included in our tables as and when they appeared in Empire trade. In this way we have obtained a clear picture of the changes which occurred in the composition of Empire trade by commodities.

The increased variety of Empire commodities imported by Britain has been particularly striking but there has been no similar increase in the variety of exports from Britain absorbed by the Empire. In 1854 Canada's main export to Britain was timber while Australia, New Zealand and the territories subsequently linked in the Union of South Africa sent principally wool. Timber accounted for

TABLE 38

UNITED KINGDOM'S* TRADE WITH THE EMPIRE 1909-1935 †

Area	Imports				Exports				Re-exports			
	1909–13	1927–29	1930–32	1933–35	1909–13	1927–29	1930–32	1933–35	1909–13	1927–29	1930–32	1933–35
					Per cent							
Five Dominions‡	54.6	58.0	63.1	64.0	50.0	49.7	49.6	53.6	71.7	56.7	51.2	50.2
India	26.0	20.7	17.6	16.4	33.5	28.7	24.6	22.3	11.4	9.4	11.4	10.7
British possessions in Asia (excluding India)	13.1	10.9	9.0	8.3	7.6	9.7	9.9	8.0	3.8	6.0	5.3	4.8
Brit. possessions in Africa (except Union of S.A.)	3.4	7.0	5.7	6.0	4.9	7.3	8.5	7.4	4.9	14.0	12.1	9.7
British West Indies	1.7	1.9	2.6	3.0	2.1	2.3	3.8	4.2	4.5	3.5	5.2	4.2
Brit. possessions in Europe	1.0	1.1	1.6	1.8	1.8	1.9	3.3	4.1	3.5	10.2	14.3	20.1
Other British possessions	0.2	0.4	0.4	0.5	0.1	0.4	0.3	0.4	0.2	0.2	0.5	0.3
Total Empire Trade	100	100	100	100	100	100	100	100	100	100	100	100
					£ 1000s							
Brit. possessions in Asia (excluding India)	22,667	33,929	20,562	20,651	12,180	27,948	15,984	12,998	485	765	418	278
Brit. possessions in Africa (except the Union of South Africa)	5,789	21,784	13,018	14,870	7,933	20,821	13,811	12,031	624	1,786	949	560
Other parts of Empire	144,222	256,410	194,364	211,987	141,044	238,232	132,036	136,482	11,670	10,244	6,447	4,947
Total Empire Trade	172,678	312,123	227,944	247,508	161,157	287,001	161,831	161,511	12,779	12,795	7,814	5,785
	Empire's Share of total U.K. trade as Percentage											
Empire territories in 1921	24.7	26.4	27.0	34.6	35.4	41.8	39.1	42.7	12.0	11.9	13.2	12.3
Empire territories in 1913	24.7	27.1	28.0	35.4	35.4	42.4	39.9	43.5	12.0	12.0	13.2	12.6

* See Table 23 of Appendix.   † 1913 Area of trade statistics [i.e. including the whole of Ireland].
‡ [i.e. Canada, Newfoundland, Australia, New Zealand, South Africa.]

82 per cent of Britain's imports from Canada and Newfoundland while wool also accounted for 82 per cent of Britain's imports from Australia and New Zealand. South Africa's wool accounted for 72 per cent of Britain's imports from that territory. It is true that these products still account for an important part of British imports from the Dominions. In time, however, additional commodities have been imported from the Empire to an increasing extent, and as far as Canada and Newfoundland are concerned, these new commodities are now actually more important than the original staple products. We do not propose to discuss this in further detail. The statistics printed in the Appendix give a picture of a progressive widening in the trade of these territories. This has been largely due to the demands of the British market.

A similar trend can be observed in Britain's Asiatic possessions (excluding India). The table in the Appendix classifies by commodities Britain's imports from Ceylon, the Straits Settlements and the Malay States. At one time nearly half of Britain's imports from these territories consisted of coffee but now no coffee is imported from them. Until about 1900 expanding imports from these territories consisted mainly of increased shipments of rubber, tin and tea. The value of these three commodities accounted in 1934 for over 80 per cent of the value of Britain's imports from these colonial territories.

There has not been any significant change in the nature of the products imported by Britain from India but there have been relative changes in the value of different groups of commodities. At one time Britain imported very large quantities of indigo and sugar but these imports had almost entirely disappeared by the 1930s. Tea, on the other hand, was once quite an insignificant import but by the 1930s had become Britain's chief import from India. Wheat, jute products, and oil-cake are virtually newcomers to the list of imports since the middle of the nineteenth century. Wheat, however, was of real significance only up to the outbreak of the first World War. The main textile fibres which India exported to Britain have been cotton and jute. In fact jute imports have risen considerably and it is rather surprising that only in quite recent times have cotton imports shown a tendency to increase. In 1854–7 Britain drew 18.7 per cent of her cotton imports from India but only 2.6 per cent in 1907–13. The percentage however had risen to 5.5 in 1927–9. It was about 8 per cent in 1932–4, 13 per cent in 1935 and 15 per cent in 1936.

The Dominions were the most important Empire territories from the point of view of Britain's overseas trade. This was just as true of Britain's exports to the Empire as it was with regard to imports from the Empire (which have already been discussed). In the last hundred years, the Dominions' share of Britain's exports to the Empire grew from about a fifth to about a half, and indeed this proportion had almost been reached before 1860.

TABLE 39

BRITISH IMPORTS OF COTTON, JUTE, WHEAT AND TEA FROM INDIA 1854–1934

[Annual Average]

Commodity	Unit	1854–57	1911–13	1927–29	1932–34
Cotton, raw	1,000 cwt.	1572	557	746	944
Jute, raw	1,000 ,,	554	5,848	4,330	3,300
Wheat	1,000 ,,	144	21,436	2,234	55
Tea	100 lb.	681	193,937	299,700	289,738

From 1800 to 1840 British exports to India and the British West Indies were of outstanding importance. As Table 25 of the Appendix shows, the products of the British textile industry largely predominated in exports to the Dominions—and to an even greater extent was this true of the dependent colonies. Even in the 1850s almost half of Britain's exports to the Empire consisted of textiles. By the 1930s indeed the proportion had dropped to a third and even less but textiles were still by far the most important single group of exports to the Empire. We must mention also iron and steel products as well as leather and leather-goods. Subsequently machinery and chemicals became important exports. In the twentieth century motor vehicles appeared and then, after the first World War, paper goods as well as the products of the electrical engineering industry (except to Canada), and such products as beer, spirits and tobacco goods. Most of the newer exports were of some importance at an early date but they were in the 1930s relatively of much greater importance than they used to be. We cannot discuss this development in further detail. We draw attention to the tables (e.g. no. 25) in which the 80 per cent of Britain's exports to the Empire which went to the Dominions, India and the British West Indies is classified by commodities.

We propose to complete our statistical picture of Britain's Empire trade by classifying this commerce according to commodities without reference to the geographical distribution of the trade. For this purpose Tables 21 and 22 of the Appendix have been compiled. The Empire's share of Britain's imports and exports of important goods has been calculated for 13 key-years for imports and 15 key-years for exports.

Manufactured articles were naturally of little significance in the imports from the Empire. The three most important manufactured imports are leather, newsprint and jute goods and they represent nearly the whole of Britain's imports of these commodities. Imports of foodstuffs and industrial raw materials from the Empire are, of course, of great importance for satisfying Britain's economic requirements. The data given in Table 21 are inadequate for ascertaining the proportions of the Empire's share in supplying the Mother Country with these two groups of commodities. The foodstuffs listed for 1934 in the Table show an average proportion of 39.2 per cent [of Empire origin] while the raw materials listed amount to 33.8 per cent. These proportions are far too high. Actually the classification which we have made does not include all the foodstuffs and raw materials which Britain imported from the Empire. Some of these products are included in the unenumerated commodities and the Empire's share of these goods is only 17.9 per cent. Since these unenumerated articles consist mainly of foodstuffs and raw materials, the correct proportion of imports [from the Empire] should be between 49.2 and 17.9 per cent for foodstuffs and between 36.0 and 17.9 per cent for raw materials. It would be only a rough approximation to the truth if we were to assume that there was an Empire share of 18 per cent for both the unenumerated foodstuffs as well as for the unenumerated raw materials in our tables but this assumption may be regarded as a satisfactory means of securing a more exact figure for the proportions we are seeking.[1] In this way we can obtain a more accurate, though by no means precise, picture of the importance of the Empire in supplying Britain with these products. The approximate percentages calculated in this way are given in Table 40.

The table shows that the Empire's share in Britain's imports of foodstuffs hardly changed until about 1900. Then an increase certainly took place and this continued after the first World War and was especially marked after 1931. In 1934 about 43 per cent of the

[1] The method of calculation is very simple one. We know the amount of the non-enumerated portion of the total imports and we know the Empire's share of that. Our totals—expressed as percentages of Britain's total imports—are the sum of the unenumerated and enumerated values i.e. (i) the values obtained by calculating the Empire's share of the *unenumerated* products, and (ii) the values obtained by adding together the *classified* imports of foodstuffs and raw materials given in Table 21. The correctness of our result actually depends upon how high a proportion of the imports have been classified in Table 21. Roughly, three-quarters of the imports (by value) of foodstuffs and raw materials have been so classified in that table.

foodstuffs imported into Britain came from her own Empire as compared with only 27 per cent in 1913. If we examine in detail the various important groups of commodities imported we find that, although there has been a very definite trend towards an increase in the Empire's share, there have been considerable differences in the rate of increase of particular products. Table 41 indicates these changes very clearly. In 1856 six out of eleven groups of foodstuffs each represented less than 10 per cent of Britain's total imports (by

TABLE 40

EMPIRE'S SHARE IN BRITISH IMPORTS OF FOODSTUFFS AND RAW MATERIALS*
1854–1934 (PER CENT)

Sample year	Food-stuffs	Raw Materials	Sample year	Food-stuffs	Raw Materials
1854	19.1	26.2	1913	27.0	28.0
1860	18.2	23.5	1925	36.4	30.7
1870	17.5	27.4	1929	30.7	28.8
1880	17.4	31.9	1931	32.3	25.8
1890	19.1	30.7	1932	39.4	28.8
1900	20.9	24.3	1933	42.3	31.1

* Old area of trade statistics [i.e. area of 1801–1923].

value) from the Empire. The other groups of foodstuffs, however, accounted for over one half and most of them actually over three quarters of Britain's total imports. In 1932–34, on an average, the groups of foodstuffs to which we have referred each accounted for over 25 per cent and seven of them accounted for more than half of Britain's total imports. Although Britain drew more and more of her foodstuffs from overseas her food supplies came largely from within the Empire.

In comparison with this remarkable increase in the importance of the Empire from the point of view of the United Kingdom's food supplies it is particularly striking that the Empire's share in Britain's imports of industrial raw materials has shown a relatively much smaller increase over the last 80 years. Narrower limits are obviously set to the expansion of the supply of industrial raw materials since their production is for the most part dependent upon natural conditions. Table 42 shows that in 1932–34 (annual average) the Empire's share of six of the seventeen groups of raw materials that we have listed was still below 25 per cent. For eight groups of raw materials the proportion was under 50 per cent. Moreover, among the products which have a low ' import proportion ', we find several which are of considerable importance in Britain's total imports.

TABLE 41

EMPIRE'S SHARE IN BRITISH IMPORTS OF IMPORTANT FOODSTUFFS 1854–1934

Proportion by value (per cent)	1854		1913		1929		1932–34	
	Commodity	Per cent	Commodity	Per cent	Commodity	Per cent	Commodity	Per cent
Between 75 to 100	Spices Rice and ground rice Coffee	94.1 91.0 76.0	Tea Cheese	87.3 81.7	Cocoa Cheese Tea	93.1 86.0 85.8	Cocoa Cheese Tea Spices	89.8 88.6 82.5 77.5
Over 50 and below 75	Raw sugar Cocoa	64.7 54.8	Spices Rice and ground rice Cocoa	72.2 60.1 50.9	Spices Rice and ground rice	67.3 51.2	Rice and ground rice Raw sugar Butter	67.4 52.6 51.6
Over 25 and below 50	—		Grain and flour	34.4	Raw sugar Coffee Butter Grain and flour	42.5 34.5 31.5 31.5	Grain and flour Coffee Fresh fruit and raw nuts Meat, game and poultry	48.6 43.0 40.7 26.7
Over 10 and below 25	—		Meat, game poultry Fresh fruit, nuts	24.7 14.3	Fresh fruit and nuts Meat, game and poultry	21.2 16.4	—	
Below 10	Fresh fruit, nuts Grain and flour Butter Meat, game and poultry Tea Cheese	3.2 2.0 1.5 0.9 0.7 Nil	Butter Sugar	9.0 8.7	—		—	

— 100 —

TABLE 42
EMPIRE'S SHARE IN IMPORTS OF IMPORTANT RAW MATERIALS 1854-1934

Proportion by Value (per cent)	1854 Commodity	per cent	1913 Commodity	per cent	1929 Commodity	per cent	1932-34 Commodity	per cent
Between 75 and 100	Indigo Jute	95.7 92.1	Jute Tin Indigo Wool	99.4 94.8 87.3 80.2	Indigo Jute Tin Wool Rubber	100.0 96.9 88.4 85.8 82.1	Jute Lead Tin Wool Rubber Zinc	98.7 89.5 85.5 84.4 82.3 80.5
Over 50 and below 75	Tin Wool Timber	71.2 70.6 55.2	Rubber Oil seeds	57.2	Lead	63.8 53.3	Copper ore Indigo Oil seeds	72.7 71.0 56.7
Over 25 and below 50	Hides Oil seeds	33.1 26.5	Hides Copper ore Lead	41.8 37.4 36.7	Oil seeds Hides Copper ore Zinc	48.6 48.0 44.3 26.1	Copper Hides	47.8 29.1
Over 10 and below 25	Rubber	11.2	Copper Tin ore Timber	21.0 18.3 16.2	Tin ore Cotton Iron ore, manganese ore Tobacco leaf	22.0 14.5 12.7 10.7	Tin Ore Tobacco leaf Timber Cotton Iron ore and manganese ore	23.2 21.2 13.1 13.8 11.4
Below 10	Copper Copper ore Cotton Tobacco leaf Lead Iron ore and manganese ore Mineral oils and tin ore	9.9 9.1 8.4 1.2 0.0 0.0 —	Iron Ore and manganese ore Mineral oils Zinc Raw tobacco	9.9 8.4 9.0 0.9	Timber Copper Mineral oils	9.3 5.4 3.9	Mineral oils	4.4

— 101 —

TABLE 43
EMPIRE'S SHARE IN EXPORTS OF HOME PRODUCTS 1830–1934

Proportion by value (per cent)	1830 Commodity	per cent	1913 Commodity	per cent	1929 Commodity	per cent	1932–34 Commodity	per cent
Between 50 and 100	Beer and ale	74.2	Motor vehicles	67.4	Motor vehicles	81.2	Paper and paper goods	71.6
	Soaps and candles	68.4	Spirituous Liquors	65.9	Paper and paper goods	72.8	Soaps	69.6
	Printers' colours	57.0	Copper ware and brass ware	64.8	Tobacco goods	71.9	Books	68.9
	Copper ware and brass ware	56.2	Paper and paper wares	62.0	Spirituous liquors	71.7	Motor vehicles	67.5
	Books	52.1	Electrical goods		Locomotives	69.5	Beer and ale	66.6
			Books	16.6	Drugs and medicines	69.4	Tobacco products	65.7
			Drugs and medicines	60.1	Beer and Ale	68.4	Copper ware and Brass ware	62.6
			Beer and ale	59.9	Books	65.6	Hardware and Cutlery	62.6
			Locomotives	59.7	Hardware and Cutlery		Drugs and medicines	61.8
			Railway carriages	58.6	Copper ware and brassware	64.2	Electrical goods	57.9
			Hardware and cutlery	58.4	Soaps	63.3	Painters' colours	56.7
			Soaps	57.2	Sugar, refined	63.3	Pottery and porcelain	56.7
				54.3	Painters' colours	57.6	Locomotives	56.5
					Electrical goods	56.7	Railway carriages	55.3
					Ships' hulls	56.5	Spirituous liquors	54.7
					Iron and ironware	52.3	Ships' hulls	54.2
						51.4	Iron and ironware	51.4
					Pottery and porcelain	50.8		

— 103 —

Over 25 and below 50	Coal, coke, etc.	43.5	Painters' colours	48.8	Arms and munitions	48.7	Soda compounds	48.9
	Iron and ironware	39.9	Arms and munitions	48.4	Railway carriages	43.8	Machines	46.7
	Machinery, arms and munitions	36.4	Iron and ironware	48.2	Machines	43.5	Tyres, rubber	45.2
		28.9	Tobacco products	44.5	Textiles	42.2	Arms and munitions	45.1
			Textiles	43.9	Tyres, rubber	40.6	Textiles	43.0
			Pottery and porcelain wares	41.9	Soda compounds	37.5	Ammonium sulphate	41.9
			Sugar, refined	41.2	Ammonium Sulphate	32.6	Candles	30.6
			Tyres, rubber	36.1	Candles	29.5	Sugar, refined	27.3
			Machines	32.5				
			Candles	36.2				
			Soda compounds	26.0				
Below 25	Textiles	22.7	Ships' hulls	20.6	Coal, coke, etc.	5.8	Coal, coke, etc.	9.7
	Pottery and porcelain	21.7	Ammonium sulphate	6.4				
	Hardwares and cutlery	21.6	Coal, coke, etc.	3.7				
	Sugar, refined	8.9						

These include mineral oils, timber, cotton and tobacco which account for more than 40 per cent of Britain's total imports of raw materials. If we make a calculation to illustrate the growth of Britain's 'import proportion' of Empire raw materials—excluding mineral oils which became of much greater significance after the first World War—we obtain the following result :

1913 : 28.5 per cent	1929 : 31.5 per cent	1932 : 33.8 per cent
1925 : 32.6 ,,	1931 : 28.9 ,,	1933 : 34.9 ,,
		1934 : 35.3 ,,

Despite the growth of the Empire's share in Britain's imports of raw materials there has therefore been no significant change in Britain's great dependence on foreign countries for these commodities.

A similar calculation has been made of the Empire's 'export proportion' of the more important groups of commodities.[1] British exports to the Empire—like Britain's total exports—consist mainly of manufactured goods but they also include certain foodstuffs, such as refined sugar, beer and spirits. The export of coal to the Empire is insignificant. Ammonium sulphate is the only raw material of any importance to be sent to Empire territories. Turning to manufactured goods we find that exports of textiles to the Empire are of most significance. The proportion of textile exports absorbed by the Empire increased considerably—especially between 1870 and 1913. The textiles sent to the Empire in 1913 amounted to 44 per cent of Britain's total textile exports. This proportion subsequently dropped and was not reached again until 1934. The Empire absorbed about one-third of Britain's exports of iron [and steel] manufactures in the nineteenth century. This proportion had increased to almost a half by 1913 and it remained between 50 and 55 per cent in the period following the first World War. A remarkably high proportion of British exports of motor vehicles, soap, books and printed matter are taken by the Empire. It is easy to understand why the Empire should be a good customer for British books and other printed matter.

The amount of Britain's re-exports to the Empire has not undergone any significant change in the eighty years under review. Re-exports have been rather insignificant and have amounted only to between 10 and 15 per cent of Britain's total re-exports. British trade in re-exports has—as far as the Empire is concerned—been chiefly with Canada and Australia. India and the Union of South Africa have also absorbed some re-exports. In the 1850's Britain's

[1] See Appendix, Table 22.

re-exports to the Empire consisted mainly of wine, spirits, tobacco-products, tea and timber. Before the first World War about 50 per cent of the textiles re-exported from Britain and about 45 per cent of the whole of British re-exports of manufactured goods went to the Empire, whilst only 20-25 per cent of re-exported foodstuffs and only an insignificant portion of re-exported raw materials were absorbed by the Empire.[1]

[1] [For developments in British Empire trade since 1938, see *A Review of Commonwealth Trade* (Commonwealth Economic Committee), 1949, London, H.M. Stationery Office].

APPENDIX OF TABLES

NOTE

As the Tables in this Appendix have been photographed from the German edition, it should be noted that in German statistics a comma is used to indicate a decimal point and that **in German usage the English comma becomes a space**, e.g. **30 000,5 (German) = 30,000.5 (English)**. This applies only to tables in this Appendix. Tables in the text have been entirely re-set.

LIST OF CONTENTS OF APPENDIX OF TABLES

Preliminary Note. A short account of the import duties on the principal foodstuffs during the transition to Free Trade (from 1819).

TABLE	PAGE
1. Official prices of imports and exports for England, Scotland and Ireland	114
2. Prices and Price Indices of Important Commodities entering into overseas trade in 1694 and their Annual Average Prices for 1854–60	115
3. Actual Overseas Trade Values of the United Kingdom 1801–1860, calculated from the volume (base-year—1913) and the Jevons Price Index	120
4. United Kingdom Imports 1854–1936. (Actual Values in £1,000s)	121
5. United Kingdom Exports of Home Products 1814–1936. (Actual values in £1,000s)	124
6. United Kingdom Re-exports 1854–1936. (Actual Values in £1,000s)	127
7. United Kingdom Imports and Exports (including Re-exports) 1697–1933. (Volumes in £1,000s)	129
7A. United Kingdom Overseas Trade 1801–1814. (Volumes in £1,000,000s)	130
8. United Kingdom Imports 1814–1933. (Volumes in £1,000s)	131
9. United Kingdom Exports of Home Products 1814–1933 (Volumes in £1,000s)	133
10. United Kingdom Re-exports 1814–1933. (Volumes in £1,000s)	136
11. United Kingdom Imports of Foodstuffs 1820–1933. (Volumes in £1,000s)	139
12. United Kingdom Imports of Raw Materials 1820–1933. (Volumes in £1,000s)	142
13. United Kingdom Imports of Finished Manufactured Goods, 1820–1933. (Volumes in £1,000s)	144
14. United Kingdom Exports of Raw Materials 1827–1933. (Volumes in £1,000s)	147
15. United Kingdom Exports of Textile Products 1827–1933. (Volumes in £1,000s)	149

TABLE		PAGE
16.	United Kingdom Exports of Finished Manufactured Goods 1827–1933. (Volumes in £1,000s)...	152
17.	British Industry, 1814–1933. (1913=100).	154
	(a) Terms of trade between finished manufactured goods and raw materials.	
	(b) Export-proportions.	
18.	United Kingdom Imports from the various Continents 1849–1936. (Per cent of total imports)	156
19.	United Kingdom Exports to the various Continents 1849–1936. (Per cent of total exports)	160
20A.	Empire share of British total Exports of Home products; the Dominions' share of British Exports to the Empire, 1814–1854. (Basis of calculation : actual values, per cent)	160
20B.	British Empire's Share of British Overseas Trade, Dominions' Share of British Trade with Empire, 1849–1936	161
21.	British Empire Share of British Imports, 1854–1934 ...	164
22.	British Empire Share of British Exports of Home Products, 1830–1934	166
23.	United Kingdom Trade with the Empire, 1854–1935 (in £1,000s)	168
24.	United Kingdom Imports from the Empire, 1854–1934 (in £1,000s)	170
25.	United Kingdom Exports of Home Products to the Empire, 1827–1934 (in £1,000s)	172
26.	Price Indices of Principal Commodity Groups in United Kingdom Overseas Trade, 1801–1933 (1913=100) ...	175

A short Account of the Import Duties on the Principal Foodstuffs during the Transition to Free Trade (from 1819).

1. *Wheat.* Imports of wheat were prohibited by the Corn Law of 1815 until home-produced wheat reached a minimum fixed price. When this price was reached imports of wheat were allowed without payment of duty. Wheat was allowed to be imported from the British North American colonies when home-produced wheat cost 67s. a quarter. This was much lower than the 80s. per quarter which was fixed as the price to be reached by home-grown wheat before wheat coming from countries other than British North America might be admitted.

The Corn Law of 1822 introduced a sliding scale by which import duties were adjusted according to the level of home prices. This scale, however, came into force only when the prohibition of the import of wheat had been dropped in accordance with the provisions of the Act of 1815—that is to say, when home prices exceeded the *new* minimum levels of 59s. (wheat from British North America) and 70s. (elsewhere).[1] It was not until May 1825, that the price of wheat produced at home actually rose to the level of 59s. per quarter at which Empire wheat could be admitted. The import of wheat from other places was still prohibited in accordance with the regulations of 1815. Even for wheat from British North America the sliding scale operated for barely a month, and on June 22, 1825 this scale was replaced by a fixed import duty of 5s. per quarter, whatever might be the price of home-grown wheat.

The later history of the Corn Laws is summarised in the following table. In 1828 all imported wheat paid import duties according to a sliding scale and the principle of not admitting imports until home-grown wheat reached a certain price-level was given up. The sliding scale of 1828 was substantially reduced, first in 1842 and again in 1846. In 1849 a fixed import duty of one shilling a quarter came into effect. After June 1, 1869, no import duty whatever was charged upon wheat.[2]

2. *Cattle and Sheep.* The prohibition of the import of live cattle—imposed as early as 1770—was replaced in 1842 by import

---
[1] [For further details, see D. G. Barnes, *History of the English Corn Laws from 1660–1846* (1930), p. 174 and C. R. Fay, *The Corn Laws and Social England* (1932), p. 124.]

[2] [For changes in duties on wheat and other cereals from 1660 to 1869, see *Customs Tariffs of the United Kingdom from 1800 to 1897*. (Cmd. 8706 of 1897, pp. 229–51)].

duties which amounted to £1 per head for oxen and bulls, 15s. for cows, 3s. per head for sheep and 2s. per head for lambs. Cattle and sheep from the colonies paid import duties that were 50 per cent lower than this. Import duties on cattle and sheep were abolished in March, 1846.

IMPORT DUTY ON WHEAT IN RELATION TO THE PRICE OF WHEAT IN THE UNITED KINGDOM 1825–1849
(shillings per quarter)

Price of Home-grown Wheat	May 15, 1825 to July 14, 1828	May 15, 1825 to June 21, 1825	June 22, 1825 to July 1, 1826	July 7, 1826 to July 14, 1828	July 15, 1828 to April 28, 1842		April 29, 1842 to June 25, 1846		June 26, 1846* to Jan. 31, 1849	
	Foreign	Colonial			Foreign	Colonial	Foreign	Colonial	Foreign	Colonial
73 and above		1	5	½	1	½	1	1	4	1
72		1	5	½	2⅔	½	2	1	4	1
71		1	5	½	6⅔	½	3	1	4	1
70		5	5	½	10⅝	½	4	1	4	1
69		5	5	½	13⅔	½	5	1	4	1
68		5	5	½	16⅔	½	5	1	4	1
67		5	5	½	18⅔	½	6	1	4	1
66		12	5	5	20⅔	5	6	1	4	1
65		12	5	5	21⅔	5	7	1	4	1
64	Pro-	12	5	5	22⅝	5	8	1	4	1
63	hib-	12	5	5	23⅔	5	9	1	4	1
62	ited	12	5	5	24⅔	5	10	1	4	1
61		12	5	5	25⅔	5	11	1	4	1
60		12	5	5	26⅔	5	12	1	4	1
59		12	5	5	27⅔	5	13	1	4	1
58			5	5	28⅔	5	14	1	4	1
57			5	5	29⅔	5	15	2	4	1
56			5	5	30⅔	5	16	3	4	1
55		Pro-	5	5	31⅔	5	17	4	4	1
54		hib-	5	5	32⅔	5	18	5	4	1
53		ited	5	5	33⅔	5	18	5	4	1
52			5	5	34⅔	5	18	5	5	1
51			5	5	35⅔	5	19	5	6	1
50			5	5	36⅔	5	20	5	7	1
49			5	5	37⅔	5	20	5	8	1
48			5	5	38⅔	5	20	5	9	1
47 and below			5	5	+ 1*s.* duty for every 1*s.* decrease in home price	5	20	5	10	1

* From January 26 to September 1, 1847, the import of grain was duty free.

3. *Ham and Bacon.* The import duty of 56s. per cwt. was reduced to 28s. from July 5, 1825. On October 10, 1842, the import duty was again reduced, this time to 14s. At the same time colonial bacon and ham had to pay an import duty of only 3s. 6d. From March 19, 1846, imports of ham were admitted duty-free while the duty on bacon was reduced to 7s. (preferential duty for colonial bacon 2s.). Bacon duties were not finally abolished until June 1, 1853.

4. *Beef and Pork.* The prohibition of the import of salt beef and pork was not lifted until July 5, 1827. The prohibition of the import of fresh and slightly salted beef and pork lasted until 1842. After 1827 a duty of 12s. per cwt. was levied on salt meat. This was reduced to 8s. on October 10, 1842. At the same time (1842) a preferential duty of 2s. was fixed for corned beef which had been produced in the Empire and had been imported direct from the Empire. After March 19, 1846, import duties on salted meat were abolished. Between 1842 and 1846 import duties were levied only on fresh meat and slightly salted meat.

5. *Butter and Cheese.* The changes in import duties are given in the following table:

IMPORT DUTIES ON BUTTER AND CHEESE ENTERING THE UNITED KINGDOM
(Shillings per cwt.)

Period	Butter		Cheese	
	from foreign countries	from British possessions	from foreign countries	from British possessions
	s. d.	s. d.	s. d.	s. d.
Until 1842	25 0*	—	13 0*	—
1842–46	20 0	5 0	10 6	2 6
1846–53	10 0	2 6	5 0	1 6
1853–60	5 0	2 6	2 6	1 6
After 1860	exempt from duty		exempt from duty	

*Imported in ' British-built ' ships : Butter, 20s. per cwt. Cheese, 10s. 6d. per cwt.

6. *Eggs.* At first there was an import duty of 10d. per 120 eggs. After Oct. 10, 1842, colonial eggs enjoyed preferential treatment and paid only 2½d. per 120. In June 1853 the import duty was reduced to 4d. but colonial eggs still paid 2½d. Between 1854 and 1860 the import duties were four and four-fifths pence per 120 on imported foreign eggs and two and two-fifths pence per 120 on colonial eggs.

Table 1. Official prices of imports and exports for England, Scotland and Ireland*

Commodity	Unit of Quantity	England			Scotland			Ireland		
		£	s	d	£	s	d	£	s	d
		Import Prices								
Coffee	cwt.	7	—	—	2	16	—	10	—	—
Sugar, raw	,,	1	7	6	1	5	6	2	5	—
Oranges, Lemons	1000 fruits	—	13	—	2	15	—	1	7	9
Hides, untanned										
dry	cwt.	3	—	—	3	10	—	3	5	—
wet	,,	3	—	—	1	15	—	3	5	—
Tallow	,,	1	1	—	1	7	6	1	10	—
Tobacco leaf	lb.	—	—	2¼	—	—	2½	—	—	6
Laths	120 pieces	1	—	—	2	10	—	1	1	3
Boards										
over 21' in length	,,	1	7	6	9	—	—	4	5	—
up to 21' ,,	,,	7	10	—	22	10	—	4	5	—
Cotton, Indian	lb.	—	—	7	—	1	—	—	—	—
other	,,	—	—	7¾						8⁴/₇
Wool, Spanish	,	—	1	2½	—	2	—			
other	,,	—	—	6						
Flax	cwt.	1	15	—	2	5	—	1	15	—
		Export Prices								
Beer	tun	5	—	—	16	16	—	4	—	—
Wheat	quarter	1	7	—	1	7	—	2	4	—
Calicoes, bleached,	yard	—	1	3	—	2	—	—	1	6
dyed	,,	—	1	6	—	2	—	—	1	6
Muslin, bleached,	,,	—	1	8	—	2	6	—	3	4
dyed	,,	—	1	10	—	2	6	—	3	4
Leather, tanned, ..	cwt.	3	10	—	6	10	8	2	16	—
Stockings, woollen	12 pairs	1	13	4	—	19	—	1	4	—

[* Source: *Imports and Exports: Official Valuation* . . . (Accounts and Papers, House of Commons (May 18, 1826), 1826, Vol. XXII, Part I, Account No. 385, pp. 47–62. Dr. Schlote gives as his reference a parliamentary paper of the previous day (May 17, 1826): *Exports and Imports*, etc. (Accounts and Papers, H. of C., 1826, Vol. XXII, Account No. 372, but this Account records the official total value of British exports and imports for the ten years ending on January 5, 1826, and does not give the official prices for 1694, by commodities.]

Table 2. Prices and Price Indices of Important Commodities entering into overseas trade in 1694 and their Average Prices for 1854–60[1]

Commodity	Unit of Quantity	Prices 1694 £ per Unit of Quantity	Prices 1854/60 £ per Unit of Quantity	Price Index (1854–60) 1694=100	Weighting Figure [see above pp. 23–4]
		I. Imported Commodities			
Foodstuffs					
Wheat	quarter	1,600	2,866	179	7,86
Rye	,,	1,400	1,711	122	0,08
Barley	,,	0,850	1,516	178	1,59
Oats	,,	0,600	1,178	196	1,25
Maize	,,	0,500	1,746	350	1,50
Flour					
Wheat	cwt.	0,448	0,947	272	2,05
Rye	,,	0,375	0,426	114	0,005
Barley	,,	0,375	0,495	132	0
Oats	,,	0,188	0,642	342	0,01
Maize	,,	0,150	0,479	320	0,002
Peas	quarter	1,050	2,075	198	0,29
Beans	,,	0,700	1,856	265	0,38
Potatoes*	cwt.	0,499	0,185	37	0,06
Rice, husked	,,	0,750	0,605	81	0,49
Cocoa	,,	2,500	2,798	112	0,16
Coffee	,,	7,000	3,118	45	1,21
Tea	lb.	0,100	0,069	69	3,28
Sugar, raw	cwt.	1,375	1,403	102	5,62
Pepper	100 lb.	1,670	1,960	118	0,11
Cassia lignea	,,	7,500	3,950	53	0,01
Cinnamon	,,	20,000	6,760	34	0,03
Cloves	,,	25,000	2,450	10	0,008
Mace	,,	62,500	8,720	14	0,005
Nutmeg	,,	20,000	10,750	54	0,02
Pepper, Jamaica	,,	2,500	1,770	71	0,02
Currants	cwt.	1,050	1,839	175	0,41
Raisins*	,,	0,702	1,783	255	0,19
Figs	,,	0,625	1,805	288	0,06
Almonds, bitter	,,	2,625	2,835	108	0,03
other	,,	2,263	3,422	151	0,008
Olive oil	Tun	32,667	54,192	166	0,59
Palm oil	cwt.	1,000	2,177	218	0,85
Brandy	gallon	0,139	0,460	330	0,52
Rum	,,	0,097	0,134	138	0,36
Gin	,,	0,058	0,130	224	0,04
Wine					
Cape of Good Hope	Tun	36,750	44,412	121	0,03
French	,,	26,250	158,142	602	0,49
Portuguese	,,	29,167	89,071	305	0,43
Bacon*	cwt.	2,253	2,613	116	0,41
Ham*	,,	2,255	3,203	142	0,04
Beef, salt*	,,	0,916	2,002	218	0,20

* 1694 prices calculated from official values.

[1] Sources:
(i) For 1694: [See note 1 to Appendix Table 1 above].
(ii) For 1854–60: *Annual Statement of The Trade . . . of the United Kingdom.* . . .

Table 2—continued

Commodity	Unit of Quantity	Prices 1694 £ per Unit of Quantity	Prices 1854/60 £ per Unit of Quantity	Price Index (1854-60) 1694=100	Weighting figure [see above pp. 23-4]
Pork, salt*	cwt.	0,942	2,400	255	0,19
Lard	,,	1,480	2,852	193	0,28
Butter	,,	1,375	4,766	347	1,94
Cheese	,,	1,375	2,543	185	0,76
Raw Materials					
Cotton, raw :					
Indian	100 lb.	2,920	1,870	64	1,60
Other	,,	3,230	2,800	86	10,63
Wool	,,	2,500	7,000	280	5,08
Flax, raw	cwt.	1,750	2,479	142	1,62
Hemp, raw	,,	0,850	1,736	204	0,53
Silk, raw					
Indian	lb.	0,367	0,856	233	4,43
European	,,	0,567	1,475	260	0,29
Hides, raw	cwt.	3,000	3,410	113	1,39
Skins and Pelts not tanned					
Bear	100	32,500	149,690	461	0,005
Beaver	,,	17,500	39,591	226	0,018
Coney (rabbit)	,,	0,417	1,706	409	0,002
Fitch (polecat)	,,	2,882	12,421	431	0,002
Fox	,,	6,250	66,574	1065	0,007
Marten	,,	25,000	66,132	265	0,030
Mink	,,	7,500	31,449	419	0,020
Musquash	,,	2,500	3,946	158	0,040
Nutria	,,	2,500	3,916	157	0,009
Otter	,,	17,500	181,806	1039	0,014
Raccoon	,,	2,500	15,630	625	0,050
Squirrel	,,	1,000	1,500	150	0,001
Deer	,,	12,500	16,112	129	0,007
Goat	,,	8,300	10,016	121	0,030
Kid	,,	1,600	4,736	296	0,0024
Lamb	,,	0,417	5,638	1352	0,034
Sheep	,,	1,670	8,616	516	0,08
Seal	,,	4,170	35,723	857	0,11
Indigo, American	cwt.	7,000	24,585	352	0,09
other	,,	15,400	30,654	199	1,11
Cochineal	,,	89,600	20,735	23	0,19
Bark and Quercitron	,,	0,250	0,340	136	0,08
Campeachy wood	,,	12,000	6,055	50	0,07
Yellow-wood	,,	9,000	5,924	66	0,03
Madder	,,	2,000	2,407	120	0,07
Madder-root	,,	9,800	2,389	24	0,26
Annatto	,,	11,200	4,236	38	0,006
Cobalt-blue	,,	2,100	4,265	203	0,004
Peruvian bark	,,	14,000	13,146	94	0,07
Jalap	lb.	0,125	0,139	111	0,008
Rhubarb	,,	0,625	0,219	35	0,02

* 1694 prices calculated from official values.

Table 2—continued

Commodity	Unit of Quantity	Prices £ per Unit of Quantity		Price Index (1854–60) 1694=100	Weighting figure [see above pp. 23–4]
		1694	1854/60		
Mahogany... ...	ton	8,000	10,557	132	0,24
Timber, hewn ...	load	1,110	3,715	335	2,10
Lath-wood ...	fathom	2,000	7,704	385	0,064
Timber, sawn* ...	load	0,280	3,097	1106	2,31
Copper	cwt.	4,000	5,292	132	0,18
Lead, smelted ...	ton	15,000	21,825	146	0,22
Zinc, smelted ...	cwt.	2,500	1,233	49	0,18
Quicksilver ...	lb.	0,200	0,095	47	0,13
Sulphur	cwt.	0,500	0,359	72	0,23
Sumac	,,	0,325	0,588	181	0,08
Paper, raw ...	ton	3,000	22,033	733	0,15
Tar	last	9,000	12,165	135	0,09
Gum arabic ...	cwt.	1,125	1,793	159	0,04
Beeswax ...	,,	4,750	7,938	167	0,05
Clover seeds ...	,,	0,500	3,259	652	0,39
Flax and linseed ...	bushel	0,1125	0,351	312	1,61
Rape seed ...	,,	0,125	0,353	282	0,37
Tobacco	cwt.	1,050	4,121	392	2,63
Hops	,,	4,000	5,034	126	0,27
Cork	,,	0,800	1,595	199	0,07
Bristles	lb.	0,019	0,122	640	0,03
Fish-glue	cwt.	12,000	28,633	238	0,04
Whalebone ...	,,	8,000	16,764	209	0,04
Ivory	,,	6,000	31,925	532	0,16
Tallow	,,	1,050	2,746	262	1,91
109 Foodstuffs and raw materials				169	75,50
II. Exports					
Foodstuffs·					
Cod, dried... ...	cwt.	1,000	1,003	100	0,02
Beer and Ale ...	tun	0,833	3,505	420	1,37
Sugar, refined ...	cwt.	2,750	2,454	89	0,17
Bread and Biscuits	,,	0,750	,1,682	225	0,04
Salt	ton	1,333	0,523	39	0,26
Raw materials					
Coal	ton	1,000	0,464	46	2,44
Iron, pig	,,	1,000	3,469	347	0,72
Iron, scrap ...	,,	1,000	4,961	496	0,012
Iron ore	,,	0,250	0,966	387	0
Steel, smelted ...	,,	28,500	32,007	112	0,73
Tin, smelted ...	cwt.	3,650	6,168	169	0,27
Finished Manufactured Goods					
Cotton yarn ...	100 lbs.	8,93	4,707	53	7,26
Cotton thread ...	lb.	0,2	0,1150	57	0,55

* 1694 prices calculated from official values.

Table 2—continued

Commodity	Unit of Quantity	Prices 1694 £ per Unit of Quantity	Prices 1854/60	Price Index (1854–60) 1694=100	Weighting figure [see above pp. 23–4]
Calicoes white or plain...	100 yards	6,25	1,22	20	16,89
Muslins, Cambrics, white or plain	,,	8,75	2,23	25	0,16
Calicoes, printed checked, etc. ...	,,	7,5	1,70	23	12,27
Muslins, Cambrics, dyed, printed, etc.	,,	9,167	2,04	22	0,07
Fustians, Velvets and similar fabrics	,,	12,5	4,05	32	0,20
Mixed cotton fabrics	,,	6,25	2,93	47	0,10
Stockings, cotton	12 prs.	1,5	0,3034	20	0,23
Woollen Yarn	100 lbs.	5,357	11,39	213	2,83
Woollen Cloth ...	piece	10,0	10,44	104	2,17
Napped clothing fabrics	,,	3,5	5,653	162	0,005
Cashmeres ...	,,	4,5	5,006	111	0,01
Baizes	,,	3,0	3,229	108	0,018
Worsted materials	,,	1,583	1,376	87	3,02
Mixed fabrics ...	100 yards	20,0	3,69	19	2,14
Flannel	,,	6,25	5,61	90	0,17
Blankets	,,	7,5	6,56	87	0,44
Carpets	,,	0,175	0,128	73	0,49
Stockings, woollen	12 prs.	1,33	0,637	48	0,12
Linen Yarn ...	100 lbs.	5,36	5,57	104	1,33
Linen Thread ...	,,	45,0	9,85	22	0,25
Linens white, plain, checked, striped, printed, stained or dyed	100 yards	5,0	3,07	61	2,88
	,,	5,0	2,92	58	0,07
Cambrics and Lawns	,,	10,0	4,45	44	0,12
Damask	,,	10,0	5,70	57	0,06
Sail-cloth ...	,,	40,0	4,59	115	0,13
Ticking	,,	50,0	3,27	65	0
Lace of thread ...	,,	10,0	3,22	32	0,01
Thrown silk ...	lb.	1,0	1,059	106	0,39
Spun silk ...	,,	1,0	0,5451	55	0,22
Silk Manufactures Laces	100 yards	10,0	6,21	62	0,043
Stockings	12 pairs	2,0	1,562	78	0,002
Silk and Cotton Goods Stockings	,,	1,5	0,919	61	0
Silk twist ...	lb.	1,0	0,926	93	0,01
Cordage and cables	cwt.	1,15	2,182	190	0,13

Table 2—continued

Commodity	Unit of Quantity	Prices		Price Index (1854–60) 1694=100	Weighting figure [see above pp. 23–4]
		1694	1854/60		
		£ per Unit of Quantity			
Iron and Steel					
Bars	ton	10,0	8,522	85	1,55
Bolts and Rods	,,	10,0	9,500	95	0,21
Cast iron Goods	,,	10,0	10,213	102	0,61
Wire	,,	40,0	20,264	51	0,18
Anchors, wrought	,,	40,0	16,063	40	0,17
Hoops	,,	15,0	10,454	70	0,32
Nails	,,	35,0	24,299	69	0,22
Hardware and Cutlery	cwt	2,75	5,234	190	2,78
Gunpowder	100 lbs.	3,0218	3,06	101	0,26
Glass					
Plate	sq. ft.	0,2	0,101	51	0,65
Window glass	cwt.	1,0	1,450	145	0,03
Optical glass wares (Flint and Phial)	,,	1,0	3,205	320	0,16
Common bottles	,,	0,5	0,546	109	0,24
Leather, tanned, unwrought	,,	3,5	8,695	248	0,30
Leather Goods (except gloves and Saddlers' Goods)	lb.	0,2133	0,201	94	1,04
Saltpetre	cwt..	3,25	1,911	59	0,07
Soap	,,	2,667	1,308	49	0,18
Candles	lb.	0,01875	0,049	261	0,21
Tobacco products	,,	0,01086	0,211	1943	0,01
Books	cwt..	4,0	14,162	354	0,36
Total of 56 Finished Manufactured Goods				43	63,73
Total of 67 Exported Goods	(including export-prices of raw materials and foodstuffs)			47	69,76

Table 3. Actual Overseas Trade Values of the United Kingdom, 1801–60, calculated from the volume (base year 1913) and the Jevons price index (in £1m.)

Year	Imports*	Exports of Home** Goods	Exports of Foreign Goods	Total	Balance of Trade
1801	69,5	40,8	14,3	55,1	—14,4
1802	50,6	46,3	13,6	59,9	+ 9,3
1803	48,3	37,1	9,3	46,4	— 1,9
1804	48,3	38,1	9,8	47,9	— 0,4
1805	55,5	38,1	9,4	47,5	— 8,0
1806	51,3	40,9	9,2	50,1	— 1,2
1807	50,1	37,2	9,1	46,3	— 3,8
1808	56,9	37,3	7,7	45,0	—11,9
1809	72,8	47,4	18,5	65,9	— 6,9
1810	92,0	48,4	13,9	62,3	—29,7
1811	55,5	32,9	8,2	41,1	—14,4
1812	54,9	41,7	12,9	54,6	— 0,3
1813	.	.	.	.	.
1814	73,7	45,5	26,6	72,1	— 1,6
1815	65,8	51,6	18,6	70,2	+ 4,4
1816	41,4	41,7	14,4	56,1	+14,7
1817	53,7	41,8	10,9	52,7	— 1,0
1818	86,3	46,5	13,4	59,9	—26,4
1819	57,5	35,2	11,4	46,6	—10,9
1820	55,2	36,4	11,0	47,4	— 7,8
1821	45,6	36,7	9,9	46,6	+ 1,0
1822	45,4	37,0	7,4	44,4	— 1,0
1823	53,1	35,4	7,3	42,7	—10,4
1824	54,7	38,4	7,9	46,3	— 8,4
1825	81,1	38,9	8,6	47,5	—33,6
1826	56,6	31,5	8,2	39,7	—16,9
1827	68,6	37,2	8,3	45,5	—23,1
1828	62,1	36,8	7,3	44,1	—18,0
1829	58,5	35,8	7,4	43,2	—15,3
1830	63,3	38,3	7,0	45,3	—18,0
1831	68,9	37,2	7,2	44,4	—24,5
1832	56,7	36,5	7,9	44,4	—12,3
1833	56,4	39,7	7,5	47,2	— 9,2
1834	65,0	41,6	8,8	50,2	—14,8
1835	62,8	47,4	8,9	56,3	— 6,5
1836	80,1	53,3	8,6	61,9	—18,2
1837	75,1	42,1	9,9	52,0	—23,1
1838	82,8	50,1	9,9	60,0	—22,8
1839	95,3	53,2	11,5	64,7	—30,6
1840	95,0	51,4	11,7	63,1	—31,9
1841	90,5	51,6	11,1	62,7	—27,8
1842	76,3	47,4	9,4	56,8	—19,5
1843	78,5	52,3	9,1	61,4	—17,1
1844	83,0	58,6	8,5	67,1	—15,9

Table 3—continued

Year	Imports*	Exports of Home**	Exports of Foreign	Total	Balance of Trade
		Goods			
1845	99,0	60,1	10,3	70,4	—28,6
1846	91,6	57,8	10,4	68,2	—23,4
1847	110,4	58,8	12,3	71,1	—39,3
1848	101,6	52,8	10,5	63,3	—38,3
1849	106,4	63,6	15,0	78,6	—27,8
1850	101,1	71,4	12,5	83,9	—17,2
1851	112,9	74,4	13,5	87,9	—25,0
1852	109,7	78,1	13,3	91,4	—18,3
1853	145,9	98,9	18,0	116,9	—29,0
1854	163,7	97,2	21,3	118,5	—45,2
1855	145,4	95,7	21,5	117,2	—28,2
1856	173,2	115,8	22,9	138,7	—34,5
1857	184,0	122,1	22,4	144,5	—39,5
1858	158,9	116,6	22,4	139,0	—19,9
1859	175,1	130,4	24,6	155,0	—20,1
1860	209,6	135,9	28,7	164,6	—45,0
		Values shown by trade statistics			
1854	152,4	97,2	18,6	115,8	—36,6
1855	143,5	95,7	21,0	116,7	—26,8
1856	172,5	115,8	23,4	139,2	—33,3
1857	187,8	122,1	24,1	146,2	—41,6
1858	164,6	116,6	23,2	139,8	—24,8
1859	179,2	130,4	25,3	155,7	—23,5
1860	210,5	135,9	28,6	164,5	—46,0

* The volumes from 1801 to 1812 were ascertained by linking the 1814 volume, calculated on value-basis of 1913, with the appropriate official values. See Table 7a.
** Values shown by trade statistics. In 1801–1804 these were published only for 'Great Britain'. Since the values for the United Kingdom in the annual average 1805–09 are higher than those for Great Britain by 2.6 per cent., the values shown here for 1801–1804 were consequently raised by that amount.
[For A. H. Imlah's 'constructed real values' for 1854–69 see his Table I in the *Journal of Economic History*, vol. viii (1948), p. 146.]

Table 4. United Kingdom Imports, 1854–1936

(Actual Values in £1000's)

Year	Livestock	Foodstuffs	Raw Materials*	Finished Manufactured Goods	Total
1854	1 582	58 915	80 330	11 562	152 389
1855	1 693	54 909	77 568	9 373	143 543
1856	1 504	64 467	93 991	12 582	172 544
1857	1 793	65 506	108 760	11 785	187 844
1858	1 494	57 874	94 937	10 279	164 584
1859	1 699	57 092	107 506	12 885	179 182

Table 4—*continued*

Year	Livestock	Foodstuffs	Raw Materials*	Finished Manufactured Goods	Total
1860	2 171	78 647	114 369	15 344	210 531
1861	2 255	84 104	112 257	18 869	217 485
1862	1 935	90 827	111 065	21 890	225 717
1863	2 701	82 782	140 057	23 379	248 919
1864	4 316	80 008	165 316	25 312	274 952
1865	6 595	78 493	159 881	26 103	271 072
1866	5 884	90 562	169 843	29 001	295 290
1867	4 190	101 329	139 052	30 612	275 183
1868	2 751	107 774	151 174	32 995	294 694
1869	5 356	107 174	149 431	33 499	295 460
1870	4 737	103 907	156 440	38 173	303 257
1871	5 748	121 609	167 692	35 966	331 015
1872	4 753	139 796	169 833	40 312	354 694
1873	6 015	146 220	176 376	42 676	371 287
1874	5 821	143 777	173 415	47 070	370 083
1875	8 329	152 871	163 307	49 433	373 940
1876	8 475	153 658	161 095	51 927	375 155
1877	6 966	173 809	160 757	52 888	394 420
1878	8 282	161 465	144 807	54 217	368 771
1879	7 489	165 915	138 956	50 632	362 992
1880	10 500	175 910	166 065	58 755	411 230
1881	8 769	170 080	162 392	55 781	397 022
1882	9 514	168 752	175 596	59 158	413 020
1883	12 226	179 744	174 971	59 951	426 892
1884	10 798	150 670	168 997	59 554	390 019
1885	8 959	151 480	151 157	59 372	370 968
1886	7 358	137 476	144 766	60 263	349 863
1887	6 376	144 539	150 028	61 285	362 228
1888	7 942	151 204	163 794	64 696	387 636
1889	10 673	163 454	181 975	71 536	427 638
1890	11 582	164 644	173 973	70 493	420 692
1891	9 715	177 480	176 278	71 968	435 441
1892	9 819	177 708	163 978	72 289	423 794
1893	6 770	171 858	154 112	71 948	404 688
1894	9 693	166 945	156 382	75 325	408 345
1895	9 948	168 452	155 750	82 540	416 690
1896	11 513	175 055	166 090	89 151	441 809
1897	12 721	180 705	165 552	92 051	451 029
1898	11 582	196 137	168 594	94 232	470 545
1899	10 705	197 943	177 303	99 085	485 036
1900	11 010	203 103	203 011	105 951	523 075
1901	10 574	213 270	195 811	102 335	521 990
1902	9 152	212 088	198 296	108 855	528 391
1903	10 427	220 267	198 683	113 223	542 600
1904	10 823	216 888	211 418	111 910	551 039
1905	10 351	219 629	218 535	116 505	565 020
1906	10 466	224 995	249 146	123 281	607 888
1907	8 737	237 132	278 687	121 252	645 808
1908	7 115	234 073	237 940	113 825	592 953
1909	6 187	246 842	251 955	119 721	624 705

Table 4—continued

Year	Livestock	Foodstuffs	Raw Materials*	Finished Manufactured Goods	Total
1910	4 590	253 695	292 997	126 975	678 257
1911	4 317	258 651	284 700	132 489	680 157
1912	1 508	276 567	318 615	147 950	744 640
1913	793	284 239	328 281	155 421	768 734
1914	394	293 543	277 913	124 785	696 635
1915	465	373 760	342 434	135 234	851 893
1916	172	414 249	389 689	144 396	948 506
1917	2 160	454 277	438 161	169 567	1 064 165
1918	5 266	556 536	523 978	230 371	1 316 151
1919	405	676 194	727 819	221 738	1 626 156
1920	402	728 960	870 344	332 943	1 932 649
1921	3 198	535 641	380 986	165 674	1 085 499
1922	1 942	448 462	380 021	172 674	1 003 099
1923	15 572	476 211	406 621	197 822	1 096 226
1924	24 577	525 845	500 654	226 363	1 277 439
1925	19 878	530 988	524 156	245 693	1 320 715
1926	19 130	493 748	499 207	229 276	1 241 361
1927	18 149	500 476	452 888	246 828	1 218 341
1928	19 092	493 261	428 694	254 551	1 195 598
1929	19 896	497 043	442 675	261 151	1 220 765
1930	21 987	440 494	343 277	238 217	1 043 975
1931	19 337	386 177	239 485	216 254	861 253
1932	12 828	347 502	224 954	116 386	701 670
1933	7 733	315 943	241 258	110 082	675 016
1934	6 635	317 942	285 027	121 810	731 414
1935	.	.	.	.	756 041
1936	.	.	.	.	848 936
Old area of trade statistics [i.e. U.K. of Great Britain and Ireland]					
1923	2 110	460 408	405 153	195 827	1 063 498
1924	2 555	513 330	499 916	223 556	1 239 357
1925	3 364	517 760	523 849	244 276	1 289 249
1926	2 375	481 914	501 405	229 740	1 215 434
1927	577	487 672	453 516	247 096	1 188 861
1928	384	479 122	428 922	255 218	1 163 646
1929	573	483 194	443 195	262 123	1 189 085
1930	680	428 453	344 639	238 585	1 012 357
1931	1 026	376 208	240 752	216 405	834 391
1932	700	341 522	226 627	116 225	685 074
1933	1 267	311 774	243 519	111 422	667 982
1934	1 372	313 000	288 414	124 460	727 246
1935	.	.	.	.	747 585
1936	.	.	.	.	847 225

* [The Brussels Register classifies semi-manufactured commodities under the same heading as raw materials. See above, page 10.]

Table 5. United Kingdom Exports of Home Products, 1814–1936
(Actual Values in £1000s)

Year	Livestock	Foodstuffs	Raw Materials*	Finished Manufactured Goods	Total
1814	.	7 741	788	36 965	45 494
1815	.	7 144	876	43 590	51 610
1816	.	5 282	1 067	35 305	41 654
1817	.	6 577	964	34 277	41 818
1818	.	5 829	965	39 677	46 471
1819	.	3 880	809	30 522	35 211
1820	.	3 976	983	31 465	36 424
1821	.	3 399	885	32 371	36 655
1822	.	2 469	824	33 673	36 966
1823	.	2 727	725	31 905	35 357
1824	.	2 445	718	35 259	38 422
1825	.	2 518	720	35 633	38 871
1826	.	2 190	800	28 547	31 537
1827	.	2 434	871	33 876	37 181
1828	.	2 557	765	33 491	36 813
1829	.	2 519	805	32 519	35 843
1830	.	2 833	923	34 516	38 272
1831	.	2 499	973	33 692	37 164
1832	.	2 326	1 203	32 922	36 451
1833	.	1 897	1 179	36 591	39 667
1834	.	2 250	1 251	38 148	41 649
1835	.	2 213	1 650	43 509	47 372
1836	.	2 073	1 718	49 503	53 294
1837	.	1 829	1 735	38 505	42 069
1838	.	2 071	2 225	45 766	50 062
1839	.	1 909	2 087	49 238	53 234
1840	85	2 240	2 491	46 590	51 406
1841	150	1 945	3 044	46 496	51 635
1842	108	1 829	3 408	42 036	47 381
1843	105	1 933	2 956	47 286	52 280
1844	117	1 862	3 007	53 598	58 584
1845	107	2 079	3 356	54 569	60 111
1846	111	1 920	3 267	52 489	57 787
1847	103	2 633	3 235	52 871	58 842
1848	40	2 104	2 754	47 951	52 849
1849	59	2 339	3 556	57 642	63 596
1850	106	2 558	4 140	64 564	71 368
1851	76	2 723	3 812	67 838	74 449
1852	119	3 084	4 484	70 390	78 077
1853	103	4 949	5 269	88 613	98 934
1854	141	5 166	6 615	85 263	97 185
1855	198	7 035	7 168	81 287	95 688
1856	137	8 424	8 237	99 029	115 827
1857	149	7 000	9 264	105 653	122 066
1858	150	6 296	7 995	102 168	116 609
1859	239	7 212	7 976	114 985	130 412
1860	242	6 752	8 638	120 259	135 891
1861	277	7 378	8 773	108 675	125 103

Table 5—continued

Year	Livestock	Foodstuffs	Raw Materials*	Finished Manufactured Goods	Total
1862	323	6 808	9 606	107 255	123 992
1863	302	7 240	10 534	128 527	146 603
1864	261	7 110	10 414	142 664	160 449
1865	218	6 969	10 958	147 691	165 836
1866	172	7 722	12 025	168 999	188 918
1867	188	7 214	12 384	161 176	180 962
1868	229	7 476	12 741	159 232	179 678
1869	174	7 323	14 294	168 163	189 954
1870	325	9 192	14 667	175 403	199 587
1871	371	12 174	17 805	192 716	223 066
1872	249	9 349	25 997	220 662	256 257
1873	281	10 498	28 288	216 097	255 164
1874	283	10 250	23 679	205 346	239 558
1875	314	9 601	20 929	192 622	223 466
1876	313	9 740	19 439	171 147	200 639
1877	190	10 405	18 382	169 916	198 893
1878	280	10 190	17 584	164 795	192 849
1879	407	9 733	19 417	161 975	191 532
1880	425	10 869	24 337	187 429	223 060
1881	508	11 029	24 577	197 909	234 023
1882	588	11 774	26 587	202 518	241 467
1883	665	11 721	26 026	201 387	239 799
1884	614	11 299	24 551	196 561	233 025
1885	513	10 949	22 688	178 894	213 044
1886	561	10 385	22 762	178 725	212 433
1887	736	10 237	24 893	185 548	221 414
1888	1 040	10 720	27 158	195 617	234 535
1889	1 173	11 403	31 160	205 199	248 935
1890	862	11 776	37 393	213 500	263 531
1891	671	11 345	34 572	200 647	247 235
1892	699	11 048	32 261	183 208	227 216
1893	630	11 164	29 201	177 265	218 260
1894	666	11 226	30 570	173 544	216 006
1895	793	11 338	29 630	184 367	226 128
1896	942	11 670	29 272	198 262	240 146
1897	1 132	11 860	32 815	188 413	234 220
1898	1 104	12 462	33 942	185 851	233 359
1899	1 002	12 893	44 050	206 547	264 492
1900	902	14 344	58 796	217 150	291 192
1901	742	15 588	48 388	215 304	280 022
1902	823	17 164	47 775	217 662	283 424
1903	998	16 026	49 058	224 718	290 800
1904	868	16 230	48 208	235 405	300 711
1905	1 248	17 559	52 662	258 348	329 817
1906	1 798	19 231	64 118	290 428	375 575
1907	1 544	20 653	78 034	325 804	426 035
1908	1 213	19 983	71 263	284 645	377 104
1909	1 395	21 264	71 535	283 986	378 180

Table 5—continued

Year	Livestock	Foodstuffs	Raw Materials*	Finished Manufactured Goods	Total
1910	1 617	25 107	75 321	328 340	430 385
1911	1 692	27 445	76 485	348 497	454 119
1912	1 711	30 175	84 869	370 468	487 223
1913	2 273	29 748	96 551	396 673	525 245
1914	1 346	24 134	76 398	328 843	430 721
1915	601	24 244	69 212	290 811	384 868
1916	859	26 325	91 887	387 209	506 280
1917	823	16 871	87 592	421 794	527 080
1918	812	10 024	79 180	411 403	501 419
1919	1 815	37 611	139 717	619 495	798 638
1920	4 819	49 903	197 986	1 081 761	1 334 469
1921	3 472	34 692	82 720	582 516	703 400
1922	1 507	31 873	127 880	558 247	719 507
1923	1 577	39 141	169 762	556 778	767 258
1924	2 559	51 156	142 689	604 563	800 967
1925	2 458	48 488	118 812	603 623	773 381
1926	1 863	43 288	77 127	530 769	653 047
1927	2 040	43 448	112 707	550 886	709 081
1928	2 172	44 482	103 946	572 979	723 579
1929	2 231	45 823	116 141	565 154	729 349
1930	1 724	39 251	91 057	438 723	570 755
1931	1 266	29 176	65 193	294 986	390 621
1932	714	26 971	62 070	275 269	365 024
1933	510	23 890	69 100	274 409	367 909
1934	642	26 462	70 108	298 773	395 985
1935	.	.	.	.	425 834
1936	.	.	.	.	440 719
Old area of trade statistics [i.e. U.K. of Great Britain and Ireland]					
1923	1 279	32 741	165 870	542 729	742 619
1924	1 943	41 975	135 765	574 956	754 639
1925	1 717	40 528	112 942	579 193	734 380
1926	1 408	36 210	73 244	508 800	619 662
1927	1 607	36 867	107 664	528 609	674 747
1928	1 485	38 343	98 780	551 616	690 224
1929	1 633	39 513	110 973	544 490	696 609
1930	1 238	33 414	86 030	419 032	539 714
1931	1 005	24 361	60 599	275 477	361 442
1932	507	23 048	58 465	258 194	340 214
1933	599	22 822	67 108	259 475	350 004
1934	695	25 559	68 374	282 985	377 613
1935	.	.	.	.	407 219
1936	.	.	.	.	421 549

* [The Brussels Register classifies semi-manufactured commodities under the same heading as raw materials. See above, page .]

Table 6. United Kingdom Re-exports, 1854–1936
(Actual Values in £1000s)

Year	Livestock	Foodstuffs	Raw Materials*	Finished Manufactured Goods	Total
1854	0	6 288	9 915	2 433	18 636
1855	0	6 186	12 841	1 976	21 003
1856	0	7 377	13 812	2 204	23 393
1857	0	6 714	15 167	2 227	24 108
1858	0	5 476	15 578	2 120	23 174
1859	0	6 025	16 386	2 870	25 281
1860	0	6 743	19 323	2 564	28 630
1861	1	8 335	24 469	2 219	35 024
1862	1	9 041	30 824	2 310	42 176
1863	2	10 362	37 311	2 625	50 300
1864	1	10 122	39 228	2 788	52 139
1865	3	11 234	38 879	2 880	52 996
1866	3	10 686	36 813	2 486	49 988
1867	4	10 465	31 821	2 551	44 841
1868	5	12 168	33 225	2 703	48 101
1869	1	11 666	32 774	2 620	47 061
1870	4	13 122	28 162	3 206	44 494
1871	6	16 952	38 342	5 209	60 509
1872	13	16 911	36 306	4 916	58 146
1873	14	17 699	33 188	4 939	55 840
1874	15	17 906	35 120	5 051	58 092
1875	12	17 275	35 523	5 336	58 146
1876	16	17 825	33 023	5 273	56 137
1877	12	17 518	30 408	5 515	53 453
1878	14	16 772	30 005	5 854	52 645
1879	20	17 043	33 503	6 686	57 252
1880	42	18 021	36 963	8 328	63 354
1881	42	16 146	38 807	8 065	63 060
1882	36	16 168	40 515	8 475	65 194
1883	51	16 238	41 126	8 223	65 638
1884	88	15 406	39 226	8 222	62 942
1885	39	13 623	36 154	8 543	58 359
1886	25	13 697	34 342	8 170	56 234
1887	23	12 722	37 508	9 096	59 349
1888	50	13 979	40 569	9 445	64 043
1889	50	13 877	42 721	10 009	66 657
1890	19	14 514	40 067	10 121	64 721
1891	43	12 919	39 090	9 827	61 879
1892	22	13 343	41 608	9 590	64 563
1893	64	12 077	37 618	9 284	59 043
1894	36	11 624	37 212	8 908	57 780
1895	77	11 319	38 830	9 478	59 704
1896	67	11 960	34 378	9 829	56 234
1897	109	12 107	37 250	10 488	59 954
1898	94	13 028	36 013	11 520	60 655
1899	61	13 311	40 611	11 059	65 042
1900	83	12 604	38 915	11 580	63 182
1901	124	12 868	42 538	12 312	67 842

Table 6—continued

Year	Livestock	Foodstuffs	Raw Materials*	Finished Manufactured Goods	Total
1902	209	10 849	42 778	11 979	65 815
1903	103	11 120	44 579	13 772	69 574
1904	76	11 863	43 312	15 053	70 304
1905	98	12 922	49 597	15 163	77 780
1906	152	12 876	55 386	16 688	85 102
1907	122	13 249	60 433	18 138	91 942
1908	116	11 941	51 756	15 811	79 624
1909	234	13 152	60 152	17 807	91 345
1910	213	14 649	69 695	19 204	103 761
1911	144	15 511	68 081	19 023	102 759
1912	137	16 349	75 548	19 703	111 737
1913	129	17 059	72 111	20 276	109 575
1914	85	18 408	59 708	17 273	95 474
1915	20	23 900	61 202	13 940	99 062
1916	79	21 947	56 303	19 237	97 566
1917	61	8 827	48 555	12 234	69 677
1918	13	4 124	18 193	8 615	30 945
1919	2	43 469	98 435	22 840	164 746
1920	79	46 265	138 008	38 401	222 753
1921	119	28 853	57 674	20 273	106 919
1922	53	21 082	62 280	20 280	103 695
1923	84	23 868	73 422	21 170	118 544
1924	151	28 273	84 968	26 578	139 970
1925	107	30 872	99 103	23 955	154 037
1926	131	25 233	80 337	19 794	125 495
1927	159	25 412	76 387	20 995	122 953
1928	270	26 204	72 748	21 061	120 283
1929	497	24 947	63 157	21 101	109 702
1930	632	22 578	44 579	19 046	86 835
1931	601	19 242	29 528	14 496	63 867
1932	316	14 308	27 380	9 017	51 021
1933	232	11 271	28 507	9 071	49 081
1934	307	11 184	31 736	8 016	51 243
1935	.	.	.	.	55 303
1936	.	.	.	.	60 416
Old area of trade statistics [i.e. U.K. of Great Britain and Ireland]					
1923	83	19 184	72 463	20 240	111 970
1924	149	20 441	83 340	24 849	128 779
1925	105	23 225	97 507	22 269	143 106
1926	127	17 827	79 037	18 103	115 094
1927	149	18 945	75 141	19 379	113 614
1928	98	19 711	71 465	19 397	110 671
1929	202	18 283	61 723	19 635	99 843
1930	260	16 500	43 034	17 737	77 531
1931	198	14 018	28 319	12 817	55 352
1932	104	10 475	26 366	8 012	44 957
1933	115	8 366	27 771	8 220	44 472
1934	119	8 238	30 410	7 243	46 010
1935	.	.	.	.	50 406
1936	.	.	.	.	55 553

— 129 —

Table 7. United Kingdom Imports and Exports (including Re-exports), 1697-1933

(Volumes [*i.e.* quantities at base year prices as explained above, p. 28 ff.] in £1000s)

Year	Imports	Exports	Year	Imports	Exports	Year	Imports	Exports
1697	3 238	1 923	1747	6 582	5 299	1797	17 786	14 022
1689	4 370	3 656	1748	7 623	6 009	1798	24 962	16 038
1699	5 257	3 328	1749	7 303	6 853	1799	23 912	18 527
1700	5 699	3 645	1750	7 113	6 682	1800	28 078	20 185
1701	5 549	3 860	1751	7 233	7 189	1801	31 583	20 763
1702	3 876	2 690	1752	7 278	6 196	1802	29 635	22 550
1703	4 176	3 466	1753	8 012	6 513	1803	26 453	16 756
1704	5 029	3 506	1754	7 435	6 232	1804	27 642	18 597
1705	3 728	2 974	1755	8 540	5 868	1805	28 378	18 238
1706	3 823	3 554	1756	7 565	6 229	1806	26 728	19 752
1707	3 943	3 627	1757	9 127	6 680	1807	26 563	18 238
1708	4 396	3 706	1758	7 973	6 864	1808	26 625	17 877
1709	4 208	3 324	1759	8 641	8 195	1809	31 548	27 228
1710	3 676	3 529	1760	9 590	8 592	1810	39 050	25 579
1711	4 361	3 348	1761	9 277	8 453	1811	26 340	16 970
1712	4 136	3 871	1762	8 619	7 551	1812	25 996	23 030
1713	5 480	3 866	1763	11 594	8 086	1813	.	.
1714	5 567	4 468	1764	10 325	9 160	1814	33 538	31 498
1715	5 218	3 817	1765	10 589	8 056	1815	34 770	33 077
1716	5 205	3 937	1766	11 135	7 656	1816	26 395	29 962
1717	5 839	4 443	1767	11 794	7 598	1817	31 217	27 948
1718	6 302	3 538	1768	11 539	8 213	1818	44 524	29 726
1719	4 955	3 786	1769	11 649	7 408	1819	34 227	24 881
1720	5 770	3 864	1770	11 972	7 881	1820	36 257	26 516
1721	5 401	4 005	1771	12 572	9 747	1821	33 848	28 429
1722	5 984	4 566	1772	13 042	9 130	1822	36 010	29 162
1723	6 106	4 017	1773	11 073	8 306	1823	41 503	28 644
1724	6 981	4 188	1774	12 794	8 771	1824	43 446	31 475
1725	6 718	4 701	1775	13 108	8 145	1825	54 760	29 798
1726	6 304	4 182	1776	10 716	7 220	1826	43 832	28 349
1727	6 451	4 015	1777	10 921	6 628	1827	53 178	33 338
1728	7 205	4 832	1778	9 433	5 541	1828	53 128	34 112
1729	7 207	4 534	1779	9 926	6 399	1829	51 274	35 514
1730	7 438	4 706	1780	9 011	6 085	1830	54 122	36 874
1731	6 639	4 252	1781	11 023	5 442	1831	58 361	38 567
1732	6 751	4 847	1782	8 788	6 517	1832	50 610	40 918
1733	7 582	4 840	1783	11 436	7 655	1833	52 698	42 119
1734	6 652	4 504	1784	13 409	8 278	1834	58 047	43 809
1735	7 694	5 026	1785	14 176	8 190	1835	54 605	47 883
1736	6 817	5 273	1786	13 528	8 421	1836	65 076	48 477
1737	6 685	5 490	1787	15 482	8 529	1837	62 630	45 016
1738	7 013	5 577	1788	15 741	8 834	1838	69 001	53 683
1739	7 370	4 797	1789	15 318	9 996	1839	72 159	56 657
1740	6 273	4 444	1790	16 451	10 482	1840	75 964	58 193
1741	7 483	5 208	1791	17 081	11 896	1841	74 164	59 850
1742	6 478	5 165	1792	16 927	13 229	1842	71 314	59 155
1743	6 940	6 135	1793	16 864	10 830	1843	76 995	66 169
1744	5 934	4 983	1794	19 414	14.248	1844	83 817	71 006
1745	6 365	4 791	1795	19 971	14 480	1845	93 389	72 305
1746	5 636	5 854	1796	20 292	14 755	1846	86 388	71 242

Table 7. —continued

Year	Imports	Exports	Year	Imports	Exports	Year	Imports	Exports
1847	98 574	71 814	1877	347 715	266 961	1907	687 246	557 760
1848	103 652	72 505	1878	346 499	271 151	1908	655 364	509 159
1849	115 672	94 509	1879	354 948	288 205	1909	678 433	532 914
1850	109 909	99 355	1880	383 995	320 095	1910	686 980	573 087
1851	118 837	106 204	1881	373 136	344 737	1911	704 200	587 801
1852	118 011	110 040	1882	392 441	353 705	1912	756 550	619 265
1853	137 555	126 480	1883	415 309	362 962	1913	768 734	634 820
1854	136 400	125 785	1884	398 942	364 608	1914	691 660	537 481
1855	126 428	127 932	1885	404 660	347 764	1915	749 755	462 022
1856	146 816	148 691	1886	404 609	363 692	1916	639 433	455 840
1857	150 795	150 618	1887	423 599	382 609	1917	534 700	362 207
1858	145 752	151 506	1888	440 688	400 182	1918	551 235	232 848
1859	159 226	166 824	1889	480 250	409 136	1919	669 135	362 686
1860	183 885	175 778	1890	478 425	407 216	1920	671 615	459 296
1861	184 390	169 976	1891	489 885	384 668	1921	585 055	343 612
1862	166 005	153 243	1892	495 272	383 718	1922	672 164	454 829
1863	176 891	162 136	1893	478 432	369 912	1923	740 388	508 223
1864	185 162	161 527	1894	525 659	376 054	1924	828 496	534 106
1865	195 956	176 715	1895	551 946	404 980	1925	853 034	530 924
1866	220 396	193 488	1896	571 546	414 718	1926	878 629	462 975
1867	215 901	200 937	1897	585 379	415 941	1927	894 799	535 976
1868	234 333	212 987	1898	613 994	418 860	1928	878 510	556 526
1869	238 297	220 414	1899	616 313	441 310	1929	919 258	554 241
1870	253 265	235 674	1900	617 491	416 524	1930	907 772	461 461
1871	287 876	273 606	1901	633 614	423 118	1931	921 991	360 901
1872	288 074	272 643	1902	642 647	443 408	1932	819 004	361 985
1873	301 656	261 254	1903	642 300	448 741	1933	825 719	363 159
1874	309 504	265 102	1904	647 327	454 534			
1875	321 284	267 628	1905	656 620	492 375			
1876	332 764	262 611	1906	675 554	524 594			

Table 7a. United Kingdom Overseas Trade, 1801–1814

(Volumes [*i.e.* quantities at base year prices as explained above, p. 28 ff.] in £1,000,000s)

Year	Imports	Export of		Total
		Home	Foreign	
		Goods		
1801	31,6	13,1	7,7	20,8
1802	29,6	13,1	9,4	22,5
1803	26,5	10,8	6,0	16,8
1804	27,6	12,0	6,6	18,6
1805	28,4	12,5	5,7	18,2
1806	26,7	14,1	5,7	19,8
1807	26,6	12,5	5,7	18,2
1808	26,6	13,6	4,3	17,9
1809	31,5	17,7	9,5	27,2
1810	39,0	18,6	7,0	25,6
1811	26,3	12,4	4,6	17,0
1812	26,0	15,8	7,2	23,0
1813	.	.	.	.
1814	33,5	17,2	14,3	31,5

Table 8. United Kingdom Imports, 1814-1933

(Volumes [*i.e.* quantities at base year prices as explained above, p. 28 ff.] in £1000s)

Year	Livestock	Foodstuffs	Raw Materials	Finished Manufactured Goods	Total
1814	.	13 616	16 138	3 784	33 538
1815	.	11 537	19 673	3 560	34 770
1816	.	8 848	15 024	2 523	26 395
1817	.	11 138	17 176	2 903	31 217
1818	.	15 272	25 334	3 918	44 524
1819	.	10 610	20 570	3 047	34 227
1820	.	11 134	21 987	3 136	36 257
1821	.	9 791	20 922	3 135	33 848
1822	.	8 943	23 925	3 142	36 010
1823	.	9 857	27 777	3 869	41 503
1824	.	11 289	28 260	3 897	43 446
1825	.	13 563	36 613	4 584	54 760
1826	.	13 764	26 570	3 498	43 832
1827	.	14 796	34 236	4 146	53 178
1828	.	15 250	33 304	4 574	53 128
1829	.	15 948	31 577	3 749	51 274
1830	.	15 429	34 518	4 175	54 122
1831	.	18 621	35 166	4 574	58 361
1832	.	12 204	34 905	3 501	50 610
1833	.	12 695	36 706	3 297	52 698
1834	.	13 841	40 547	3 659	58 047
1835	.	12 343	38 975	3 287	54 605
1836	.	15 107	46 188	3 781	65 076
1837	.	15 238	43 459	3 933	62 630
1838	.	16 934	48 040	4 027	69 001
1839	.	21 965	46 037	4 157	72 159
1840	.	20 890	50 823	4 251	75 964
1841	.	21 244	49 041	3 879	74 164
1842	.	20 799	46 608	3 907	71 314
1843	.	16 590	56 050	4 355	76 995
1844	.	19 887	59 339	4 591	83 817
1845	.	21 148	66 384	5 857	93 389
1846	.	25 491	54 408	6 489	86 388
1847	.	40 141	52 323	6 110	98 574
1848	.	32 676	62 453	8 523	103 652
1849	.	39 647	67 615	8 410	115 672
1850	.	36 999	65 056	7 854	109 909
1851	.	39 526	72 337	6 974	118 837
1852	2 410	33 743	74 796	7 062	118 011
1853	3 261	43 157	80 447	10 690	137 555
1854	2 921	42 677	79 604	11 198	136 400
1855	2 394	37 444	76 915	9 675	126 428
1856	2 094	44 582	88 522	11 618	146 816
1857	2 342	42 122	95 837	10 494	150 795
1858	2 299	45 259	88 943	9 251	145 752
1859	2 284	43 333	102 286	11 323	159 226
1860	2 816	56 858	110 735	13 476	183 885
1861	2 877	63 624	102 279	15 610	184 390

Table 8—continued

Year	Livestock	Foodstuffs	Raw Materials	Finished Manufactured Goods	Total
1862	2 644	72 534	73 064	17 763	166 005
1863	3 957	71 041	81 687	20 206	176 891
1864	5 914	64 967	91 930	22 351	185 162
1865	7 799	64 524	100 480	23 153	195 956
1866	6 482	71 388	117 777	24 749	220 396
1867	4 756	73 058	112 643	25 444	215 901
1868	3 554	78 119	123 489	29 171	234 333
1869	5 989	85 338	116 849	30 121	238 297
1870	5 656	83 886	126 826	36 897	253 265
1871	7 012	93 889	154 030	32 945	287 876
1872	5 414	105 307	142 031	35 322	288 074
1873	6 469	110 070	148 708	36 409	301 656
1874	6 078	108 673	152 997	41 756	309 504
1875	8 268	119 815	149 402	43 799	321 284
1876	9 017	124 101	153 200	46 446	332 764
1877	6 811	131 431	158 893	50 580	347 715
1878	7 882	135 295	152 346	50 976	346 499
1879	7 402	145 967	153 919	47 660	354 948
1880	10 102	149 207	172 059	52 627	383 995
1881	8 566	142 997	171 204	50 369	373 136
1882	9 311	140 709	187 185	55 236	392 441
1883	12 137	155 849	191 371	55 952	415 309
1884	10 906	142 197	189 536	56 303	398 942
1885	9 494	154 666	181 223	59 277	404 660
1886	8 785	147 835	187 229	60 760	404 609
1887	8 226	157 167	193 909	64 297	423 599
1888	9 868	161 087	202 995	66 738	440 688
1889	13 231	170 212	223 905	72 902	480 250
1890	14 627	177 886	214 291	71 621	478 425
1891	11 898	180 163	224 698	73 126	489 885
1892	11 346	189 733	219 358	74 835	495 272
1893	7 692	186 868	205 750	78 122	478 432
1894	11 530	202 496	226 051	85 582	525 659
1895	11 663	211 661	234 795	93 827	551 946
1896	14 462	220 700	234 857	101 527	571 546
1897	15 752	225 198	236 940	107 489	585 379
1898	14 521	237 136	251 237	111 100	613 994
1899	13 110	245 992	241 536	115 675	616 313
1900	12 895	247 690	241 031	115 875	617 491
1901	12 476	254 380	248 506	118 252	633 614
1902	10 438	249 898	258 009	124 302	642 647
1903	12 445	258 226	245 621	126 008	642 300
1904	12 701	257 893	254 997	121 736	647 327
1905	12 540	251 868	268 141	124 071	656 620
1906	12 478	258 022	273 306	131 748	675 554
1907	10 560	258 596	292 431	125 659	687 246
1908	8 575	250 345	279 568	116 876	655 364
1909	7 322	256 860	291 885	122 366	678 433

— 133 —

Table 8—continued

Year	Livestock	Foodstuffs	Raw Materials	Finished Manufactured Goods	Total
1910	5 132	259 667	292 910	129 271	686 980
1911	4 689	267 478	296 254	135 779	704 200
1912	1 554	272 212	332 202	150 582	756 550
1913	793	284 239	328 281	155 421	768 734
1914	415	274 596	292 263	124 386	691 660
1915	397	285 531	341 274	122 553	749 755
1916	96	268 644	269 439	101 254	639 433
1917	1 333	217 566	225 206	90 595	534 700
1918	2 982	229 216	216 923	102 114	551 235
1919	175	270 153	301 537	97 270	669 135
1920	175	258 441	298 025	114 974	671 615
1921	1 547	265 653	240 504	77 351	585 055
1922	1 118	286 552	283 261	101 233	672 164
1923	15 392	313 871	287 978	123 147	740 388
1924	24 924	339 188	323 442	140 942	828 496
1925	18 914	333 604	334 912	165 604	853 034
1926	18 126	328 276	380 803	151 424	878 629
1927	17 911	343 673	360 884	172 331	894 799
1928	19 265	343 444	340 628	175 173	878 510
1929	19 726	351 508	362 236	185 788	919 258
1930	23 316	358 167	345 055	181 234	907 772
1931	20 473	390 084	328 041	183 393	921 991
1932	16 373	373 775	321 041	107 815	819 004
1933	14 649	364 287	340 672	106 111	825 719
Old area of trade statistics [i.e. U.K. of Great Britain and Ireland]					
1923	2 085	303 499	286 936	121 935	714 455
1924	2 591	338 385	322 942	139 200	803 118
1925	3 201	325 226	334 728	164 606	827 761
1926	2 251	320 422	382 536	151 744	856 953
1927	570	334 940	361 367	172 553	869 430
1928	387	333 650	340 955	175 649	850 641
1929	568	341 721	362 680	186 432	891 401
1930	721	348 336	346 371	181 572	877 000
1931	1 086	380 008	329 797	183 550	894 441
1932	894	367 228	323 291	107 715	799 128
1933	2 400	359 601	343 953	107 446	813 400

Table 9. United Kingdom Exports of Home Products, 1814–1933
(Volumes [i.e. quantities at base year prices as explained above, p. 28 ff.] in £1000s)

Year	Livestock	Foodstuffs	Raw Materials	Finished Manufactured Goods	Total
1814	.	3 531	637	13 058	17 226
1815	.	3 476	729	17 250	21 455
1816	.	3 089	1 170	14 927	19 186
1817	.	3 574	1 123	15 726	20 423
1818	.	3 273	947	17 312	21 532
1819	.	2 584	828	13 478	16 890

Table 9—continued

Year	Livestock	Foodstuffs	Raw Materials	Finished Manufactured Goods	Total
1820	.	2 635	1 011	14 405	18 051
1821	.	2 600	926	16 175	19 701
1822	.	2 791	975	18 385	22 151
1823	.	2 868	766	18 259	21 893
1824	.	2 656	814	20 460	23 930
1825	.	2 493	755	19 625	22 873
1826	.	2 253	981	17 628	20 862
1827	.	2 668	1 141	21 978	25 787
1828	.	2 799	1 118	22 695	26 612
1829	.	2 945	1 170	23 678	27 793
1830	.	3 274	1 482	24 974	29 730
1831	.	2 847	1 549	25 917	30 313
1832	.	2 604	1 967	27 961	32 532
1833	.	2 283	1 800	29 860	33 943
1834	.	2 754	1 771	29 909	34 434
1835	.	2 598	2 374	33 697	38 669
1836	.	2 276	2 385	35 530	40 191
1837	.	2 144	2 527	30 655	35 326
1838	.	2 428	2 126	38 475	44 029
1839	.	2 303	3 069	40 921	46 293
1840	59	2 720	3 653	40 766	47 198
1841	117	2 399	4 500	42 045	49 061
1842	69	2 328	5 192	41 245	48 834
1843	59	2 503	4 785	48 226	55 573
1844	64	2 395	4 502	53 737	60 698
1845	58	2 564	4 916	53 400	60 938
1846	59	2 337	4 649	52 549	59 594
1847	53	2 991	4 666	50 966	58 676
1848	21	2 583	4 455	52 789	59 848
1849	31	2 978	5 848	66 447	75 304
1850	48	3 176	6 778	73 310	83 312
1851	40	3 770	6 473	79 056	89 339
1852	66	4 314	7 322	81 513	93 215
1853	50	6 094	7 635	92 715	106 494
1854	62	5 738	8 338	90 498	104 636
1855	132	7 449	9 282	88 833	105 696
1856	131	8 811	10 437	106 226	125 605
1857	134	7 666	11 573	109 567	128 940
1858	106	6 861	10 935	109 239	127 141
1859	147	8 125	10 834	121 335	140 441
1860	150	7 429	11 813	126 483	145 875
1861	168	7 622	12 504	115 791	136 085
1862	213	7 219	13 532	99 362	120 326
1863	202	7 966	14 535	103 198	125 901
1864	177	7 706	13 823	103 952	125 658
1865	160	7 553	14 594	114 323	136 630
1866	112	7 895	15 489	128 579	152 075
1867	125	7 446	16 243	135 471	159 285
1868	178	7 784	17 181	143 990	169 133
1869	149	7 683	19 724	150 480	178 036

— 135 —

Table 9—*continued*

Year	Livestock	Foodstuffs	Raw Materials	Finished Manufactured Goods	Total
1870	353	10 251	20 560	161 245	192 409
1871	375	13 040	24 676	175 858	213 949
1872	188	9 934	23 981	184 612	218 715
1873	173	10 725	20 801	179 152	210 851
1874	160	10 703	21 236	179 498	211 597
1875	144	10 483	23 418	177 366	211 411
1876	124	10 846	24 955	171 307	207 232
1877	95	10 775	25 646	176 713	213 229
1878	154	11 128	26 276	178 196	215 754
1879	242	10 562	31 229	184 254	226 287
1880	255	12 121	35 697	204 484	252 557
1881	309	12 100	37 921	226 259	276 589
1882	379	12 162	40 898	229 142	282 581
1883	525	12 566	40 548	233 184	286 823
1884	427	12 909	39 681	235 517	288 534
1885	366	12 781	38 120	224 207	275 474
1886	381	12 755	39 737	233 722	286 595
1887	474	12 970	43 205	244 975	301 624
1888	577	13 362	44 521	254 110	312 570
1889	623	13 466	44 676	260 959	319 724
1890	628	13 773	44 836	260 618	319 855
1891	522	13 151	42 961	244 431	301 065
1892	556	13 528	43 528	233 312	290 924
1893	597	13 365	42 334	227 390	283 686
1894	943	13 963	42 918	234 153	291 977
1895	1 122	14 065	45 227	255 574	315 988
1896	1 146	15 181	46 869	267 905	331 101
1897	1 290	14 799	51 716	257 153	324 958
1898	1 305	15 697	49 639	258 602	325 243
1899	1 213	14 571	56 921	272 485	345 190
1900	1 098	15 846	54 559	256 774	328 277
1901	942	17 491	53 726	257 460	329 619
1902	1 048	18 974	59 061	272 017	351 100
1903	1 289	18 000	61 174	275 028	355 491
1904	1 386	19 633	61 433	279 534	361 986
1905	1 613	20 815	66 120	305 323	393 871
1906	2 120	21 483	75 468	325 089	424 160
1907	2 039	23 115	83 228	344 779	453 161
1908	1 750	22 816	81 122	307 623	413 311
1909	1 856	23 338	87 180	316 313	428 687
1910	1 988	26 935	87 318	352 787	469 028
1911	2 066	28 324	88 801	364 051	483 242
1912	2 052	30 785	91 299	383 830	507 966
1913	2 273	29 748	96 551	396 673	525 245
1914	1 241	24 292	79 258	330 186	434 977
1915	255	21 612	59 612	274 900	356 379
1916	385	18 603	58 069	292 853	369 910
1917	298	9 497	48 467	250 951	309 213
1918	232	4 209	37 568	170 844	212 853
1919	641	14 949	49 032	209 317	273 939

Table 9—continued

Year	Livestock	Foodstuffs	Raw Materials	Finished Manufactured Goods	Total
1920	1810	17 304	49 061	294 055	362 230
1921	1447	15 511	42 616	198 692	258 266
1922	638	15 784	88 839	257 049	362 310
1923	1544	20 664	98 085	285 958	406 251
1924	2298	26 085	85 517	307 977	421 877
1925	1607	24 881	78 550	313 163	418 201
1926	1265	23 280	53 814	297 342	375 701
1927	1373	24 187	82 495	332 035	440 090
1928	1416	24 795	82 316	347 493	456 020
1929	1593	26 866	94 316	346 266	469 041
1930	1396	24 460	80 078	279 586	385 520
1931	1100	20 786	63 580	208 787	294 253
1932	607	20 921	62 133	215 596	299 257
1933	242	18 622	68 453	221 571	308 888
Old area of trade statistics [i.e. U.K. of Great Britain and Ireland]					
1923	1253	17 287	95 823	278 751	393 114
1924	1744	21 405	81 345	292 897	397 391
1925	1127	20 794	74 643	300 567	397 131
1926	956	19 478	50 513	285 042	355 989
1927	1081	20 527	78 817	318 631	419 056
1928	968	21 373	78 211	334 516	435 068
1929	1166	23 161	90 149	333 634	448 110
1930	1002	20 819	75 664	267 070	364 555
1931	873	17 351	59 121	194 959	272 304
1932	431	17 908	58 524	202 188	279 051
1933	284	17 788	66 509	209 592	294 173

Table 10. United Kingdom Re-exports, 1814–1933

(Volumes [i.e. quantities at base year prices as explained above, p. 28 ff.] in £1000s)

Year	Livestock	Foodstuffs	Raw Materials	Finished Manufactured Goods	Total
1814	.	8 249	2 997	3 026	14 272
1815	.	5 927	2 603	3 092	11 622
1816	.	4 698	3 481	2 597	10 776
1817	.	3 732	1 859	1 934	7 525
1818	.	4 023	2 130	2 041	8 194
1819	.	3 388	2 717	1 886	7 991
1820	.	3 820	2 582	2 063	8 465
1821	.	3 812	2 829	2 087	8 728
1822	.	2 966	2 209	1 836	7 011
1823	.	2 811	2 224	1 716	6 751
1824	.	3 377	2 426	1 742	7 545
1825	.	2 679	2 522	1 724	6 925
1826	.	2 864	3 322	1 301	7 487
1827	.	3 290	2 968	1 293	7 551
1828	.	3 359	2 924	1 217	7 500
1829	.	2 956	3 490	1 275	7 721

Table 19—continued

Year	Livestock	Foodstuffs	Raw Materials	Finished Manufactured Goods	Total
1830	.	2 609	2 938	1 597	7 144
1831	.	3 240	3 440	1 574	8 254
1832	.	3 595	3 161	1 630	8 386
1833	.	3 547	3 229	1 400	8 176
1834	.	3 706	4 062	1 607	9 375
1835	.	3 400	4 473	1 341	9 214
1836	.	3 083	4 083	1 120	8 286
1837	.	3 276	5 094	1 320	9 690
1838	.	3 470	4 468	1 716	9 654
1839	.	4 139	4 475	1 750	10 364
1840	.	4 383	4 781	1 831	10 995
1841	.	4 109	5 240	1 440	10 789
1842	.	3 340	5 670	1 311	10 321
1843	.	3 474	5 669	1 453	10 596
1844	.	3 253	5 510	1 545	10 308
1845	.	4 103	5 611	1 653	11 367
1846	.	3 206	6 567	1 875	11 648
1847	.	4 173	7 192	1 773	13 138
1848	.	3 775	6 746	2 136	12 657
1849	.	4 959	10 730	3 516	19 205
1850	0	3 794	9 391	2 858	16 043
1851	0	4 328	10 690	1 847	16 865
1852	0	4 430	10 450	1 945	16 825
1853	0	5 909	11 837	2 240	19 986
1854	0	6 494	11 721	2 934	21 149
1855	0	6 181	13 499	2 556	22 236
1856	0	7 050	13 671	2 365	23 086
1857	0	6 092	13 433	2 153	21 678
1858	0	6 565	15 612	2 188	24 365
1859	1	6 689	16 963	2 730	26 383
1860	0	7 327	20 136	2 440	29 903
1861	3	7 948	23 541	2 399	33 891
1862	6	9 449	21 122	2 340	32 917
1863	4	11 140	22 353	2 738	36 235
1864	3	10 542	22 524	2 800	35 869
1865	8	11 059	26 239	2 779	40 085
1866	26	10 655	27 874	2 858	41 413
1867	4	10 339	28 478	2 831	41 652
1868	5	12 358	28 564	2 927	43 854
1869	1	12 169	27 511	2 697	42 378
1870	13	14 010	25 813	3 429	43 265
1871	10	16 749	36 961	5 937	59 657
1872	23	17 016	31 354	5 535	53 928
1873	32	16 618	28 224	5 529	50 403
1874	26	15 702	32 035	5 742	53 505
1875	8	15 510	34 614	6 085	56 217
1876	26	16 481	32 408	6 464	55 379
1877	23	16 543	29 980	7 186	53 732
1878	27	16 528	31 009	7 833	55 397
1879	16	17 065	35 391	9 446	61 918

Table 10—continued

Year	Livestock	Foodstuffs	Raw Materials	Finished Manufactured Goods	Total
1880	67	17 888	37 541	12 042	67 538
1881	42	16 490	39 988	11 628	68 148
1882	31	16 382	43 640	11 071	71 124
1883	30	17 620	47 286	11 203	76 139
1884	61	16 664	46 863	12 486	76 074
1885	24	15 776	44 141	12 349	72 290
1886	41	16 224	49 095	11 737	77 097
1887	45	15 027	52 264	13 649	80 985
1888	88	16 287	57 123	14 114	87 612
1889	63	16 181	58 750	14 418	89 412
1890	48	17 559	56 352	13 402	87 361
1891	34	15 386	55 183	13 000	83 603
1892	22	16 491	63 173	13 108	92 794
1893	7	14 420	58 238	13 561	86 226
1894	17	14 622	55 425	14 013	84 077
1895	198	15 073	59 079	14 642	88 992
1896	166	16 264	51 986	15 201	83 617
1897	286	16 486	57 235	16 976	90 983
1898	220	17 744	56 334	19 319	93 617
1899	82	18 251	59 652	18 135	96 120
1900	65	16 281	53 130	18 771	88 247
1901	73	16 486	57 919	19 021	93 499
1902	109	13 755	59 866	18 578	92 308
1903	90	14 015	59 704	19 441	93 250
1904	77	15 180	55 519	21 772	92 548
1905	97	16 567	61 754	20 086	98 504
1906	109	15 800	62 824	21 701	100 434
1907	123	15 442	66 661	22 373	104 599
1908	123	13 898	63 193	18 634	95 848
1909	221	15 171	67 601	21 234	104 227
1910	222	16 214	66 351	21 272	104 059
1911	150	16 343	67 796	20 270	104 559
1912	148	16 209	74 341	20 601	111 299
1913	129	17 059	72 111	20 276	109 575
1914	94	18 791	66 767	16 852	102 504
1915	18	21 840	70 411	13 374	105 643
1916	29	17 734	51 746	16 421	85 930
1917	39	5 969	38 140	8 846	52 994
1918	8	2 393	12 512	5 082	19 995
1919	1	21 639	56 480	10 627	88 747
1920	29	25 225	59 713	12 099	97 066
1921	41	22 258	54 016	9 031	85 346
1922	15	17 049	65 607	9 848	92 519
1923	41	18 484	71 833	11 614	101 972
1924	146	18 814	78 221	15 048	112 229
1925	42	20 042	79 624	13 015	112 723
1926	45	15 914	59 071	12 244	87 274
1927	42	16 379	66 575	12 890	95 886
1928	59	16 422	70 943	13 082	100 506
1929	87	16 138	55 200	13 775	85 200

Table 10—continued

Year	Livestock	Foodstuffs	Raw Materials	Finished Manufactured Goods	Total
1930	93	16 074	46 673	13 101	75 941
1931	83	16 146	38 310	12 109	66 648
1932	95	12 887	41 632	8 114	62 728
1933	59	10 416	34 480	9 316	54 271

Old area of trade statistics [*i.e.* U.K. of Great Britain and Ireland]

1923	41	14 860	70 903	11 103	96 907
1924	144	13 600	76 740	14 071	104 555
1925	41	15 081	78 319	12 096	105 537
1926	44	11 240	58 115	11 195	80 594
1927	39	12 215	65 511	11 896	89 661
1928	21	12 350	69 722	12 048	94 141
1929	35	11 826	53 954	12 817	78 632
1930	38	11 744	45 062	12 199	69 043
1931	27	11 760	36 730	10 708	59 225
1932	31	9 437	40 070	7 212	56 750
1933	29	7 732	33 580	8 439	49 780

Table 11. United Kingdom Imports of Foodstuffs, 1820–1933
(Volumes [*i.e.* quantities at base year prices as explained above, p. 28 ff.] in £1000s)

Year	Grain	Rice Vegetables Fruit	Tropical and subtropical products	Sugar, raw	Vegetable Foodstuffs total	Animal Foodstuffs	Processed Food-	Other Foodstuffs	Total Foodstuffs
1820	1 586	701	2 601	2 155	7 043	687	3 404		11 134
1821	294	545	2 458	2 239	5 536	970	3 285		9 791
1822	150	486	2 469	1 932	5 037	976	2 930		8 943
1823	62	597	2 578	2 152	5 389	1 058	3 410		9 857
1824	516	661	2 893	2 259	6 329	1 458	3 502		11 289
1825	1 302	654	2 730	2 015	6 701	2 319	4 543		13 563
1826	2 346	1 004	2 763	2 211	8 324	1 733	3 707		13 764
1827	2 337	1 017	3 303	2 104	8 761	1 887	4 148		14 796
1828	1 776	1 059	2 685	2 543	8 063	1 909	5 278		15 250
1829	3 865	808	2 510	2 486	9 669	1 450	4 829		15 948
1830	3 523	653	2 611	2 517	9 304	1 038	5 087		15 429
1831	4 648	1 020	2 674	2 747	11 089	1 200	6 332		18 621
1832	907	842	2 792	2 492	7 033	1 256	3 915		12 204
1833	597	813	2 711	2 426	6 547	1 311	4 837		12 695
1834	482	1 208	2 844	2 428	6 962	1 341	5 538		13 841
1835	235	771	3 049	2 277	6 332	1 207	4 804		12 343
1836	521	1 146	3 536	2 380	7 583	2 134	5 390		15 107
1837	1 347	1 379	2 910	2 295	7 931	2 489	4 818		15 238
1838	2 519	1 038	3 085	2 577	9 219	2 348	5 367		16 934
1839	6 449	1 696	3 110	2 394	13 649	2 137	6 179		21 965

Table 11—continued

Year	Grain	Rice Vegetables Fruit	Tropical and sub-tropical products	Sugar, raw	Vegetable Foodstuffs total	Animal Foodstuffs	Processed Food-	Other Foodstuffs	Total Foodstuffs
1840	4 984	1 702	2 997	2 066	11 749	2 425	6 716		20 890
1841	5 151	2 024	2 855	2 512	12 542	2 762	5 940		21 244
1842	5 774	1 714	3 131	2 435	13 054	2 011	5 734		20 799
1843	2 103	1 434	3 383	2 570	9 490	1 995	5 105		16 590
1844	3 400	1 828	3 905	2 498	11 631	2 377	5 879		19 887
1845	2 598	2 160	4 012	2 980	11 750	2 834	6 564		21 148
1846	4 649	2 706	4 044	2 879	14 278	3 585	7 628		25 491
1847	11 693	3 544	4 156	4 203	23 596	4 518	12 027		40 141
1848	8 779	3 453	3 874	3 516	19 622	5 600	7 454		32 676
1849	12 779	3 502	4 278	3 551	24 110	5 789	9 748		39 647
1850	10 896	3 334	3 873	3 221	21 324	5 582	10 093		36 999
1851	11 456	3 101	4 877	4 061	23 495	4 754	11 277		39 526
1852	9 201	3 096	4 729	3 506	20 532	3 624	9 587		33 743
1853	13 257	3 499	4 997	3 729	25 482	5 405	12 270		43 157
1854	9 742	2 901	6 078	4 665	23 386	6 909	12 194	188	42 677
1855	7 894	3 410	5 875	3 749	20 928	5 890	10 400	226	37 444
1856	11 814	4 430	5 964	3 973	26 181	6 535	11 595	271	44 582
1857	11 159	4 602	4 797	4 295	24 853	5 979	10 960	330	42 122
1858	13 584	5 241	5 647	4 613	29 085	5 036	10 872	266	45 259
1859	12 467	3 873	5 471	4 657	26 468	5 412	11 031	422	43 333
1860	17 606	4 322	6 663	4 513	33 104	9 371	14 046	337	56 858
1861	19 865	5 848	7 084	5 323	38 120	11 161	13 999	344	63 624
1862	23 595	5 832	8 303	5 060	42 790	14 282	15 083	379	72 534
1863	18 785	6 082	9 942	5 490	40 299	15 582	14 633	527	71 041
1864	15 113	5 268	9 134	5 505	35 020	13 929	15 484	534	64 967
1865	15 858	4 783	9 630	5 247	35 518	12 968	15 232	806	64 524
1866	19 556	5 310	10 235	5 446	40 547	14 005	15 988	848	71 388
1867	22 066	6 341	9 943	5 398	43 748	13 469	15 159	682	73 058
1868	22 192	7 715	12 061	6 038	48 006	13 162	16 103	848	78 119
1869	26 226	7 718	11 392	5 648	50 984	14 959	18 438	957	85 338
1870	23 534	7 126	11 642	6 551	48 853	14 172	19 849	1 012	83 886
1871	27 832	8 368	13 304	6 208	55 712	17 676	19 528	973	93 889
1872	33 338	11 573	13 183	7 052	65 146	18 406	20 582	1 173	105 307
1873	30 778	10 943	12 878	7 290	61 889	23 167	23 780	1 234	110 070
1874	30 180	11 217	12 189	7 233	60 819	24 200	22 433	1 221	108 673
1875	35 631	11 898	14 377	8 326	70 232	24 368	23 802	1 413	119 815
1876	36 157	12 865	13 195	7 992	70 209	27 077	25 288	1 527	124 101
1877	39 880	14 098	14 051	8 508	76 537	27 141	26 223	1 530	131 431
1878	41 040	12 973	13 637	7 637	75 287	33 476	24 689	1 843	135 295
1879	43 303	14 009	13 981	9 078	80 371	35 863	27 744	1 989	145 967
1880	41 736	14 694	14 836	8 651	79 917	38 879	28 291	2 120	149 207
1881	40 029	14 092	13 747	9 548	77 416	35 917	27 751	1 913	142 997
1882	41 347	13 105	14 351	10 157	78 960	29 277	30 273	2 199	140 709
1883	46 305	15 318	15 307	10 427	87 357	34 942	31 069	2 481	155 849
1884	35 534	14 252	13 952	10 045	73 783	35 271	30 244	2 899	142 197
1885	44 108	13 897	13 620	9 940	81 565	37 380	32 599	3 122	154 666

Table 11—continued

Year	Grain	Rice Vegetables Fruit	Tropical and sub-tropical products	Sugar, raw	Vegetable Foodstuffs total	Animal Foodstuffs	Processed Food-	Other Foodstuffs	Total Foodstuffs
1886	38 019	13 973	14 231	8 260	74 483	37 717	32 655	2 980	147 835
1887	42 044	14 355	14 145	9 220	79 764	37 350	36 897	3 156	157 167
1888	44 971	15 150	14 041	9 141	83 303	38 616	35 966	3 202	161 087
1889	46 265	15 213	14 022	8 984	84 484	45 457	37 031	3 240	170 212
1890	47 792	15 322	13 602	8 046	84 762	50 828	38 782	3 514	177 886
1891	46 643	16 679	13 676	8 295	85 293	49 974	41 587	3 309	180 163
1892	47 344	17 559	14 040	8 342	87 285	53 584	45 311	3 553	189 733
1893	49 051	16 881	14 583	8 208	88 723	50 702	43 430	4 013	186 868
1894	54 929	19 723	14 324	7 324	96 300	57 347	44 567	4 282	202 496
1895	56 712	18 617	14 981	8 707	99 017	62 699	45 616	4 329	211 661
1896	58 024	18 804	14 828	8 060	99 716	68 573	47 845	4 566	220 700
1897	54 083	20 629	15 039	6 938	96 689	75 015	48 814	4 680	225 198
1898	57 760	19 817	15 972	7 521	101 070	79 656	51 745	4 665	237 136
1899	57 665	21 027	16 680	6 718	102 090	84 393	53 852	5 657	245 992
1900	57 434	22 244	16 466	6 776	102 920	84 794	54 389	5 587	247 690
1901	59 496	21 145	16 624	6 854	104 119	88 704	56 718	4 839	254 380
1902	60 376	23 037	16 796	6 769	106 978	85 747	52 999	4 174	249 898
1903	65 540	25 083	17 608	6 475	114 706	89 092	51 103	3 325	258 226
1904	67 009	25 461	18 246	7 517	118 233	90 548	45 847	3 265	257 893
1905	65 594	22 854	17 318	7 503	113 279	92 281	43 151	3 157	251 868
1906	64 429	23 199	17 069	7 811	112 508	96 153	46 188	3 173	258 022
1907	65 792	24 428	18 043	7 658	115 921	94 455	45 146	3 074	258 596
1908	58 486	23 948	17 694	7 517	107 645	95 286	44 305	3 109	250 345
1909	65 070	23 707	18 920	8 346	116 043	91 324	46 669	2 824	256 860
1910	66 233	22 718	18 627	9 021	116 599	90 704	49 590	2 774	259 667
1911	66 215	22 976	18 762	9 841	117 794	96 603	49 964	3 117	267 478
1912	70 838	24 824	19 133	9 284	124 079	95 041	50 209	2 883	272 212
1913	71 683	25 218	19 675	10 715	127 291	100 214	53 406	3 328	284 239
1914	64 441	22 505	21 292	11 255	119 493	99 499	51 731	3 873	274 596
1915	59 848	24 677	28 161	10 000	122 686	102 615	57 659	2 571	285 531
1916	60 898	22 208	26 999	11 497	121 602	88 798	56 197	2 047	268 644
1917	52 880	12 453	15 744	12 470	93 547	77 280	44 545	2 194	217 566
1918	33 879	12 378	21 527	13 148	80 932	94 689	50 984	2 611	229 216
1919	42 670	21 241	31 474	11 696	107 081	87 355	72 575	3 142	270 153
1920	61 521	23 934	26 460	12 815	124 730	83 155	45 060	5 496	258 441
1921	52 791	26 992	24 658	8 344	112 785	104 829	42 755	5 284	265 653
1922	58 318	27 312	25 789	14 187	125 606	109 263	44 929	6 754	286 552
1923	61 178	32 211	24 884	11 960	130 233	131 500	44 729	7 409	313 871
1924	70 371	35 075	28 028	11 873	145 347	131 076	55 019	7 746	339 188
1925	56 087	32 817	27 846	13 849	130 599	134 827	59 602	8 576	333 604
1926	55 456	34 097	26 480	10 917	126 950	134 410	57 254	9 662	328 276
1927	65 697	32 215	29 980	12 052	139 944	137 250	55 681	10 798	343 673
1928	59 163	34 021	27 552	17 501	138 237	140 272	52 920	12 015	343 444
1929	62 533	35 024	30 176	20 961	148 694	138 521	52 605	11 688	351 508
1930	61 458	35 076	29 437	19 023	144 994	146 410	54 031	12 732	358 167
1931	73 499	41 189	29 359	18 199	162 246	161 036	51 956	14 846	390 084
1932	62 275	39 860	30 559	24 070	156 764	159 151	44 472	13 388	373 775
1933	69 288	36 769	27 926	20 566	154 549	153 168	44 651	11 919	364 287

Table 12. United Kingdom Imports of Raw Materials, 1820–1933

(Volumes [*i.e.* quantities at base year prices as explained above, p. 28 ff.] in £1000s)

Year	Ores and scrap	Metals	Timber	Wood Pulp	Mineral oils	Chemical Raw Materials	Textile Raw Materials	Skins and Hides	Other Raw Materials	Raw Materials Total
1820		139	2 042	24	.	552	8 553	445	10 232	21 987
1821	3	70	2 032	23	.	445	8 415	623	9 311	20 922
1822	8	126	2 356	30	.	327	9 957	645	10 476	23 925
1823	2	273	2 398	40	.	807	11 511	969	11 777	27 777
1824	2	117	2 855	42	.	764	11 471	1 459	11 550	28 260
1825	16	398	3 354	49	.	759	15 849	1 561	14 627	36 613
1826	11	131	2 711	30	.	884	10 937	1 082	10 784	26 570
1827	11	196	2 506	38	.	686	15 711	1 121	13 967	34 236
1828	51	121	2 571	37	.	1 083	15 275	1 470	12 696	33 304
1829	23	162	2 716	43	.	763	13 838	1 635	12 397	31 577
1830	27	301	2 432	45	.	909	15 931	1 752	13 121	34 518
1831	48	191	2 707	34	.	812	16 409	1 733	13 232	35 166
1832	74	342	2 527	32	.	738	16 515	1 381	13 296	34 905
1833	111	454	2 418	45	.	772	17 446	1 577	13 883	36 706
1834	.	480	2 774	52	.	535	18 745	2 163	15 798	40 547
1835	.	523	3 253	53	.	551	19 674	1 656	13 265	38 975
1836	.	597	3 293	53	.	949	24 701	2 164	14 431	46 188
1837	.	530	3 277	62	.	829	22 173	1 909	14 679	43 459
1838	.	512	3 247	38	.	899	26 300	2 027	15 017	48 040
1839	.	642	3 335	44	.	728	23 186	2 080	16 022	46 037
1840	788	446	3 672	44	.	972	28 021	1 897	14 983	50 823
1841	913	557	3 459	31	.	987	25 782	2 519	14 793	49 041
1842	937	481	2 586	31	.	1 295	25 806	2 486	12 986	46 608
1843	1 253	691	4 125	38	.	1 033	30 547	2 752	16 611	56 050
1844	1 097	736	4 602	33	.	1 921	32 666	2 767	15 517	59 339
1845	1 065	730	6 104	35	.	2 815	35 269	3 357	17 009	66 384
1846	970	675	6 317	48	.	1 612	26 780	2 515	15 491	54 408
1847	779	813	5 777	31	. .	1 683	26 085	2 770	14 385	52 323
1848	940	706	5 431	34	.	1 443	34 538	2 284	17 077	62 453
1849	891	1 218	5 222	33	.	1 808	38 222	2 943	17 278	67 615
1850	861	1 383	5 294	38	.	1 886	35 654	3 049	16 891	65 056
1851	792	1 631	6 518	50	.	2 782	40 114	3 349	17 101	72 337
1852	809	1 675	6 431	37	.	2 121	43 722	2 772	17 229	74 796
1853	1 089	1 858	7 858	46	.	1 801	47 400	3 720	16 675	80 447
1854	1 267	1 473	7 859	54	.	2 649	44 985	2 912	18 405	79 604
1855	1 948	1 887	5 868	45	0	2 868	44 239	2 488	17 572	76 915
1856	2 109	1 403	7 612	49	2	2 508	51 244	2 985	20 610	88 522
1857	2 470	1 710	8 173	58	19	2 903	55 459	3 921	21 124	95 837
1858	2 440	1 888	7 318	54	22	3 304	50 490	3 101	20 326	88 943
1859	2 453	3 008	8 518	69	4	1 878	60 861	3 724	21 771	102 286
1860	2 806	2 926	8 875	76	0	2 374	67 190	3 724	22 764	110 735
1861	2 691	3 290	9 810	97	8	2 554	61 838	3 429	18 562	102 279
1862	3 138	3 105	9 406	113	124	2 306	35 595	3 871	15 406	73 064
1863	3 040	3 164	10 692	215	198	2 864	40 594	4 228	16 692	81 687
1864	2 958	5 188	11 011	320	118	2 294	49 412	3 947	16 682	91 930
1865	3 638	4 522	12 165	336	79	2 847	54 363	3 896	18 634	100 480
1866	3 906	4 618	11 619	449	173	2 510	68 766	4 380	21 356	117 777
1867	3 328	5 734	10 776	355	126	2 973	63 927	3 970	21 454	112 643

— 143 —

Table 12—continued

Year	Ores and scrap	Metals	Timber	Wood Pulp	Mineral oils	Chemical Raw Materials	Textile Raw Materials	Skins and Hides	Other Raw Materials	Raw Materials Total
1868	3 580	6 445	11 823	541	96	2 966	68 974	4 109	24 955	123 489
1869	3 824	6 047	11 509	502	120	3 085	63 923	3 812	24 027	116 849
1870	4 128	6 025	12 542	628	152	3 436	70 035	4 909	24 971	126 826
1871	4 515	7 101	13 031	857	199	4 235	90 468	5 640	27 984	154 030
1872	6 043	8 824	14 147	650	142	3 853	77 065	6 116	25 191	142 031
1873	5 449	7 308	16 063	618	370	4 286	81 269	5 775	27 570	148 708
1874	4 909	7 813	18 379	691	477	4 283	83 736	5 459	27 250	152 997
1875	4 524	9 552	14 985	800	432	4 587	79 407	5 475	29 640	149 402
1876	5 085	9 168	18 376	764	560	5 043	81 452	5 120	27 632	153 200
1877	7 035	9 724	19 339	997	752	3 846	79 616	5 422	32 162	158 893
1878	6 557	10 190	15 384	870	672	4 488	77 291	5 464	31 430	152 346
1879	6 250	10 916	13 600	983	962	4 256	82 951	5 354	28 647	153 919
1880	8 635	10 403	18 037	1 222	862	3 741	91 380	6 493	31 286	172 059
1881	8 267	10 542	16 311	1 253	1 316	5 228	91 020	6 240	31 027	171 204
1882	9 361	11 245	18 157	1 290	1 328	5 909	98 151	7 438	34 306	187 185
1883	9 887	11 871	19 058	1 500	1 569	6 087	97 016	7 863	36 520	191 371
1884	10 146	12 826	17 790	1 405	1 178	5 424	98 144	7 829	34 794	189 536
1885	10 612	13 181	18 187	1 582	1 643	5 574	85 607	8 012	36 825	181 223
1886	9 579	12 899	15 898	1 653	1 584	4 652	97 523	7 677	35 764	187 229
1887	11 306	12 070	16 295	1 789	1 721	4 833	101 828	7 680	36 387	193 909
1888	12 661	14 019	18 682	2 222	2 099	5 130	104 871	7 970	35 341	202 995
1889	14 869	14 429	22 597	2 026	2 288	5 304	115 388	8 723	38 281	223 905
1890	14 933	14 652	20 791	2 072	2 337	5 060	106 074	8 646	39 726	214 291
1891	14 812	14 828	19 668	2 078	2 905	4 311	116 629	8 923	40 544	224 698
1892	15 191	14 251	22 303	2 145	2 896	4 715	107 370	9 143	41 344	219 358
1893	14 910	15 705	20 518	2 141	3 451	4 164	93 132	9 556	42 173	205 750
1894	14 068	17 571	22 957	2 462	3 625	4 537	106 491	9 407	44 933	226 051
1895	14 016	17 111	21 576	2 525	3 940	5 047	112 821	11 413	46 346	234 795
1896	13 828	18 639	25 133	2 647	4 225	4 978	107 865	9 218	48 324	234 857
1897	14 421	17 146	29 150	3 021	4 130	4 856	108 517	10 728	44 971	236 940
1898	13 898	17 272	25 966	3 035	4 876	4 652	120 264	11 051	50 223	251 237
1899	16 303	17 892	28 330	3 123	5 341	5 340	102 285	11 523	51 399	241 536
1900	15 125	20 547	29 390	3 430	5 672	4 998	99 156	12 187	50 526	241 031
1901	14 627	21 376	27 703	3 192	5 645	4 873	109 649	11 820	49 621	248 506
1902	14 935	24 769	28 642	3 585	6 335	4 440	108 714	11 827	54 762	258 009
1903	15 346	22 068	29 843	3 737	6 358	3 865	102 622	10 387	51 395	245 621
1904	14 301	26 298	27 903	3 806	6 720	3 929	107 795	9 530	54 715	254 997
1905	18 318	25 322	26 896	3 815	6 675	4 028	119 157	11 319	52 611	268 141
1906	19 768	25 359	29 865	3 947	6 655	4 077	114 876	14 026	54 733	273 306
1907	19 899	24 907	28 913	4 301	6 765	4 374	133 761	12 541	56 970	292 431
1908	18 688	29 206	28 537	4 582	7 643	4 460	119 428	11 959	55 065	279 568
1909	18 677	28 854	27 607	4 620	7 965	3 817	126 227	14 136	59 982	291 885
1910	20 008	28 120	29 062	5 136	7 684	4 491	119 515	14 330	64 564	292 910
1911	18 755	29 813	28 170	4 835	8 133	4 736	126 736	12 773	62 303	296 254
1912	18 908	30 078	29 072	5 540	9 194	5 115	151 009	14 876	68 410	332 202
1913	20 027	32 068	33 789	5 816	10 857	5 075	128 574	15 067	77 008	328 281
1914	17 816	32 246	24 976	5 713	14 385	5 345	109 787	13 285	68 710	292 263
1915	18 356	33 968	22 263	5 235	13 089	5 097	148 366	14 119	80 781	341 274

10*

Table 12—*continued*

Year	Ores and scrap	Metals	Timber	Wood Pulp	Mineral oils	Chemical Raw Materials	Textile Raw Materials	Skins and Hides	Other Raw Materials	Raw Materials Total
1916	17 339	22 554	17 841	3 847	10 044	3 165	114 704	11 635	68 310	269 439
1917	16 026	23 477	8 261	2 111	18 392	2 158	92 674	11 020	51 087	225 206
1918	15 003	25 348	7 350	2 076	29 460	2 538	79 749	9 786	45 613	216 923
1919	12 745	21 652	20 095	4 807	16 046	3 194	123 157	14 582	85 259	301 537
1920	15 956	23 060	20 745	6 038	19 560	4 092	114 898	12 899	80 777	298 025
1921	8 024	20 025	12 117	3 187	25 825	2 397	80 151	8 362	80 416	240 504
1922	11 443	17 395	21 947	5 251	26 988	3 081	110 300	12 240	74 616	283 261
1923	16 116	22 398	27 268	6 479	29 483	3 730	87 783	13 617	81 104	287 978
1924	17 593	29 409	29 468	7 064	34 944	4 068	100 032	16 439	84 425	323 442
1925	15 568	31 806	28 899	7 091	35 903	3 597	107 147	16 708	88 193	334 912
1926	12 366	33 263	24 702	7 572	42 565	3 042	104 921	14 899	137 473	380 803
1927	15 545	34 388	32 011	8 271	45 630	4 133	103 662	16 461	100 783	360 884
1928	16 895	31 133	27 789	7 510	46 913	3 611	97 814	15 988	92 975	340 628
1929	19 187	31 815	30 241	9 369	48 835	4 059	101 423	14 410	102 897	362 236
1930	17 033	32 495	29 651	8 658	53 469	3 392	87 232	14 984	98 141	345 055
1931	11 845	31 948	24 070	8 281	49 097	3 314	87 198	15 040	97 248	328 041
1932	10 310	24 828	23 678	9 985	50 023	2 393	95 309	18 024	86 491	321 041
1933	9 728	25 002	28 024	10 517	54 317	2 213	103 658	18 783	88 430	340 672

Table 13. United Kingdom Imports of Finished Manufactured Goods, 1820-1933

(Volumes [*i.e.* quantities at base year prices as explained above, p. 28 ff.] in £1000s)

Year	Textiles	Leather, Leather Goods, Furs and Skins	Iron and Steel Goods	Other Finished Manufactured Goods	Finished Manufactured Goods Total
1820	2 012	138	60	926	3 136
1821	1 810	138	60	1 127	3 135
1822	1 994	138	76	934	3 142
1823	2 165	170	75	1 459	3 869
1824	2 506	171	79	1 141	3 897
1825	3 246	201	129	1 008	4 584
1826	2 189	154	74	1 081	3 498
1827	2 569	182	102	1 293	4 146
1828	3 143	202	84	1 145	4 574
1829	2 474	173	86	1 016	3 749
1830	2 493	235	83	1 364	4 175
1831	3 057	210	97	1 210	4 574
1832	1 808	250	107	1 336	3 501
1833	1 757	244	98	1 198	3 297
1834	1 854	268	91	1 446	3 659
1835	1 831	241	107	1 108	3 287
1836	2 229	234	136	1 182	3 781
1837	2 246	243	106	1 338	3 933
1838	2 350	237	126	1 314	4 027
1839	2 466	187	115	1 389	4 157

— 145 —

Table 13—continued

Year	Textiles	Leather, Leather Goods, Furs and Skins,	Iron and Steel Goods	Other Finished Manufactured Goods	Finished Manufactured Goods Total
1840	2 637	238	104	1 272	4 251
1841	2 159	214	130	1 376	3 879
1842	2 386	288	103	1 130	3 907
1843	2 594	303	71	1 387	4 355
1844	2 891	356	135	1 209	4 591
1845	3 543	410	183	1 721	5 857
1846	4 215	519	190	1 565	6 489
1847	4 030	476	182	1 422	6 110
1848	6 238	558	134	1 593	8 523
1849	5 879	639	160	1 732	8 410
1850	5 246	657	185	1 766	7 854
1851	4 073	716	219	1 966	6 974
1852	4 217	808	182	1 855	7 062
1853	6 139	1 554	249	2 748	10 690
1854	6 738	1 268	237	2 955	11 198
1855	6 029	1 176	210	2 260	9 675
1856	7 354	1 196	291	2 777	11 618
1857	6 011	1 425	285	2 773	10 494
1858	5 192	1 208	150	2 701	9 251

Year	Textiles	Leather	Leather Goods, Furs and Skins	Iron and Steel Goods	Other Metal Goods	Chemicals	Paper Goods	Other Finished Manufactured Goods	Finished Manufactured Goods Total
1859	6 405	842	649	250	282	.	17	2 878	11 323
1860	7 758	789	780	329	359	.	41	3 420	13 476
1861	9 237	814	768	246	411	.	85	4 049	15 610
1862	10 300	886	881	322	315	.	162	4 897	17 763
1863	11 911	942	997	339	411	.	167	5 439	20 206
1864	12 709	1 123	1 108	486	398	.	198	6 329	22 351
1865	14 115	1 286	1 105	565	446	.	187	5 449	23 153
1866	15 491	1 583	1 174	600	453	.	230	5 218	24 749
1867	15 140	1 550	1 239	593	429	.	241	6 252	25 444
1868	18 705	1 731	1 245	566	521	.	252	6 151	29 171
1869	19 616	1 615	1 326	599	585	.	265	6 115	30 121
1870	25 514	1 591	1 367	679	495	.	260	6 991	36 897
1871	18 750	2 267	1 727	691	481	.	206	8 823	32 945
1872	19 422	3 254	1 859	910	664	.	278	8 935	35 322
1873	19 821	3 552	1 928	778	621	.	266	9 443	36 409
1874	23 227	3 614	2 083	986	687	.	272	10 887	41 756
1875	22 705	5 071	2 878	1 143	748	.	254	11 000	43 799
1876	24 408	5 643	2 792	1 228	706	.	328	11 341	46 446
1877	27 875	5 665	2 568	1 414	733	.	327	11 998	50 580
1878	27 727	5 841	2 585	1 693	868	.	317	11 945	50 976
1879	25 946	4 452	2 485	1 812	815	.	327	11 823	47 660

Table 13—continued

Year	Textiles	Leather	Leather Goods, Furs and-Skins	Iron and Steel Goods	Other Metal Goods	Chemicals	Paper Goods	Other Finished Manufactured Goods	Finished Manufactured Goods Total
1880	27 813	6 113	2 866	2 294	953		359	12 229	52 627
1881	24 223	6 810	2 797	2 435	1 031	3 255	315	9 503	50 369
1882	24 028	6 951	3 474	2 557	854	3 303	568	13 501	55 236
1883	23 821	7 091	3 746	2 690	942	3 472	606	13 584	55 952
1884	24 465	7 350	3 239	2 558	898	3 635	737	13 421	56 303
1885	26 254	7 664	3 069	2 480	848	3 656	735	14 571	59 277
1886	28 426	7 422	3 132	2 416	790	4 026	794	13 754	60 760
1887	28 838	8 269	3 627	2 410	868	4 360	867	15 058	64 297
1888	30 009	8 778	3 653	2 656	848	4 462	1 019	15 313	66 738
1889	32 542	10 359	3 763	2 627	848	5 008	1 109	16 646	72 902
1890	30 797	10 013	3 850	2 489	849	5 334	1 222	17 067	71 621
1891	31 394	10 572	4 177	2 458	918	4 899	1 414	17 294	73 126
1892	31 972	10 405	4 416	2 336	836	5 267	1 619	17 984	74 835
1893	33 377	11 472	4 464	2 300	881	5 207	1 628	18 793	78 122
1894	36 569	12 773	4 545	2 350	988	5 368	1 916	21 073	85 582
1895	42 570	13 777	4 947	2 480	1 076	5 713	2 055	21 209	93 827
1896	45 458	13 637	5 506	2 782	1 250	6 114	2 383	24 397	101 527
1897	48 020	14 041	5 280	2 610	1 413	6 057	2 811	27 257	107 489
1898	47 618	13 934	5 144	3 241	1 598	6 783	2 828	29 954	111 100
1899	48 698	15 353	5 323	3 306	1 589	6 834	2 993	31 579	115 675
1900	48 339	15 591	5 468	4 785	2 089	7 329	3 625	28 649	115 875
1901	46 153	14 765	5 998	5 831	1 779	8 129	3 548	32 049	118 252
1902	49 364	13 794	6 049	6 632	2 078	8 954	3 651	33 780	124 302
1903	48 563	12 825	5 819	9 582	2 013	9 148	4 067	33 991	126 008

Year	Textiles	Leather	Leather Goods, Furs and-Skins	Iron and Steel products	Machinery (including electrical)	Other Metal Goods	Chemicals	Paper Goods	Other Finished Manufactured Goods	Finished Manufactured Goods Total
1904	45 937	13 225	5 641	7 450	5 244	2 128	9 243	4 225	28 643	121 736
1905	48 308	12 313	6 600	6 857	5 013	1 972	10 159	4 724	28 125	124 071
1906	51 250	13 261	6 362	6 683	5 706	1 832	10 707	5 256	30 691	131 748
1907	49 519	10 993	4 803	5 791	5 703	1 645	11 905	5 141	30 159	125 659
1908	43 807	12 613	4 713	6 336	4 649	1 460	10 401	5 501	27 396	116 876
1909	46 251	11 914	5 257	6 861	4 225	1 427	11 119	5 456	29 856	122 366
1910	47 406	11 319	5 927	7 788	4 152	1 513	11 575	6 562	33 029	129 271
1911	47 511	11 486	5 953	9 708	5 202	1 793	11 694	6 596	35 836	135 779
1912	51 574	12 845	6 622	10 608	6 216	2 002	12 986	7 301	40 428	150 582
1913	54 016	10 572	6 435	12 680	6 729	2 112	12 880	7 691	42 306	155 421
1914	41 736	11 208	4 359	9 413	5 836	1 623	11 042	7 059	32 110	124 386
1915	36 184	14 213	3 396	5 667	6 999	5 384	12 328	6 983	31 399	122 553
1916	32 127	10 240	2 906	4 610	5 231	2 353	12 317	5 350	26 120	101 254
1917	18 435	5 436	1 393	2 843	4 634	1 666	9 731	1 617	44 840	90 595
1918	18 174	5 223	890	2 057	4 535	681	11 497	1 220	57 837	102 114
1919	22 896	16 712	2 001	3 366	5 295	491	8 075	4 397	34 037	97 270

Table 13—continued

Year	Textiles	Leather	Leather Goods, Furs and Skins	Iron and Steel products	Machinery (including electrical)	Other Metal Goods	Chemicals	Paper Goods	Other Finished Manufactured Goods	Finished Manufactured Goods Total
1920	31 489	5 580	2 513	6 074	7 058	2 529	10 757	9 583	39 391	114 974
1921	22 480	3 776	1 868	7 671	4 077	2 072	6 296	4 982	24 129	77 351
1922	33 412	5 912	3 525	5 946	3 536	1 883	7 562	8 082	31 375	101 233
1923	41 641	6 888	4 697	7 441	4 091	2 227	9 219	9 672	37 271	123 147
1924	49 312	7 965	4 778	11 525	4 540	2 271	9 986	10 449	40 116	140 942
1925	56 890	7 764	4 986	14 901	5 441	2 688	10 005	11 108	51 821	165 604
1926	45 430	7 219	5 423	18 155	5 920	3 153	10 102	12 110	43 912	151 424
1927	53 139	7 983	5 957	21 449	7 578	3 541	10 153	13 487	49 044	172 331
1928	52 317	8 802	6 776	17 084	7 539	3 820	10 885	14 628	53 322	175 173
1929	57 356	7 165	6 193	17 172	8 639	4 224	11 335	15 534	58 170	185 788
1930	57 452	7 679	6 352	16 197	8 080	4 226	10 394	15 860	54 994	181 234
1931	61 277	8 061	9 098	16 462	6 973	3 861	11 224	15 921	50 516	183 393
1932	28 585	5 123	4 126	8 044	4 052	1 871	8 068	13 277	34 669	107 815
1933	30 038	5 618	3 838	5 338	3 137	2 067	8 493	14 048	33 534	106 111

Table 14. United Kingdom Exports of Raw Materials, 1827–1933
(Volumes [*i.e.* quantities at base year prices as explained above p. 28 ff.] in £1000s)

Year	Coal	Metals	Other Raw Materials	Raw Materials Total
1827	259	741	141	1 141
1828	251	601	266	1 118
1829	260	669	241	1 170
1830	355	707	420	1 482
1831	358	714	477	1 549
1832	413	969	585	1 967
1833	447	715	638	1 800
1834	433	953	385	1 771
1835	517	1 191	666	2 374
1836	644	1 152	589	2 385
1837	783	1 252	492	2 527
1838	923	1 363	840	3 126
1839	1 018	1 328	723	3 069
1840	1 128	1 712	813	3 653
1841	1 299	2 016	1 185	4 500
1842	1 406	2 621	1 165	5 192
1843	1 312	2 229	1 244	4 785
1844	1 234	1 935	1 333	4 502
1845	1 778	1 799	1 339	4 916
1846	1 778	1 856	1 015	4 649
1847	1 745	1 870	1 051	4 666
1848	1 959	1 616	880	4 455
1849	1 988	2 157	1 703	5 848
1850	2 367	2 213	2 198	6 778
1851	2 459	2 098	1 916	6 473

Table 14—continued

Year	Coal	Metals	Other Raw Materials	Raw Materials Total
1852	2 574	2 271	2 477	7 322
1853	2 851	2 491	2 293	7 635
1854	3 092	2 202	3 044	8 338
1855	3 598	2 496	3 188	9 282
1856	4 212	2 956	3 269	10 437
1857	4 823	3 355	3 395	11 573
1858	4 654	3 030	3 251	10 935
1859	4 981	2 860	2 993	10 834
1860	5 223	3 128	3 462	11 813
1861	5 595	2 961	3 948	12 504
1862	5 898	3 710	3 924	13 532
1863	5 863	4 733	3 939	14 535
1864	6 254	3 942	3 627	13 823
1865	6 534	4 040	4 020	14 594
1866	7 147	3 860	4 482	15 489
1867	7 445	4 560	4 238	16 243
1868	7 710	4 707	4 764	17 181
1869	7 571	6 152	6 001	19 724

Year	Coal	Metals	Fertilisers	Textile Raw Materials	Other Raw Materials	Raw Materials Total
1870	8 225	6 123	.	.	6 212	20 560
1871	8 950	7 754	.	.	7 972	24 676
1872	9 228	9 003	.	.	5 750	23 981
1873	8 828	7 674	.	.	4 299	20 801
1874	9 718	6 152	.	.	5 366	21 236
1875	10 173	6 656	.	.	6 589	23 418
1876	11 391	6 449	.	.	7 115	24 955
1877	10 783	6 734	.	.	8 129	25 646
1878	10 805	7 259	.	.	8 212	26 276
1879	11 507	8 604	.	.	11 118	31 229
1880	13 123	10 367	.	.	12 207	35 697
1881	13 709	11 022	.	.	13 190	37 921
1882	14 668	11 805	.	.	14 425	40 898
1883	15 956	10 309	.	.	14 283	40 548
1884	16 343	8 808	.	.	14 530	39 681
1885	16 649	7 436	.	.	14 035	38 120
1886	16 335	8 605	.	.	14 797	39 737
1887	17 155	10 174	.	.	15 876	43 205
1888	18 926	8 962	.	.	16 633	44 521
1889	20 309	10 724	2 285	.	11 358	44 676
1890	21 123	11 455	2 211	.	10 047	44 836
1891	21 809	9 407	2 241	.	9 504	42 961
1892	21 323	9 803	2 362	.	10 040	43 528
1893	20 328	8 927	2 405	.	10 674	42 334
1894	23 128	8 016	2 287	.	9 487	42 918
1895	23 169	8 792	2 296	.	10 970	45 227
1896	23 963	9 446	2 548	.	10 912	46 869

Table 14—*continued*

Year	Coal	Metals	Fertilisers	Textile Raw Materials	Other Raw Materials	Raw Materials Total
1897	26 007	9 771	2 992	.	12 946	51 716
1898	25 589	9 525	2 955	.	11 570	49 639
1899	30 180	11 190	2 970	.	12 581	56 921
1900	32 273	10 374	2 883	.	9 029	54 559
1901	30 622	8 485	3 025	.	11 594	53 726
1902	31 380	9 585	3 335	.	14 761	59 061
1903	32 562	9 459	3 210	.	15 943	61 174
1904	33 747	7 814	3 332	.	16 540	61 433
1905	34 495	9 889	3 895	.	17 841	66 120
1906	40 380	12 604	4 095	.	18 389	75 468
1907	46 155	13 719	4 497	.	18 857	83 228
1908	45 588	10 610	4 406	8 215	12 303	81 122
1909	45 938	10 642	5 115	10 878	14 607	87 180
1910	45 082	11 407	5 501	9 751	15 577	87 318
1911	47 032	11 038	5 582	9 176	15 973	88 801
1912	46 851	12 182	5 144	11 117	16 005	91 299
1913	53 660	11 873	5 745	10 151	15 122	96 551
1914	43 300	9 518	5 405	8 907	12 128	79 258
1915	32 091	8 508	4 712	5 898	8 403	59 612
1916	29 034	11 411	3 930	5 605	8 089	58 069
1917	26 701	10 736	1 031	3 510	6 489	48 467
1918	24 104	6 914	494	2 258	3 798	37 568
1919	27 249	8 114	1 543	5 233	6 893	49 032
1920	20 748	9 866	2 030	6 559	9 858	49 061
1921	18 466	8 327	1 907	8 022	5 894	42 616
1922	47 772	14 262	2 284	12 046	12 475	88 839
1923	59 536	13 074	3 856	11 445	10 174	98 085
1924	46 152	10 286	4 300	11 418	13 361	85 517
1925	38 093	11 024	4 193	10 356	14 884	78 550
1926	15 383	12 291	2 733	9 972	13 435	53 814
1927	38 198	12 716	4 173	12 020	15 388	82 495
1928	37 900	11 854	5 880	10 739	15 943	82 316
1929	45 421	14 719	8 547	10 283	15 346	94 316
1930	41 089	10 293	8 261	7 428	13 007	80 078
1931	32 437	6 852	5 879	7 098	11 314	63 580
1932	29 620	6 947	6 210	8 943	10 413	62 133
1933	29 818	10 812	4 988	12 007	10 828	68 453

Table 15. **United Kingdom Exports of Textiles, 1827-1933**
(Volumes [*i.e.* quantities at base year prices as explained above, p. 28 ff.] in £1000s)

Year	Cotton	Wool	Linen	Jute	Other Textiles	Textiles Total
1827	8 364	5 768	2 027	.	438	16 597
1828	8 628	5 746	2 209	.	536	17 119
1829	9 744	5 468	2 106	.	742	18 060

Table 15—*continued*

Year	Cotton	Wool	Linen	Jute	Other Textiles	Textiles Total
1830	10 617	5 487	2 253	.	967	19 324
1831	10 235	6 315	2 525	.	729	19 804
1832	11 517	7 239	1 826	.	748	21 330
1833	11 923	7 627	2 363	.	793	22 706
1834	13 015	6 193	2 566	.	1 175	22 949
1835	13 356	7 716	2 984	.	1 149	25 205
1836	14 902	6 193	3 207	.	2 762	27 064
1837	13 730	5 128	2 526	.	1 596	22 980
1838	16 951	6 802	3 533	.	1 876	29 162
1839	17 306	7 378	3 897	.	1 993	30 574
1840	18 866	6 964	4 105	22	2 419	32 376
1841	18 426	7 800	4 520	17	2 132	32 895
1842	18 611	7 543	3 969	21	2 001	32 145
1843	21 669	9 674	4 283	21	2 140	37 787
1844	23 662	11 296	4 692	17	2 230	41 897
1845	24 106	11 031	4 436	26	2 560	42 159
1846	24 715	9 192	4 131	37	3 386	41 461
1847	21 338	10 254	3 982	69	2 968	38 611
1848	24 426	8 768	3 956	65	3 278	40 493
1849	29 049	12 859	5 098	77	4 055	51 138
1850	28 705	16 269	5 620	97	4 726	55 417
1851	31 757	16 200	5 754	113	6 076	59 900
1852	31 505	17 336	6 234	145	6 010	61 230
1853	33 112	17 632	6 269	177	11 275	68 465
1854	33 795	17 173	5 118	194	9 960	66 240
1855	38 469	15 781	5 340	191	7 771	67 552
1856	41 349	19 480	6 663	279	11 256	79 027
1857	40 313	20 630	6 332	327	11 371	78 973
1858	45 625	19 072	6 218	361	9 929	81 205
1859	48 863	20 983	6 457	315	11 738	88 356
1860	52 190	21 611	6 972	293	11 772	92 838
1861	47 718	19 782	5 783	490	10 959	84 732
1862	30 322	21 569	7 600	568	6 051	66 110
1863	29 106	25 082	8 821	688	4 584	68 281
1864	29 693	26 396	9 844	744	3 848	70 525
1865	35 256	28 330	10 780	827	4 248	79 441
1866	45 589	28 632	10 785	977	7 553	93 536
1867	50 930	28 050	9 254	1 248	8 517	97 999
1868	53 346	29 970	8 821	1 699	9 353	103 189
1869	51 745	31 873	9 296	1 902	8 666	103 482
1870	58 039	31 413	9 882	2 057	9 923	111 314
1871	61 250	38 710	9 881	2 412	11 396	123 649
1872	64 569	41 819	10 262	3 065	13 523	133 238
1873	64 155	37 219	8 987	3 536	13 427	127 324
1874	65 618	36 651	8 565	3 985	12 592	127 411
1875	64 922	35 427	8 889	3 399	12 030	124 667
1876	66 975	32 327	7 179	3 872	11 733	122 086
1877	69 840	30 711	7 419	4 122	12 125	124 217
1878	68 605	31 701	6 927	4 290	12 804	124 327
1879	69 240	32 383	6 902	4 925	11 924	125 374

Table 15—continued

Year	Cotton	Wool	Linen	Jute	Other Textiles	Textiles Total
1880	80 165	32 861	6 994	5 298	14 301	139 619
1881	86 971	34 808	7 387	5 842	17 581	152 589
1882	81 063	35 285	7 576	5 625	18 349	147 898
1883	84 947	34 095	6 962	5 885	16 618	148 507
1884	83 188	38 559	7 182	6 153	15 738	150 820
1885	80 807	36 633	6 885	5 543	14 776	144 644
1886	88 616	37 915	7 452	5 602	15 852	155 437
1887	90 182	38 458	7 699	5 762	16 944	159 045
1888	91 783	36 193	8 199	5 764	18 312	160 251
1889	90 318	35 673	8 377	6 281	19 233	159 882
1890	92 042	32 907	8 678	6 267	18 837	159 331
1891	88 769	30 275	7 667	6 351	18 985	152 047
1892	88 111	29 313	8 028	5 729	17 509	148 690
1893	84 075	27 956	7 598	5 866	15 675	141 170
1894	94 246	25 089	7 403	5 483	14 687	146 908
1895	93 455	34 008	9 400	5 830	16 099	158 792
1896	96 791	32 022	8 567	6 017	17 289	160 686
1897	90 933	29 530	8 250	5 787	15 984	150 484
1898	96 445	25 871	7 551	5 386	15 764	151 017
1899	99 671	27 484	8 513	5 305	16 017	156 990
1900	91 980	26 829	7 687	4 619	16 504	147 628
1901	95 835	24 608	7 144	5 335	16 334	149 256
1902	96 651	26 319	7 779	4 977	17 608	153 334
1903	95 066	28 146	7 556	5 423	17 270	153 461
1904	100 303	29 928	7 766	5 382	15 029	158 408
1905	111 135	30 121	8 559	4 791	15 925	170 531
1906	113 417	31 539	8 863	5 018	17 357	176 194
1907	118 211	32 673	8 814	5 489	18 754	183 941
1908	102 741	26 900	7 423	5 030	16 330	158 424
1909	106 547	29 735	10 154	5 534	17 787	169 757
1910	109 544	34 818	10 558	5 441	21 401	181 762
1911	120 094	33 152	9 622	5 194	22 091	190 153
1912	125 413	32 929	10 294	5 230	23 735	197 601
1913	124 906	32 053	9 463	5 339	24 044	195 805
1914	101 867	26 485	8 645	4 223	20 820	162 040
1915	88 134	23 512	6 190	4 206	17 243	139 285
1916	97 650	30 443	6 866	4 329	19 136	158 424
1917	89 241	27 327	6 296	3 797	13 724	140 385
1918	67 586	16 997	4 638	1 019	10 041	100 281
1919	69 376	26 633	4 449	3 607	12 221	116 286
1920	87 982	30 303	5 551	4 021	20 566	148 423
1921	57 142	15 580	3 009	2 437	10 469	88 637
1922	80 055	24 376	5 100	3 528	16 002	129 061
1923	78 326	27 334	5 912	3 759	19 833	135 164
1924	82 182	29 294	7 158	4 254	22 552	145 440
1925	84 837	24 011	5 665	4 412	24 244	143 169
1926	73 661	21 582	5 504	3 764	29 067	133 578
1927	79 694	24 089	5 944	4 038	31 791	145 556
1928	74 947	23 616	5 357	4 526	36 392	144 838
1929	72 031	21 895	5 684	3 844	33 346	136 800

Table 15—*continued*

Year	Cotton	Wool	Linen	Jute	Other Textiles	Textiles Total
1930	51 142	16 142	4 833	2 671	26 163	100 951
1931	40 633	12 771	4 518	2 133	19 971	80 026
1932	49 542	12 646	4 562	2 140	23 476	92 366
1933	46 773	14 515	5 097	2 490	24 755	93 630

Table 16. United Kingdom Exports of Manufactured Goods, 1827–1933
(Volumes in £1000s)

Year	Textiles	Iron and Steel Goods	Machinery	Other Metal Goods	Paper and Paper Goods	Chemicals	Leather, Leather Goods Furs and Skins	Other Finished Manufactured Goods	Total
1827	16 597	2 386	181	323	.	.	364	2 127	21 978
1828	17 119	2 422	242	282	.	.	350	2 280	22 695
1829	18 060	2 570	258	359	.	.	352	2 079	23 678
1830	19 324	2 743	230	416	.	.	390	1 871	24 974
1831	19 804	3 054	119	400	.	.	329	2 211	25 917
1832	21 330	3 259	118	470	.	.	344	2 440	27 961
1833	22 706	3 561	160	424	.	.	401	2 608	29 860
1834	22 949	3 556	259	452	.	.	405	2 288	29 909
1835	25 205	4 395	390	532	.	.	530	2 645	33 697
1836	27 064	4 249	284	450	.	.	528	2 955	35 530
1837	22 980	3 666	525	550	.	.	441	2 493	30 655
1838	29 162	4 618	723	583	.	.	501	2 888	38 475
1839	30 574	4 845	753	599	.	.	642	3 508	40 921
1840	32 376	3 545	562	678	.	.	624	2 981	40 766
1841	32 895	4 286	555	577	.	.	670	3 062	42 045
1842	32 145	4 062	616	729	.	.	631	3 062	41 245
1843	37 787	4 459	788	968	.	.	742	3 482	48 226
1844	41 897	5 476	832	1 094	.	.	666	3 772	53 737
1845	42 159	4 909	804	899	.	.	594	4 035	53 400
1846	41 461	4 862	924	916	.	.	565	3 821	52 549
1847	38 611	5 673	1 050	1 004	.	.	613	4 015	50 966
1848	40 493	5 819	772	985	.	.	513	4 207	52 789
1849	51 138	7 342	744	1 436	.	.	733	5 054	66 447
1850	55 417	8 505	1 118	1 489	.	.	985	5 796	73 310
1851	59 900	9 345	1 280	1 296	.	.	922	6 313	79 056
1852	61 230	9 794	1 339	1 215	.	.	1 269	6 666	81 513
1853	68 465	11 529	1 689	1 244	.	.	2 037	7 751	92 715
1854	66 240	11 224	1 521	1 230	.	.	2 015	8 268	90 498
1855	67 552	9 856	1 915	1 297	.	1 652	1 550	5 011	88 833
1856	79 027	13 112	2 297	1 754	.	1 823	2 310	5 903	106 226
1857	78 973	14 229	3 411	1 897	.	1 710	2 743	6 604	109 567
1858	81 205	12 741	3 340	2 033	.	1 672	2 431	5 817	109 239
1859	88 356	15 066	3 593	1 874	.	2 044	2 550	7 852	121 335

— 153 —

Table 16—*continued*

Year	Textiles	Iron and Steel Goods	Machinery	Other Metal Goods	Paper and Paper Goods	Chemicals	Leather, Leather Goods Furs and Skins	Other Finished Manufactured Goods	Total
1860	92 838	14 973	3 720	2 208	.	2 133	2 539	8 072	126 483
1861	84 732	12 686	4 177	1 978	.	1 846	2 505	7 867	115 791
1862	66 110	13 563	3 193	2 671	164	2 491	2 645	8 525	99 362
1863	68 281	15 464	3 461	3 461	206	2 557	2 365	7 403	103 198
1864	70 525	14 442	3 798	3 497	213	2 734	2 467	6 276	103 952
1865	79 441	15 186	3 967	3 008	188	2 884	2 827	6 822	114 323
1866	93 536	16 145	3 409	2 661	277	3 003	2 175	7 373	128 579
1867	97 999	16 692	3 568	3 182	259	3 172	2 039	8 560	135 471
1868	103 189	17 458	3 797	3 398	242	3 541	2 910	9 455	143 990
1869	103 482	21 574	3 798	3 537	320	3 936	3 348	10 485	150 480
1870	111 314	22 385	3 980	3 324	233	4 282	3 339	12 388	161 245
1871	123 649	21 362	4 257	2 991	299	5 005	4 809	13 486	175 858
1872	133 238	21 913	4 759	2 447	399	4 683	4 704	12 469	184 612
1873	127 324	20 241	5 269	2 722	408	4 411	4 188	14 589	179 152
1874	127 411	18 932	5 188	3 075	366	5 407	4 162	14 957	179 498
1875	124 667	18 174	5 530	3 115	392	6 014	4 491	14 983	177 366
1876	122 086	16 096	4 935	2 939	363	6 307	4 138	14 443	171 307
1877	124 217	17 411	4 904	3 314	399	6 814	4 082	15 572	176 713
1878	124 327	16 914	5 742	3 345	421	7 228	4 628	15 591	178 196
1879	125 374	17 616	6 311	3 716	457	8 075	5 518	17 187	184 254
1880	139 619	21 998	7 250	3 822	560	8 403	4 886	17 946	204 484
1881	152 589	24 328	8 359	3 899	660	9 740	6 093	20 591	226 259
1882	147 898	29 323	10 699	4 036	706	10 075	5 837	20 568	229 142
1883	148 507	29 521	12 374	4 213	702	9 656	6 225	21 986	233 184
1884	150 820	27 645	12 606	4 671	779	8 922	5 924	24 150	235 517
1885	144 644	26 953	10 994	4 751	844	9 026	5 456	21 539	224 207
1886	155 437	27 420	11 123	4 330	844	8 790	4 600	21 178	233 722
1887	159 045	31 742	13 296	4 300	875	9 143	5 497	21 077	244 975
1888	160 251	35 324	15 134	2 187	1 143	10 321	5 461	24 289	254 110
1889	159 882	36 121	16 704	3 956	1 054	11 133	5 288	26 821	260 959
1890	159 331	34 756	15 329	3 907	1 025	11 274	6 009	28 986	260 618
1891	152 047	30 740	15 540	3 829	1 070	9 943	6 020	25 242	244 431
1892	148 690	26 416	14 884	3 858	989	9 574	5 607	23 294	233 312
1893	141 170	25 952	15 750	3 960	966	10 191	5 636	23 765	227 390
1894	146 908	24 407	16 807	3 890	964	11 122	5 300	24 755	234 153
1895	158 792	26 573	18 688	3 828	970	12 831	5 797	28 095	255 574
1896	160 686	32 005	20 916	3 588	1 134	12 839	5 576	31 161	267 905
1897	150 484	32 341	19 831	3 439	1 073	12 803	6 014	31 168	257 153
1898	151 017	30 020	22 202	3 199	1 014	12 294	5 763	33 093	258 602
1899	156 990	31 712	24 819	2 690	1 005	11 783	5 667	37 819	272 485
1900	147 628	29 700	20 755	2 826	1 134	11 497	5 387	37 847	256 774
1901	149 256	28 957	19 891	2 897	1 123	9 027	5 431	40 878	257 460
1902	153 334	33 561	20 800	3 569	1 155	10 308	5 994	43 296	272 017
1903	153 461	35 161	21 005	4 030	1 227	12 422	6 390	41 332	275 028
1904	158 408	34 940	21 511	4 511	1 346	12 196	6 197	40 425	279 534
1905	170 531	38 566	24 787	4 528	1 438	12 612	7 205	45 656	305 323
1906	176 194	42 954	28 450	3 831	1 527	13 109	7 671	51 353	325 089

Table 16—continued

Year	Textiles	Iron and Steel Goods	Machinery	Other Metal Goods	Paper and Paper Goods	Chemicals	Leather, Leather Goods Furs and Skins	Other Finished Manufactured Goods	Total
1907	183 941	45 345	33 131	3 761	1 872	13 371	7 576	55 782	344 779
1908	158 424	40 135	31 438	4 728	2 236	12 144	6 714	51 804	307 623
1909	169 757	43 386	27 688	4 105	2 511	12 870	7 464	48 532	316 313
1910	181 762	49 728	29 046	5 297	3 164	13 835	8 697	61 258	352 787
1911	190 153	49 289	30 111	5 411	3 324	14 396	9 112	62 255	364 051
1912	197 601	52 531	31 610	4 661	3 550	15 101	10 041	68 735	383 830
1913	195 805	55 328	33 670	5 201	3 679	14 984	10 695	77 311	396 673
1914	162 040	45 077	25 780	4 324	3 228	13 828	9 472	66 437	330 186
1915	139 285	36 096	13 291	3 128	2 920	14 048	6 620	59 512	274 900
1916	158 424	33 108	13 748	2 427	3 189	13 126	8 048	60 783	292 853
1917	140 385	21 091	11 119	1 048	1 349	10 329	6 443	59 187	250 951
1918	100 281	15 576	7 593	760	871	8 781	2 215	34 767	170 844
1919	116 286	26 378	13 310	3 512	1 193	10 421	5 299	32 918	209 317
1920	148 423	38 787	24 501	8 347	3 145	14 144	7 664	49 044	294 055
1921	88 637	23 092	26 128	3 993	1 842	7 452	4 267	43 281	198 692
1922	129 061	36 511	21 412	5 196	2 741	10 674	5 120	46 334	257 049
1923	135 164	47 520	21 085	5 650	4 601	13 439	6 732	51 767	285 958
1924	145 440	47 383	21 387	6 202	5 055	14 110	8 354	60 046	307 977
1925	143 169	47 486	24 182	5 378	5 070	14 080	7 889	65 909	313 163
1926	133 578	41 595	21 763	4 971	4 932	13 703	7 711	69 089	297 342
1927	145 556	54 561	23 009	5 261	4 619	14 641	9 245	75 143	332 035
1928	144 838	55 405	26 741	5 411	4 949	15 584	9 394	85 171	347 493
1929	136 800	56 282	26 902	5 039	5 478	16 000	8 616	91 149	346 266
1930	100 951	42 410	23 816	4 371	4 747	13 444	6 019	83 828	279 586
1931	80 026	26 883	15 784	3 148	3 740	11 571	4 424	63 211	208 787
1932	92 366	26 482	14 173	3 547	4 277	12 451	4 255	58 045	215 596
1933	93 630	27 936	12 578	4 479	4 183	12 914	4 926	60 925	221 571

Table 17. British Industry, 1814–1944 (1913=100)

(a) Terms of trade between finished manufactured goods and raw materials
(b) Export-proportions †

Year Trade	Terms of Trade	Export Proportion	Year	Terms of Trade	Export Proportion	Year	Terms of Trade	Export Proportion
1814	129	53	1854	93	72	1894	107	87
1815	134	61	1855	91	74	1895	108	91
1816	150	56	1856	88	80	1896	103	91
1817	127	53	1857	85	80	1897	103	88
1818	118	55	1858	88	84	1898	107	85
1819	134	44	1859	90	85	1899	104	86
1820	143	47	1860	92	84	1900	105	83
1821	148	48	1861	86	79	1901	108	84
1822	145	52	1862	71	74	1902	105	87
1823	137	49	1863	73	74	1903	101	88

† [These two terms are defined below at the end of this table]

Table 17—continued

Year	Terms of Trade	Export Proportion	Year	Terms of Trade	Export Proportion	Year	Terms of Trade	Export Proportion
1824	137	50	1864	76	71	1904	100	90
1825	123	44	1865	81	73	1905	103	90
1826	126	43	1866	91	78	1906	97	96
1827	119	48	1867	96	83	1907	99	100
1828	126	42	1868	90	83	1908	107	96
1829	120	45	1869	87	86	1909	102	96
1830	118	44	1870	88	87	1910	92	102
1831	110	44	1871	101	89	1911	100	102
1832	105	49	1872	100	91	1912	101	105
1833	114	49	1873	102	85	1913	100	100
1834	113	46	1874	101	83	1914	105	89
1835	112	51	1875	99	84	1915	105	73
1836	113	49	1876	95	81	1916	91	81
1837	105	45	1877	95	81	1917	86	73
1838	99	51	1878	97	87	1918	100	56
1839	91	50	1879	97	94	1919	123	60
1840	91	52	1880	95	86	1920	126	78
1841	91	53	1881	92	98	1921	185	82
1842	95	56	1882	94	93	1922	162	89
1843	96	60	1883	94	93	1923	138	92
1844	101	58	1884	94	96	1924	127	88
1845	96	55	1885	96	94	1925	123	89
1846	94	55	1886	96	100	1926	136	94
1847	93	55	1887	95	101	1927	132	83
1848	93	52	1888	93	97	1928	131	88
1849	95	64	1889	96	94	1929	134	84
1850	96	71	1890	101	95	1930	158	73
1851	91	73	1891	105	89	1931	194	60
1852	93	71	1892	104	90	1932	182	61
1853	91	75	1893	103	90	1933	175	59

(a) Terms of trade :

1814–1853 $\quad \dfrac{\text{Export price index of manufactured goods}}{\text{Price index for total imports.}}$

1854–1933 $\quad \dfrac{\text{Export price index of manufactured goods}}{\text{Price index for raw materials imports}}$

(b) Export-proportion :

1814–1826 $\quad \dfrac{\text{Index of exports of home products.}}{\text{Index of industrial production (1913=100)}}$

1827–1933 $\quad \dfrac{\text{Index of exports of manufactured goods, metals, coal, coke, etc., and processed food stuffs.}}{\text{Index of industrial production (1913=100).}}$

[For a comment on this table see Imlah : 'The terms of trade of the United Kingdom, 1798–1913 (*Journal of Economic History*), Vol. X, Nov. 1950, No. 2, p. 175, footnote 1. Imlah observes : 'Schlote constructed his index on net barter terms of trade by diving a price index of exports of manufactured goods by the price index of *gross* imports for the years 1814–1853, and by the price index of imported raw materials from 1854 on. His index numbers show the general trends but are not very precise on short-term variations, and the series is not strictly continuous. Reduced to the same base, his index numbers for net barter terms of trade for 1814 is 136 to my 149; for 1815, 141 to my 153, and for 1824 it is 144 to my 164 ; and for 1825, 129 to my 138 '].

— 156 —

Table 18. United Kingdom Imports by Continents, 1949-1936
(percentage of total imports)

Year	Europe	Africa	Asia	North America	South America	Australia
1849	35,0	3,5	18,0	27,3	14,9	1,3
1850	36,5	4,4	20,5	22,7	14,4	1,5
1851	32,8	4,8	21,5	23,3	16,1	1,5
1852	30,2	6,2	19,9	28,7	13,4	1,6
1853	35,8	5,6	20,8	24,2	12,2	1,4
1854	39,7	5,5	15,3	24,4	12,3	2,8
1855	38,9	6,4	17,0	21,4	13,1	3,2
1856	36,3	7,2	17,3	24,9	10,8	3,5
1857	36,3	7,9	18,0	21,5	13,1	3,2
1858	36,3	7,2	15,6	23,8	13,9	3,2
1859	39,6	8,0	15,8	22,4	10,8	3,4
1860	40,7	7,9	13,9	24,7	9,7	3,1
1861	35,9	6,7	17,0	26,9	10,3	3,2
1862	38,3	7,8	23,4	16,3	10,9	3,3
1863	35,8	9,3	28,6	12,4	11,0	2,9
1864	36,2	9,3	27,6	10,9	12,3	3,7
1865	41,2	10,5	20,9	11,6	11,9	3,9
1866	41,9	7,7	18,6	18,3	9,6	3,9
1867	43,6	8,1	15,4	17,5	10,6	4,8
1868	41,6	8,5	17,6	17,0	10,9	4,4
1869	41,8	8,1	18,3	17,1	10,5	4,2
1870	43,7	7,1	14,8	19,3	10,4	4,7
1871	41,3	7,5	16,1	21,4	9,2	4,5
1872	42,2	7,4	16,9	18,1	10,9	4,5
1873	41,0	6,6	15,1	22,4	10,0	4,9
1874	42,2	5,6	14,9	23,3	8,8	5,2
1875	42,4	5,6	15,7	21,5	9,1	5,7
1876	41,3	5,7	15,7	23,3	8,0	6,0
1877	42,9	5,7	15,7	23,0	7,2	5,5
1878	41,7	4,1	14,7	26,9	6,9	5,7
1879	39,5	5,0	13,7	28,3	7,4	6,1
1880	39,1	4,9	14,1	29,5	6,1	6,3
1881	38,4	5,0	14,9	29,0	5,9	6,8
1882	42,1	4,7	16,5	24,0	6,6	6,1
1883	41,3	5,0	15,8	26,3	5,4	6,2
1884	41,2	5,3	15,9	25,1	5,2	7,3
1885	42,4	4,9	15,2	26,3	4,9	6,3
1886	42,6	4,6	16,0	26,5	4,3	6,0
1887	43,6	4,6	14,6	26,0	4,8	6,4
1888	46,3	4,4	14,4	23,1	5,1	6,7
1889	45,1	4,6	14,5	25,3	4,2	6,3
1890	44,4	4,7	13,3	26,2	4,4	7,0
1891	43,3	5,0	13,3	27,0	4,1	7,3
1892	41,6	5,0	12,6	29,0	4,5	7,3
1893	45,0	4,7	11,7	26,1	5,0	7,5
1894	45,5	4,7	11,7	25,2	5,1	7,8
1895	46,3	4,7	11,3	24,1	5,5	8,1

Table 18—continued

Year	Europe	Africa	Asia	North America	South America	Australia
1896	45,4	4,5	10,3	27,9	5,2	6,7
1897	45,6	4,3	9,9	29,5	4,1	6,6
1898	43,4	4,4	10,0	31,2	4,8	6,2
1899	43,8	4,7	10,3	29,1	5,1	7,0
1900	42,4	4,3	9,9	30,9	5,7	6,8
1901	42,7	4,4	9,7	31,0	5,4	6,8
1902	44,9	4,9	9,8	28,5	5,9	6,0
1903	44,7	4,7	10,3	27,7	6,8	5,8
1904	42,8	5,1	11,3	25,8	8,3	6,7
1905	42,7	5,1	10,9	25,1	8,9	7,3
1906	41,5	5,2	11,1	26,7	8,0	7,5
1907	40,1	6,5	11,9	25,2	8,3	8,0
1908	40,8	5,8	10,0	25,5	10,5	7,4
1909	41,1	6,3	10,7	23,4	10,3	8,2
1910	40,6	6,4	12,1	21,5	10,6	8,8
1911	41,4	6,4	12,8	22,1	8,8	8,5
1912	39,8	6,6	13,6	22,1	10,1	7,8
1913	40,5	6,1	12,7	22,8	10,1	7,8
1914	36,0	6,2	14,0	24,8	10,2	8,8
1915	22,4	6,9	15,6	33,1	13,0	9,0
1916	20,4	7,3	16,2	37,4	11,3	7,4
1917	15,5	7,2	14,1	43,6	10,7	8,9
1918	13,6	8,2	12,5	49,1	11,2	5,4
1919	15,5	8,6	14,7	41,0	9,9	10,3
1920	23,6	8,2	13,1	34,9	11,9	8,3
1921	28,6	7,4	10,4	32,1	10,6	10,9
1922	30,5	7,6	11,3	28,6	10,5	11,5
1923	35,3	7,6	13,0	24,9	10,7	8,5
1924	36,0	7,5	12,2	24,6	11,2	8,5
1925	34,9	7,5	13,1	24,5	10,4	9,6
1926	38,7	6,7	12,1	24,2	9,6	8,7
1927	39,2	6,9	13,0	21,6	11,0	8,3
1928	39,0	7,5	11,8	20,9	12,0	8,8
1929	39,8	7,1	12,3	20,2	11,9	8,7
1930	43,8	6,1	11,5	18,8	10,7	9,1
1931	47,3	5,1	10,3	16,4	10,9	10,0
1932	38,1	6,8	11,3	18,7	13,0	12,1
1933	37,0	6,9	11,8	18,5	12,9	12,9
1934	35,5	6,1	13,7	18,5	13,7	12,5
1935	35,5	7,2	12,8	19,3	12,6	12,4
1936	34,3	7,5	12,8	20,1	12,7	12,6

Table 19. United Kingdom Exports by Continents, 1849-1936
(percentage of total exports)

Year	Europe	Africa	Asia	North America	South America	Australia
1805	37,8	2,1	8,0	52,1		.
1806	29,3	3,0	7,6	60,1		.
1807	25,4	2,2	9,5	62,9		.

Table 19—*continued*

Year	Europe	Africa	Asia	South America	North America	Australia
1808	25,8	1,8	10,1	62,3		.
1809	35,4	1,8	6,4	56,4		.
1810	34,2	1,3	6,5	58,0		.
1811	42,9	1,2	9,8	46,1		.
1812	.	.	.	.		.
1813	.	.	.	.		.
1814	59,1	0,8	5,1	25,1	9,9	.
1815	40,1	0,6	5,6	46,5	7,2	.
1816	44,6	1,0	7,4	39,8	7,2	.
1817	46,0	1,0	8,9	34,7	9,4	.
1818	42,0	0,9	8,5	37,3	11,3	.
1819	48,1	0,9	7,7	33,8	9,5	.
1820	51,0	1,1	10,5	26,6	10,8	.
1821	43,6	1,4	11,8	32,2	11,0	.
1822	45,4	1,1	10,9	31,7	10,9	.
1823	42,1	1,4	11,0	30,5	15,0	.
1824	41,6	1,0	9,6	31,0	17,4	.
1825	37,7	1,0	9,3	33,2	18,8	.
1826	44,0	1,0	13,6	29,3	12,1	.
1827	38,6	2,1	12,0	22,6	23,8	0,9
1828	37,1	2,2	12,1	20,4	27,0	1,2
1829	40,2	2,7	10,9	17,9	27,4	0,9
1830	40,5	2,6	10,8	20,9	24,4	0,8
1831	36,2	2,5	10,0	29,8	20,5	1,0
1832	42,4	2,8	10,3	20,6	22,6	1,3
1833	39,1	2,7	10,5	24,4	21,9	1,4
1834	42,9	2,7	9,4	20,4	22,9	1,7
1835	38,7	2,7	10,0	26,9	20,2	1,5
1836	35,2	3,0	11,2	28,3	20,7	1,6
1837	45,0	3,8	11,0	16,1	21,9	2,2
1838	43,1	3,9	11,6	19,2	19,5	2,7
1839	38,2	2,8	11,6	22,4	21,8	3,2
1840	40,9	2,9	14,5	15,9	21,8	4,0
1841	44,0	3,0	14,1	19,6	16,7	2,6
1842	50,2	3,1	14,5	12,4	17,8	2,0
1843	46,4	3,5	16,9	12,8	17,9	2,5
1844	42,6	3,0	18,9	18,8	15,4	1,3
1845	42,5	3,3	17,3	17,8	17,0	2,1
1846	44,5	3,4	15,5	17,6	16,4	2,6
1847	40,9	3,7	13,4	24,1	15,1	2,8
1848	41,7	4,0	13,8	21,8	15,9	2,8
1849	39,3	3,6	14,4	22,5	16,9	3,3
1850	37,1	3,8	14,9	25,9	14,6	3,7
1851	35,5	3,9	15,2	25,0	16,5	3,9
1852	35,3	4,0	14,2	25,5	15,6	5,4
1853	29,1	3,7	11,3	29,5	11,7	14,7
1854	30,3	4,0	12,8	28,5	12,1	12,3
1855	39,5	4,9	14,7	21,6	12,7	6,6
1856	38,4	4,2	14,0	23,2	11,6	8,6
1857	37,7	4,9	14,4	19,6	13,8	9,6
1858	38,6	4,9	20,0	15,5	12,0	9,0
1859	33,2	4,8	22,2	20,5	10,6	8,7

Table 19—continued

Year	Europe	Africa	Asia	North America	South America	Australia
1860	36,0	5,1	20,2	19,1	12,4	7,2
1861	42,3	5,3	20,5	10,7	12,6	8,6
1862	40,8	5,4	17,2	15,6	11,3	9,7
1863	39,0	5,5	19,9	15,3	11,7	8,6
1864	37,4	6,5	18,9	15,5	14,2	7,5
1865	38,3	6,1	18,4	16,8	12,3	8,1
1866	34,9	6,1	19,2	19,4	13,1	7,3
1867	38,4	7,0	21,0	15,7	12,6	5,3
1868	40,6	5,7	20,6	15,1	11,2	6,8
1869	41,4	6,4	18,0	16,1	11,0	7,1
1870	39,7	6,8	18,9	18,1	11,5	5,0
1871	43,7	5,5	15,8	19,5	11,0	4,5
1872	41,8	5,6	14,6	20,2	12,3	5,5
1873	43,4	5,6	15,2	17,0	11,9	6,9
1874	42,6	4,8	17,6	16,2	10,9	7,9
1875	42,1	4,9	19,5	14,2	10,6	8,7
1876	43,7	5,1	20,1	12,3	9,9	8,9
1877	39,4	5,1	22,6	12,6	10,5	9,8
1878	41,4	5,4	21,5	11,3	10,1	10,3
1879	40,9	6,0	21,0	14,0	9,4	8,7
1880	35,9	5,9	23,4	17,9	9,4	7,5
1881	35,7	5,9	22,1	17,1	10,0	9,2
1882	35,5	5,7	20,1	17,7	10,5	10,5
1883	36,6	5,2	21,6	15,9	10,5	10,2
1884	37,4	5,0	21,6	14,6	11,1	10,3
1885	36,1	5,2	23,3	14,1	9,4	11,9
1886	34,5	4,7	23,0	16,8	10,4	10,6
1887	33,9	5,2	23,2	17,5	11,3	8,9
1888	32,4	5,4	23,4	16,1	11,8	10,9
1889	34,1	6,6	21,0	16,1	12,9	9,3
1890	34,8	6,7	21,8	15,7	12,2	8,8
1891	35,6	6,9	22,0	14,8	10,3	10,4
1892	35,7	7,0	21,3	15,6	12,0	8,4
1893	36,5	7,8	21,9	14,8	12,0	7,0
1894	38,1	8,2	22,9	12,2	11,1	7,5
1895	36,5	8,5	20,2	15,5	11,5	7,8
1896	35,9	9,9	22,5	11,6	10,9	9,2
1897	37,8	10,4	21,8	12,1	8,8	9,1
1898	39,7	10,0	22,5	9,7	9,0	9,1
1899	40,7	9,2	22,6	10,4	8,5	8,6
1900	41,0	9,5	21,0	10,3	8,8	9,4
1901	36,5	11,8	23,6	10,1	8,3	9,7
1902	35,2	13,9	20,8	13,0	8,1	9,0
1903	34,9	14,5	20,9	12,5	9,1	8,1
1904	34,3	11,8	24,7	11,1	10,2	7,9
1905	34,2	10,5	25,9	11,6	10,7	7,1
1906	34,9	9,6	24,0	11,8	12,2	7,5
1907	36,9	8,7	22,9	12,1	11,7	7,7
1908	38,2	9,2	23,5	9,6	11,0	8,5
1909	36,4	9,4	21,3	12,8	11,7	8,4

Table 19—continued

Year	Europe	Africa	Asia	North America	South America	Australia
1910	34,9	10,6	20,5	12,7	12,8	8,5
1911	35,3	10,5	22,4	11,1	11,6	9,1
1912	35,0	10,3	22,2	11,7	11,4	9,4
1913	34,7	9,9	25,2	10,7	10,8	8,7
1914	33,5	10,2	25,5	12,2	8,5	10,1
1915	41,2	11,1	19,9	10,4	7,4	10,0
1916	42,5	11,3	19,0	10,2	7,5	9,5
1917	47,5	11,1	18,7	9,7	7,4	5,6
1918	42,5	14,9	18,6	7,8	9,4	6,8
1919	55,0	9,4	17,9	6,5	6,7	4,5
1920	37,8	11,4	25,7	9,4	9,0	6,7
1921	31,7	11,5	29,7	9,8	8,7	8,6
1922	35,0	9,7	25,1	11,7	7,9	10,6
1923	36,5	9,8	22,4	12,0	9,0	10,3
1924	37,2	9,8	22,8	10,9	8,9	10,4
1925	35,5	11,0	21,6	11,0	10,0	10,9
1926	30,2	11,4	23,8	12,2	9,8	12,6
1927	33,8	11,4	22,4	11,1	9,9	11,4
1928	33,3	11,3	22,5	11,9	10,6	10,4
1929	34,7	11,2	21,4	11,7	10,6	10,4
1930	39,3	12,1	18,6	10,9	10,3	8,8
1931	43,3	12,9	17,9	10,6	8,6	6,7
1932	41,7	12,5	19,9	9,4	8,0	8,5
1933	39,4	13,3	18,2	11,0	9,6	8,5
1934	38,3	14,2	18,4	10,1	9,4	9,6
1935	37,0	15,4	17,7	11,0	8,7	10,2
1936	35,8	16,1	16,0	11,9	8,8	11,4

Table 20 a. Empire share of British Exports of Home Products; the Dominions'* share of British Exports to the Empire, 1814–1854
(Basis of calculation: actual values, per cent)

[* i. e. those territories which were Dominions in 1938, including Newfoundland.]

Year	Empire Share of Total Exports	Dominions' Share of Exports to the Empire	Year	Empire Share of Total Exports	Dominions' Share of Exports to the Empire
1814	35,4	29,0	1835	23,2	29,0
1815	29,9	24,1	1836	25,8	29,5
1816	28,2	23,3	1837	29,6	28,5
1817	29,5	14,6	1838	26,5	29,8
1818	27,4	15,7	1839	29,8	32,7
1819	29,5	21,8	1840	33,0	31,3
1820	29,3	18,0	1841	28,8	31,4
1821	29,9	14,1	1842	28,2	27,4
1822	28,2	16,6	1843	28,8	23,6
1823	29,8	20,3	1844	28,2	25,8
1824	29,2	21,1	1845	28,0	32,1
1825	26,1	23,4	1846	27,7	32,7

Table 20a.—continued

Year	Empire Share of Total Exports	Dominions' Share of Exports to the Empire	Year	Empire Share of Total Exports	Dominion's Share of Exports to the Empire
1826	30,8	18,4	1847	25,4	37,3
1827	29,7	17,7	1848	24,3	31,9
1828	30,2	21,2	1849	26,1	29,4
1829	28,5	21,6	1850	27,2	34,1
1830	25,5	25,6	1851	27,4	36,1
1831	24,8	29,8	1852	26,0	41,2
1832	26,0	29,9	1853	33,7	61,9
1833	24,3	31,6	1854	34,8	55,7
1834	22,3	29,0			

Table 20b. British Empire share of British Overseas Trade, Dominions'* share of British Trade with Empire, 1849–1936

Year	Imports		Exports		Re-exports	
	Share of British Possessions	Dominions' Share of Imports from the Empire	Share of British Possessions	Dominions' Share of Exports to the Empire	Share of British Possessions	Dominions, Share of Re-exports to the Empire
	Proportions (percentages) based on official values					
1849	23,0	13,2	.	.	11,7	32,1
1850	25,8	12,8	.	.	12,1	38,7
1851	25,8	13,3	.	.	10,6	37,3
1852	24,5	13,3	.	.	11,3	50,6
1853	23,5	13,0	.	.	12,5	64,5
1854	24,5	12,1	.	.	10,4	53,1
	Proportions (percentages) based on actual values					
1854	22,4	35,7	34,8	55,7	16,1	61,3
1855	23,4	30,2	27,2	38,2	11,0	51,7
1856	24,9	32,8	28,6	46,4	14,5	61,6
1857	24,6	30,6	30,4	48,0	13,6	60,1
1858	23,5	30,3	34,5	38,1	12,9	51,8
1859	22,0	32,9	35,4	36,4	13,9	49,2
1860	20,4	34,9	32,1	35,5	10,0	43,5
1861	24,2	32,3	33,8	38,7	8,4	49,1
1862	28,9	26,2	33,8	42,6	8,4	51,2
1863	34,0	20,4	34,7	37,0	8,1	48,0
1864	34,1	20,1	32,2	38,1	7,6	46,4
1865	26,9	26,2	29,1	41,0	6,3	56,8
1866	24,4	29,1	28,4	40,7	6,9	55,6
1867	22,1	36,9	27,5	34,9	7,9	47,3
1868	22,7	32,9	27,8	37,1	8,0	46,2
1869	23,8	32,1	25,3	41,9	8,1	46,9

[* i. e. those territories which were Dominions in 1938, including Newfoundland.]

Table 20b.—*continued*

Year	Imports		Exports		Re-exports	
	Share of British Possessions	Dominions' Share of Imports from the Empire	Share of British Possessions	Dominions' Share of Exports to the Empire	Share of British Possessions	Dominions, Share of Re-exports to the Empire
1870	21,4	39,3	26,0	35,8	8,0	48,7
1871	22,0	36,6	23,0	40,0	7,1	47,2
1872	22,4	35,9	23,6	46,3	8,7	54,6
1873	21,8	40,9	26,0	46,1	8,6	55,6
1874	22,2	42,2	30,2	45,2	9,7	51,2
1875	22,6	41,8	31,8	47,0	9,6	50,7
1876	22,5	44,1	32,3	45,3	9,4	52,4
1877	22,7	42,5	35,2	44,4	10,9	55,7
1878	21,1	44,6	34,3	46,7	10,9	53,8
1879	21,7	46,9	31,8	45,2	9,6	52,3
1880	22,5	48,3	33,7	41,6	9,9	51,0
1881	23,1	47,7	33,9	46,4	11,6	56,3
1882	24,1	42,1	35,1	50,2	11,5	61,9
1883	23,1	44,7	34,8	45,4	10,5	58,1
1884	24,6	47,3	34,7	45,3	11,8	58,9
1885	22,7	45,2	36,6	46,4	12,8	59,6
1886	23,4	44,0	35,5	44,5	11,7	62,4
1887	23,1	46,5	34,0	43,6	11,6	59,4
1888	22,4	46,9	35,9	46,3	11,7	64,3
1889	22,7	46,4	33,4	48,1	11,3	63,9
1890	22,9	49,8	33,1	45,0	11,0	58,6
1891	22,8	50,4	34,8	47,4	11,9	60,8
1892	23,1	51,7	32,9	46,4	10,2	61,0
1893	22,7	53,1	33,0	42,9	10,9	62,2
1894	23,0	53,0	33,7	42,3	10,0	62,6
1895	22,9	56,6	31,0	47,7	9,8	66,4
1896	21,1	54,8	35,0	49,3	11,6	68,2
1897	20,8	57,3	34,4	49,8	10,5	69,6
1898	21,2	56,0	35,7	47,3	11,0	69,4
1899	22,0	56,3	33,1	47,1	10,2	67,7
1900	21,0	56,2	32,4	50,8	12,1	67,4
1901	20,2	57,1	37,4	49,9	12,3	71,5
1902	20,2	56,0	38,5	55,4	12,9	73,1
1903	20,9	56,0	38,2	53,4	12,0	71,9
1904	21,8	54,1	37,2	46,7	12,6	71,2
1905	22,6	56,5	34,4	45,9	12,0	69,7
1906	23,4	57,8	32,3	47,0	11,0	70,2
1907	24,3	56,4	32,4	46,7	11,1	71,4
1908	21,6	59,3	33,6	44,9	12,5	68,1
1909	23,2	59,1	33,6	48,9	11 6	73,2
1910	25,1	56,4	34,2	51,8	11,7	74,0
1911	25,2	53,8	35,0	51,1	12,7	71,1
1912	24,9	51,5	36,3	51,3	12,9	69,1
1913	24,9	53,4	37,2	47,2	12,4	72,0

Table 20b.—continued

Year	Imports		Exports		Re-exports	
	Share of British Possessions	Dominions' Share of Imports from the Empire	Share of British Possessions	Dominions' Share of Exports to the Empire	Share of British Possessions	Dominions, Share of Re-exports to the Empire
1914	26,9	55,0	39,8	46,5	12,8	75,0
1915	29,3	51,6	36,5	50,1	12,0	67,6
1916	29,1	50,9	34,6	51,2	14,3	67,3
1917	30,6	58,3	29,9	41,1	10,3	66,3
1918	27,9	56,3	31,1	45,7	15,9	69,4
1919	32,0	58,5	23,3	38,5	5,3	51,3
1920	25,3	56,4	34,3	39,7	10,9	65,5
1921	27,8	66,1	39,1	40,1	11,8	53,1
1922	28,4	65,4	37,0	47,4	14,4	67,4
1923*	27,4	55,9	36,6	49,4	12,8	66,3
1924	27,2	57,5	38,0	49,4	11,8	68,2
1925	30,0	57,9	39,6	49,2	10,7	64,9
1926	27,6	57,7	45,1	50,6	11,4	56,2
1927	27,3	55,3	43,1	48,6	11,2	56,4
1928	27,5	58,3	42,5	48,6	11,9	56,5
1929	26,5	56,3	41,5	50,1	12,9	55,5
1930	25,9	58,4	39,7	49,7	13,8	52,8
1931	25,4	62,6	38,8	49,0	13,6	52,2
1932	32,7	65,1	41,1	46,9	12,1	44,7
1933	35,0	64,6	41,3	50,1	13,1	48,0
1934	35,3	61,4	44,0	53,2	12,6	52,6
1935	36,1	61,9	45,3	53,6	12,0	47,6
1936	37,3	63,2	46,5	57,0	10,6	49,4
New Area of Trade Statistics						
1923	29,6	50,2	38,7	45,3	17,6	45,4
1924	30,2	49,7	41,7	42,4	18,9	39,2
1925	32,4	51,9	42,8	43,2	17,0	37,7
1926	30,2	51,3	48,1	45,1	18,7	31,3
1927	30,1	48,6	46,1	43,3	17,9	32,4
1928	30,4	50,9	45,3	43,4	18,9	32,6
1929	29,4	49,1	44,5	44,5	21,0	31,0
1930	29,1	50,0	43,5	42,7	23,6	27,5
1931	28,7	53,1	43,7	40,3	25,1	24,4
1932	35,4	57,9	45,3	39,6	22,6	21,1
1933	36,9	59,6	44,4	44,3	21,3	26,7
1934	37,1	57,2	46,8	47,6	21,6	27,5
1935	37,5	57,9	47,9	48,3	19,8	26,2
1936	39,1	59,2	49,2	51,4	17,9	26,9

* 1923–36: old area of trade statistics.

— 164 —

Table 21. British Empire share

Commodity	1854 Imports £1000s	1860	1870	1880	1890	1900
		Empire Proportion per cent				
Wheat	11 694	0,5	3,1	9,8	20,3	22,0	15,1
Wheaten flour**	3 971	5,1	7,9	9,8	7,1	6,6	6,5
Rice and Ground Rice***	983	91,0	83,2	88,4	83,5	78,8	69,6
Other Grain, Flour, etc.†	6 225	2,8	4,3	4,6	2,6	7,5	10,1
Total Grain, Flour	22 873	5,8	6,7	12,6	15,7	16,5	13,6
Fresh Fruit and Nuts	780	3,2	3,5	3,9	6,5	9,4	12,1
Coffee	1 575	76,0	86,4	73,7	62,2	33,0	22,3
Tea	5 541	0,7	3,5	11,4	26,7	71,7	91,2
Cocoa	73	54,8	47,3	55,9	52,4	55,9	45,1
Spices	491	94,1	90,5	87,2	79,2	79,0	58,0
Sugar, raw	9 616	64,7	59,8	35,8	28,7	15,8	12,9
Meat, Game and Poultry	1 706	0,9	1,0	7,6	3,0	15,4	20,1
Butter	2 171	1,5	11,6	4,3	4,8	2,2	18,1
Cheese	906	0	0	5,3	15,1	39,8	58,8
Imported Foodstuffs listed	45 732	20,4	20,1	19,8	18,5	21,5	23,7
Copper Ore	1 236	9,1	12,6	19,0	17,4	12,8	15,2
Tin Ore	.	.	18,2	40,9	0	11,3	2,9
Iron Ore, Pyrites, Manganese Ore	71	0	0	0	0,3	0,5	2,4
Copper, smelted...††	181	9,9	33,2	79,4	28,7	22,9	23,3
Lead, raw, and sheet lead	255	0	0	0	0	25,2	29,1
Tin, smelted	267	71,2	78,6	49,1	91,0	94,4	88,3
Zinc, smelted	357	0	0	0	0	0,5	0,4
Mineral oils	.	.	0	3,4	0	0	0,3
Timber and Joinery	11 849	55,2	46,1	35,2	43,1	26,7	24,9
Raw Cotton	20 175	8,4	9,8	19,1	11,3	11,2	1,7
Sheep's wool, lambswool	6 372	70,6	68,5	88,5	87,0	88,8	84,5
Jute, raw	554	92,1	98,8	99,6	99,8	99,9	99,3
Hides, raw	1 514	33,1	33,4	44,7	54,7	41,0	50,5
Oil seeds	2 906	26,5	47,4	37,0	42,8	42,3	34,0
Rubber, raw	250	11,2	17,2	21,9	19,5	14,2	12,6
Tobacco leaf	1 069	0,2	0,7	26,5	1,8	2,8	0,3
Indigo	1 670	95,7	88,2	66,2	74,1	91,2	84,9
Imported raw materials listed	48 726	33,8	30,7	35,9	39,9	37,6	28,8
Jute Yarn and Jute Goods	.	.	.	.	.	94,2	88,9
Leather, Tanned Hides	382	9,4	14,7	38,5	24,5	39,1	43,1
Printing Paper	.	.	.	.	.	.	3,2
Imports listed	94 840	27,3	25,8	28,9	28,0	29,8	26,9
Remainder	57 549	14,4	10,1	8,4	12,4	11,6	11,8
Imports. Total	152 389	22,4	20,4	21,4	22,5	22,9	21,0

** Including coarse flour.
*** Ground rice, ground rice powder, rice husked or unhusked.

* Old area of trade statistics after 1925

of British Imports, 1854-1934

1913		1925	1929		1931	1932	1933	1934	
Imports in £1000s	Empire Proportion per cent		Imports in £1000s	Empire Proportion per cent				Imports in £1000s	Empire proportion per cent

43 849	48,5	54,8	60 555	36,0	46,3	69,4	72,1	30 038	63,3
6 440	38,1	61,1	7 223	51,2	55,8	71,6	66,1	4 374	62,0
3 209	60,1	55,3	3 735	51,2	47,4	54,8	77,1	1 874	70,2
51 997	8,8	31,5	33 085	18,8	13,1	20,7	16,3	25 311	17,2
105 495	35,3	48,6	104 598	32,1	34,8	51,0	52,0	61 597	44,4
11 626	14,3	23,4	35 450	21,2	27,8	38,9	40,3	26 590	43,0
2 519	18,7	42,1	3 763	34,5	43,6	45,0	50,4	2 459	34,0
13 783	87,3	89,1	37 598	85,8	86,5	89,1	89,4	27 990	88,9
2 283	50,9	86,4	3 811	93,1	88,9	87,4	91,2	1 778	90,7
687	72,2	70,2	2 382	67,3	71,6	80,8	73,6	1 841	77,6
10 716	8,7	27,7	22 732	42,5	44,4	41,3	52,2	13 277	64,2
56 421	24,7	23,8	108 074	16,4	20,0	21,5	26,0	79 774	32,1
24 084	19,0	44,1	50 129	35,4	44,8	50,2	51,1	32 113	53,5
7 035	81,7	88,5	13 884	86,0	82,9	87,6	89,4	7 015	88,9
234 649	30,3	43,3	382 421	36,0	38,7	45,2	47,9	254 434	49,2
2 454	37,4	55,3	1 604	44,3	69,9	68,6	69,4	965	80,0
3 309	18,3	16,1	10 712	22,0	24,0	20,2	25,4	5 191	23,9
9 705	8,4	13,6	7 974	12,7	11,0	9,6	11,7	4 633	13,0
7 346	21,0	11,6	12 583	5,4	16,8	40,0	55,9	7 862	47,4
3 718	36,7	60,0	6 928	63,8	63,1	84,4	94,8	3 549	89,4
9 252	94,8	84,5	3 031	88,4	95,9	97,9	98,2	2 366	60,3
3 451	0,9	11,4	3 657	26,1	66,6	75,6	86,4	1 955	79,5
10 857	7,6	5,1	43 927	3,9	3,5	2,8	4,5	32 345	5,9
33 789	16,2	11,9	46 618	9,3	8,3	9,7	12,7	40 641	16,8
60 295	3,0	10,2	75 865	14,5	11,7	11,3	13,1	35 308	17,1
34 226	80,2	86,0	59 225	85,8	82,4	86,1	83,6	36 840	83,4
9 247	99,4	98,8	6 623	96,9	97,9	98,8	98,5	2 902	98,8
5 848	41,8	36,5	4 810	48,0	31,1	27,2	26,6	3 228	33,6
15 888	53,3	56,0	21 732	48,6	38,5	46,6	63,1	8 879	60,5
20 524	57,2	80,5	16 831	82,1	81,3	85,3	81,8	11 873	79,7
6 709	0,9	7,7	17 319	10,7	17,5	27,3	23,4	16 149	13,0
55	87,3	100,0	8	100,0	98,0	81,3	50,0	2	81,8
236 673	34,5	35,4	339 447	34,1	32,5	33,5	35,5	214 688	36,8
2 972	82,3	82,2	3 596	79,0	69,9	93,8	94,0	1 615	94,3
10 572	35,9	41,8	14 366	38,9	29,3	46,9	54,0	7 151	58,3
2 344	19,6	36,5	5 936	57,2	56,3	59,7	64,7	4 049	65,2
487 210	32,7	39,5	745 766	35,4	36,4	41,4	43,2	481 937	44,1
281 524	11,3	12,0	443 320	11,4	10,5	16,0	18,5	245 309	17,9
768 734	24,9	30,0	1 189 086	26,5	25,4	32,7	35,0	727 246	35,3

† Including bran waste products.
†† Before 1890 includes also semi-manufactured copper.

Table 22. British Empire share of

Commodity	1830 Exports in £1000s	1840	1850	1860	1870	1880	1890	1900
		\multicolumn{7}{c}{Empire proportion per cent}						
Sugar, refined	1 288	8,9	39,7	33,1	36,0	26,8	23,5	23,9	35,6
Spirituous Liquors	.	.	.	.	31,4	41,0	82,7	81,0	75,7
Beer and Ale	213	74,2	83,4	70,1	77,6	68,0	69,2	74,2	69,1
Coal, Coke, Briquettes	184	43,5	25,6	14,9	16,3	12,4	14,9	12,5	9,8
Cotton Yarn	4 134	9,0	12,8	17,4	23,8	21,1	31,8	24,5	22,3
Cotton Goods (Bales)	14 120	21,2	36,6	31,2	37,7	34,7	44,1	47,4	45,8
Woollen Yarn	.	.	2,9	0,6	0,4	0,5	1,2	1,7	2,0
Other Woollen Goods	4 851	28,1	21,8	17,3	26,2	14,0	25,4	20,8	29,4
Linen Yarn and Goods	2 066	25,5	22,4	11,9	10,4	8,2	12,5	14,2	18,5
Jute Yarn, Jute Goods	.	.	.	.	.	19,1	7,6	9,0	13,9
Silk Goods	521	26,7	36,6	17,8	12,4	9,6	31,3	25,6	28,2
Artificial Silk Goods	.	.	.	.	.	.	.	.	.
Clothing, all kinds	983	67,2	78,5	52,6	46,1	55,5	61,7	72,3	80,9
Manufactured textiles	26 675	22,7	29,0	26,7	30,6	26,6	36,8	37,2	39,7
Pig Iron and Iron Goods	1 079	39,9	36,3	22,5	30,4	21,7	31,2	33,5	36,7
Hardware and Cutlery	1 412	21,6	33,7	20,5	30,0	28,3	35,5	42,1	48,6
Copper Goods, Brass Goods	867	56,2	32,7	36,9	51,6	42,3	44,9	53,8	45,9
Machinery	209	36,4	24,5	13,7	30,7	19,0	18,3	24,6	22,3
Locomotives	.	.	.	.	.	16,0	67,5	27,8	49,5
Railway Carriages	.	.	.	.	.	6,3	56,9	33,9	55,9
Motor Vehicles	.	.	.	.	.	.	.	.	(38,7)
Steamships	.	.	.	.	.	.	.	.	7,0
Electrical Engineering Goods	.	.	.	.	29,8	65,4	43,0	51,8	25,2
Drugs and Medicines	.	..	.	.	38,5	49,7	59,0	61,8	67,7
Sodium Compounds	.	.	.	.	33,3	5,4	6,3	7,0	21,0
Ammonium Sulphate	.	.	.	.	48,4	32,5	15,1	18,2	11,4
Dye-stuffs	100	57,0	52,9	32,7	34,7	38,8	43,0	41,2	46,3
Soaps	} 247	68,4	76,9	73,9	76,0	57,3	54,5	60,9	63,2
Candles					92,2	82,7	76,9	57,9	51,0
Pottery and Porcelain	442	21,7	26,5	17,7	23,0	22,8	25,3	29,8	33,4
Paper and Paper Goods	.	.	.	.	76,9	71,5	79,0	69,6	63,7
Books	96	52,1	63,3	44,5	45,5	42,0	57,2	59,2	60,6
Arms and Munitions	242	28,9	52,7	·42,0	41,3	13,2	39,8	42,2	49,2
Rubber Tyres, etc.	.	.	.	.	.	.	.	.	.
Tobacco products	.	.	.	.	78,6	39,3	53,1	67,7	84,6
Enumerated	33 054	24,7	31,1	26,6	31,9	26,7	34,8	34,6	33,2
Unenumerated	5 218	35,0	40,3	33,2	33,1	21,5	28,9	27,2	29,4
Total	38 272	26,1	32,3	27,2	32,1	26,0	33,7	33,1	32,4

* Old area of trade statistics after 1925 [*i.e.* U.K. of Great Britain and Ireland].

British Exports of Home Products, 1830-1934*

1913			1925	1929		1931	1932	1933	1934	
Exports in £1000s	Empire Proportion per cent		Exports in £1000s	Exports in £1000s	Empire Proportion per cent				Exports in £1000s	Empire proportion per cent
335	41,2	63,7	1 769	57,6	26,0	34,7	29,2		3 227	17,9
4 188	65,9	68,5	8 891	71,7	60,7	58,3	62,7		7 529	41,7
2 135	59,7	64,5	1 626	68,4	63,0	66,6	65,1		835	68,2
53 659	3,7	6,1	50 425	5,8	5,6	9,4	9,9		33 699	9,8
15 006	19,3	11,1	20 695	17,7	16,5	23,1	18,4		10 105	19,2
97 776	51,7	46,3	98 214	50,0	45,4	53,2	49,5		38 805	53,2
8 040	10,2	15,0	10 663	18,0	17,4	20,4	19,2		6 324	16,5
27 669	33,5	31,8	40 821	31,8	26,8	29,7	33,8		17 701	37,7
9 463	22,7	26,6	10 028	30,1	27,4	28,1	26,9		6 612	32,1
5 339	18,1	19,2	5 246	19,2	19,9	21,8	18,4		2 227	22,1
2 157	31,2	46,8	2 101	42,0	48,3	51,4	42,8		1 007	38,7
.	.	54,5	8 214	63,6	68,7	70,3	69,1		4 381	69,4
20 973	68,6	66,6	22 252	63,6	58,9	61,6	62,9		9 850	66,5
186 423	43,9	39,5	218 234	42,2	37,6	43,4	41,4		97 012	44,2
53 405	48,2	53,1	65 693	51,4	50,4	46,9	51,9		33 727	55,3
2 218	57,2	72,6	2 627	64,2	57,1	62,5	61,4		2 214	63,8
4 660	64,8	63,8	5 370	63,3	55,7	62,3	65,0		3 141	68,2
33 602	32,5	46,7	53 145	43,5	39,6	40,7	48,1		31 609	51,2
2 782	58,6	74,7	5 258	69,5	58,8	60,5	40,2		972	65,3
4 240	58,4	50,7	3 882	43,8	46,2	35,4	60,3		795	68,3
2 396	67,4	77,0	4 248	81,2	72,5	66,4	64,5		5 080	71,7
5 867	20,6	34,8	5 823	52,3	47,2	25,6	89,7		550	47,0
5 386	61,6	55,3	12 762	56,5	55,1	56,0	56,5		7 649	61,1
2 352	59,9	70,4	2 941	69,4	64,8	65,5	66,6		3 403	53,4
1 788	26,0	37,7	3 742	37,5	44,1	47,6	48,0		3 098	50,4
4 391	6,4	14,5	5 434	32,6	23,9	34,8	47,9		1 578	43,0
3 232	48,8	55,9	3 740	56,7	55,3	57,4	58,7		2 338	54,1
2 093	54,3	64,4	3 432	63,3	66,2	69,7	67,5		1 617	71,6
435	26,2	29,9	281	29,5	30,4	30,2	31,5		222	30,0
3 797	41,9	48,5	5 996	50,8	50,3	56,8	54,6		3 032	58,0
3 679	62,0	73,4	9 010	72,8	67,2	70,3	73,0		5 613	71,5
2 800	60,1	63,3	4 291	65,6	62,9	66,6	69,1		2 954	71,1
4 707	48,4	48,1	4 968	48,7	42,1	40,4	38,4		3 142	56,5
1 294	36,1	50,5	3 959	40,6	39,0	42,9	42,3		3 005	50,3
3 376	44,5	75,1	9 529	71,9	65,5	67,6	65,4		4 351	64,0
395 240	38,9	42,1	497 076	43,7	39,3	41,9	43,2		262 392	45,4
130 005	31,8	32,3	199 533	35,9	37,8	39,3	37,1		115 221	41,0
525 245	37,2	39,6	696 609	41,5	38,8	41,1	41,2		377 613	44,0

— 168 —

Table 23. United Kingdom Trade with the Empire, 1854-1935 (in £1000)

Area	Old area of trade statistics [i.e. U.K. of Great Britain and Ireland]						New Area of Trade Statistics		
	1854/57	1877/79	1898/1901	1909/13	1927/29	1930/32	1933/35	1927/29	1930/32	1933/35

Imports

Australia–New Zealand	5 116	21 517	33 116	56 334	101 754	86 612	90 847	101 450	85 938	89 508
Union of S. Africa...	1 234	4 422	5 347	10 676	23 274	16 297	13 349	23 260	16 270	13 333
Canada–Newfoundland	6 285	10 671	21 029	27 260	56 026	40 866	54 265	55 021	40 163	53 140
5 old Dominions	12 635	36 610	59 492	94 270	181 054	143 775	158 461	179 731	142 311	155 981
India	14 814	27 798	27 498	44 837	64 432	40 092	40 557	64 386	40 021	40 194
British Asia (excludg. India)	2 236	7 938	11 753	22 667	35 237	22 028	22 765	35 235	22 018	22 719
British Africa (excl. S.A.)	2 277	1 805	2 572	5 789	28 174	16 226	18 311	28 173	16 226	18 307
British West Indies	6 448	6 927	2 315	2 868	6 031	5 833	7 442	6 031	5 832	7 416
British Europe	822	992	1 652	1 818	3 587	3 661	4 459	48 079	39 008	22 372
Other British Possessions	4	74	163	429	1 394	1 114	1 153	1 394	1 112	1 154
Other Possessions	26 601	45 534	45 953	78 408	138 855	88 954	94 687	183 298	124 217	112 162
Total Imports from Empire	39 236	82 144	105 445	172 678	319 909	232 729	253 148	363 029	266 528	268 143*

Re-exports.

Australia–New Zealand	1 430	1 953	2 389	4 221	3 100	1 397	981	3 100	1 397	981
Union of S. Africa...	68	483	1 202	1 724	1 570	944	633	1 570	944	633
Canada–Newfoundland	275	638	1 471	3 221	2 566	1 659	1 290	2 565	1 659	1 289
5 old Dominions	1 773	3 074	5 062	9 166	7 236	4 000	2 904	7 235	4 000	2 903
India	475	1 334	726	1 462	1 202	889	618	1 202	889	618
British Asia (excludg. India)	74	366	305	485	790	446	328	790	446	328
British Africa (excl. S.A.)	104	156	392	624	1 853	992	607	1 853	992	607
British West Indies	218	308	388	570	452	408	244	452	408	244

Table 24—continued

Commodity	1854	1876	1900	1913	1929	1934
Australia-New Zealand (continued)						
Lead	.	.	1 031	1 308	2 114	1 838
Apples, fresh	.	.	113	296	1 079	2 143
Currants and Raisins, dried	.	.	.	14	2 061	1 348
Sugar, raw	.	.	.	.	2 851	2 817
Eggs	.	.	.	.	316	1 186
Other Goods	497	2 013	4 636	7 041	7 534	6 725
Total	4 304	21 951	35 417	58 403	103 743	91 520
Union of South Africa*						
Wool and Mohair	497	2 857	1 733	6 008	13 475	5 248
Skins and Furs	25	302	422	1 420	1 048	504
Hides, raw	20	156	40	825	1 115	379
Feathers, ornamental	6	361	847	2 420	12	19
Sugar, raw	.	35	—	0	1 293	645
Fruits, fresh	.	.	6	103	1 785	2 462
Maize	.	.	—	10	1 815	282
Other Goods	143 **	481	925	1 523	3 767	2 353
Total	691	4 192	3 973	12 309	24 310	11 892
Ceylon Straits Settlement and Malay States						
Coffee	1 007	2 681	45	2	—	—
Coconut oil	306	237	355	324	366	220
Tin	138	569	3 365	8 103	2 599	1 108
Sago and Sago Flour	126	233	182	222	278	172
Gutta percha	113	145	1 381	552	20	3
Gambir and Cutch	110	460	261	121	43	17
Spices	51	589	505	193	864	1 099
Rubber, raw	18	49	188	11 138	13 055	9 133
Tea	10	7	4 097	4 179	11 984	9 506
Graphite	.	48	215	163	24	19
Mineral oils	.	.	.	191	457	110
Fruit, preserves	.	.	.	.	1 022	857
Other Goods	422	758	1 905	1 982	2 084	1 461
Total	2 301	5 776	12 499	27 170	32 796	23 705
British West Indies***						
Sugar, raw, and Molasses	3 891	4 635	625	698	1 426	2 310
Rum	1 306	907	341	307	273	218
Mahogany	257	54	153	133	100	76
Coffee, raw	95	311	48	27	28	22
Dyewoods	75	371	57	45	2	—
Spices of all kinds	64	111	122	96	184	72
Cocoa, raw	40	288	629	483	245	98
Cotton, raw	10	22	8	209	191	47
Asphalt, Bitumen	.	12	49	98	302	95
Gutta percha, raw	.	.	100	142	67	10
Bananas	.	.	1	133	1 210	2 260
Mineral oils	.	.	.	.	1 215	1 716
Other goods	443 †	415	351	570	844	518
Total	6 181	7 126	2 484	2 941	6 087	7 442

* 1854 and 1876: Cape of Good Hope and Natal, excluding diamond exports.
** Of these (in £1000s): Wine 49, Copper Ore, 21.
*** British West Indies with Bahamas, British Honduras and British Guiana.
† This includes: Cochineal 235 (in £1000s).

Table 25. United Kingdom Exports of Home Products to the Empire, 1827-1934

(in £1000s)

Commodity	1827	1854	1876	1900	1913	1929	1934
Canada-Newfoundland							
Manufactured textiles	785	2 930	3 767	4 010	11 389	13 266	7 301
Iron and Steel Goods (including bicycles and cutlery)	152	1 815	1 434	993	2 539	3 051	2 887
Leather and Leather Goods	60	87	56	58	460	627	270
Pottery and Porcelain	16	105	90	154	502	949	494
Coal, Coke, etc.	13	64	112	41	70	986	2 264
Chemicals	12	98	222	314	659	835	1 243
Books	8	16	68	79	247	362	242
Machinery	2	111	57	207	900	1 616	833
Vegetable oils, crude and refined	.	28	8	95	40	486	146
Spirituous liquors, British and Irish production	.	12	35	216	741	1 910	578
Electrical engineering products	.	2	48	251	236	251	69
Paper, Cardboard, and derivatives	.	.	81	68	270	385	253
Ships	.	.	.	.	.	3 941	41
Other Goods	349	713	1 380	1 641	6 622	7 340	3 912
Total	1397	5 981	7 358	8 127	24 675	36 005	20 533
India							
Manufactured textiles	2648	7 191	15 961	19 069	40 729	32 340	11 373
Iron and Steel Goods, including bicycles and cutlery	330	584	1 864	3 280	9 801	10 099	4 070
Other metals and derivatives	330	203	799	713	1 733	1 701	1 343
Arms, Munitions	284	33	53	120	200	810	497
Tobacco, beer, spirituous liquors, sugar	74	308	501	626	914	3 034	1 007
Leather, Leather Goods	44	37	101	200	632	476	235
Books	30	33	80	131	309	397	305
Machinery (1854 including locomotives)	22	101	724	1 529	4 558	9 182	5 689
Chemicals	21	67	232	683	1 309	2 559	2 424
Coal, coke, etc.	4	36	298	129	177	25	2
Locomotives, Railway Carriages	.	10	155	867	2 200	3 429	515
Paper, Cardboard and derivatives	.	1	110	167	513	988	557
Electrical engineering products	.	.	145	76	362	1 347	1 071
Soap	.	.	22	114	433	1 010	444
Instruments, Tools, Scientific apparatus	.	.	.	13	219	504	562
Rubber Goods	.	.	.	13	67	791	125
Cement	.	.	.	8	52	200	89
Ships	.	.	.	.	242	255	37
Motor vehicles, and parts, including tyres	.	.	.	288	260	125	.
Other Goods	486	524	1 326	1 786	679	1 945	1 745
					4 623	7 595	4 639
Total	4273	9 128	22 405	30 116	70 273	78 308	36 729

Table 25—continued

Commodity	1827	1854	1876	1900	1913	1929	1934
Australia—New Zealand							
Manufactured textiles	171	4 826	7 418	10 353	13 334	24 094	12 975
Iron and Steel Goods (including bicycles, cutlery)	35	1 397	3 012	4 608	8 891	10 906	5 231
Beer	21	541	476	398	354	17	854
Pottery, Porcelain and glass-wares	17	353	471	566	736	1 762	851
Other Metalwares	11	241	215	363	1 158	1 487	787
Leather, Leather Goods, boots and shoes	9	858	774	682	957	1 130	240
Chemicals	4	193	393	1 297	1 725	2 706	2 098
Books	3	154	334	481	772	1 416	909
Arms, Munitions	2	34	158	554	1 246	861	590
Machinery	1	266	525	1 422	3 063	5 157	2 379
Spirituous liquors (British and Irish production)	.	99	169	814	1 087	1 930	855
Paper, Cardboard and derivatives		42	466	549	949	3 610	1 904
Instruments, Tools, Scientific Apparatus	.	14	112	270	659	907	685
Tobacco	.	2	3	63	289	1 159	280
Ships [ducts	.	.	.	311	1 036	1 347	99
Electrical engineering pro-	.	.	.	238	939	3 243	1 282
Motor vehicles and parts, including tyres	.	.	.	.	908	3 828	2 781
Other Goods	66	2 911	3 156	4 093	7 205	10 305	2 899
Total	340	11 931	17 682	27 062	45 308	75 865	37 699
Union of South Africa							
Manufactured textiles	135	480	1 664	3 851	6 886	10 342	8 828
Pig iron and Iron Goods	19	103	745	1 767	3 642	5 108	4 435
Leather and Leather Goods	8	77	396	814	1 436	1 015	68
Soaps and candles	5	27	62	284	77	34	28
Beer	3	21	107	121	17	—	—
Books	2	12	40	144	250	368	372
Coal, coke, etc.	1	5	34	714	54	—	—
Machinery	0	4	74	520	1 397	2 739	4 094
Pickles, Sauces, Vinegar, Confectionery, etc.	—	14	39	241	271	201	163
Chemicals	.	12	52	376	995	1 072	1 350
Locomotives and Railway carriages	.	6	106	281	397	864	404
Spirituous liquors (British and Irish production)	—	3	11	283	212	364	379
Paper, Cardboard and derivatives	.	3	39	179	306	684	622
Instruments, Tools, Scientific apparatus [ducts	.	1	36	128	329	355	487
Electrical engineering pro-	.	.	.	122	338	829	1 375
Motor-vehicles and parts, including tyres	.	.	.	.	570	1 323	1 676
Other Goods	.	154	964	2 933	5 008	7 272	6 028
Total	217	922	4 369	12 758	22 185	32 570	30 309

British West Indies

Commodity	1827	1854	1876	1900	1913	1929	1934
British West Indies							
Manufactured textiles ...	1915	892	1 317	1 022	1 131	1 516	1 265
Pig iron and Iron Goods, including bicycles, cutlery	221	150	296	191	243	578	777
Soaps (1854, including candles)	156	82	71	73	135	193	162
Leather and Leather Goods	155	107	139	112	98	185	187
Beer	56	57	119	94	102	190	116
Coal, coke, etc.	31	67	95	90	61	56	112
Machinery	27	56	152	94	131	335	392
Chemicals	21	32	74	78	103	291	326
Books	12	10	15	18	25	48	32
Tobacco	.	2	—	26	66	176	102
Paper, Cardboard and derivatives			5	18	23	100	103
Electrical engineering products	.	.	1	3	.	32	52
Spirituous liquors, British and Irish production	.	.	.	46	64	528	144
Instruments, Tools, Scientific Apparatus ...	.	.	.	22	28	65	64
Motor vehicles and parts, including tyres ...	.	.	.	.	.	100	90
Other Goods	989	553	760	654	1 211	2 498	2 329
Total	3583	2 008	3 044	2 541	3 421	6 891	6 253

— 175 —

Table 26. Price Indices of Principal Commodity Groups in United Kingdom's Foreign Trade, 1801-1933

(1913=100)

Year	Foodstuffs and Livestock		Raw Materials and semi-manufactured Goods			Manufactured Goods			Weighted average of Total Trade			Sauerbeck Index
	Imports	Exports*	Imports	Exports*	Turnover†	Imports	Exports*	Turnover†	Imports	Exports*	Turnover†	
1801	.	.	.	.	.	.	.	.	220	311	247	200
1802	.	.	.	.	.	.	.	.	171	353	227	156
1803	.	.	.	.	.	.	.	.	182	344	229	167
1804	.	.	.	.	.	.	.	.	175	317	218	159
1805	.	.	.	.	.	.	.	.	195	304	229	178
1806	.	.	.	.	.	.	.	.	192	290	226	174
1807	.	.	.	.	.	.	.	.	188	298	223	172
1808	.	.	.	.	.	.	.	.	214	274	234	194
1809	.	.	.	.	.	.	.	.	231	268	244	210
1810	.	.	.	.	.	.	.	.	236	260	244	214
1811	.	.	.	.	.	.	.	.	211	265	228	191
1812	.	.	.	.	.	.	.	.	211	264	231	192
1813	.	.	.	.	.	.	.	.	.	.	.	194
1814	.	219	.	124	.	.	283	.	220	265	235	200
1815	.	206	.	120	.	.	253	.	189	241	209	172
1816	.	171	.	91	.	.	237	.	157	217	182	143
1817	.	184	.	86	.	.	218	.	172	205	185	156
1818	.	178	.	102	.	.	229	.	194	216	201	167
1819	.	150	.	98	.	.	226	.	168	208	181	142
1820	.	151	.	97	.	.	218	.	152	201	168	132
1821	.	131	.	96	.	.	200	.	135	186	154	125
1822	.	88	.	85	.	.	183	.	126	167	142	119
1823	.	95	.	95	.	.	175	.	128	162	140	122
1824	.	92	.	88	.	.	172	.	126	160	138	125
1825	.	101	.	95	.	.	182	.	148	170	154	138
1826	.	97	.	82	.	.	162	.	129	151	136	118
1827	.	91	.	76	.	.	154	.	129	144	134	115
1828	.	91	.	68	.	.	148	.	117	138	124	115
1829	.	86	.	69	.	.	137	.	114	129	119	111
1830	.	87	.	62	.	.	138	.	117	129	121	107
1831	.	88	.	63	.	.	130	.	118	123	120	109
1832	.	89	.	61	.	.	118	.	112	112	112	105

* Home Products.
† Excluding Re-exports.

No calculations have been made of a price index for the total trade in foodstuffs since in imports there was a considerable preponderance of unprocessed foodstuffs; in exports, of processed foodstuffs. No calculation of a price index for re-exports has been made, as re-exported goods are already contained in imports—though not necessarily in the imports of the same year. The price index of Sauerbeck—given for comparison—was taken back to 1818 by linking it with Jevon's price-index for 1818-27 (annual average). Sauerbeck's index was continued in *The Statist*.

— 176 —

Table 26—*continued*

Year	Foodstuffs and Livestock		Raw Materials and semi-manufactured Goods			Manufactured Goods			Weighted average of Total Trade			Sauerbeck Index
	Imports	Exports*	Imports	Exports*	Turnover†	Imports	Exports*	Turnover†	Imports	Exports*	Turnover†	
1833	.	83	.	65	.	.	123	.	107	117	111	107
1834	.	82	.	71	.	.	128	.	112	121	115	106
1835	.	85	.	70	.	.	129	.	115	123	118	109
1836	.	91	.	72	.	.	139	.	123	133	127	120
1837	.	85	.	69	.	.	126	.	120	119	120	110
1838	.	85	.	71	.	.	119	.	120	114	118	116
1839	.	83	.	68	.	.	120	.	132	115	125	122
1840	.	84	.	68	.	.	114	.	125	109	119	122
1841	.	83	.	68	.	.	111	.	122	105	115	118
1842	.	81	.	66	.	.	102	.	107	97	103	107
1843	.	80	.	62	.	.	98	.	102	94	99	97
1844	.	80	.	67	.	.	100	.	99	97	98	99
1845	.	83	.	68	.	.	102	.	106	99	103	103
1846	.	85	.	70	.	.	100	.	106	97	102	105
1847	.	90	.	69	.	.	104	.	112	100	108	112
1848	.	82	.	62	.	.	91	.	98	88	94	92
1849	.	80	.	61	.	.	87	.	92	84	89	87
1850	.	83	.	61	.	.	88	.	92	86	89	91
1851	.	73	.	59	.	.	86	.	95	83	90	88
1852	.	73	.	61	.	.	86	.	93	84	89	92
1853	.	82	.	69	.	.	96	.	106	93	100	112
1854	133	92	101	79	99	103	94	95	112	93	104	120
1855	142	95	101	77	98	97	92	92	114	91	103	119
1856	141	96	106	79	103	108	93	95	118	92	106	119
1857	151	92	113	80	110	112	96	98	125	95	111	123
1858	125	93	107	73	103	111	94	95	113	92	103	107
1859	129	91	105	74	102	114	95	96	113	93	103	110
1860	135	92	103	73	100	114	95	97	114	93	105	116
1861	130	87	110	70	105	121	94	97	118	92	107	114
1862	123	96	152	71	139	123	108	110	136	103	122	119
1863	114	92	171	72	156	116	125	123	141	116	131	122
1864	119	94	180	75	166	113	137	133	148	128	140	123
1865	118	93	159	75	148	113	129	126	138	121	131	119
1866	124	99	144	78	136	117	131	129	134	124	129	120
1867	136	98	123	76	117	120	119	119	127	114	122	118
1868	135	97	122	74	117	113	111	111	126	106	118	116
1869	123	96	128	72	120	111	112	112	124	107	117	116
1870	121	90	123	71	116	103	109	108	120	104	113	113
1871	126	94	109	72	104	109	110	110	115	104	110	118
1872	131	95	120	108	118	114	120	119	123	117	121	128
1873	131	99	119	136	121	117	121	120	123	121	122	131
1874	130	97	113	112	113	113	114	114	120	113	117	120
1875	126	93	109	89	107	113	109	109	116	106	112	113

* Home Products.   † Excluding Re-exports.

Table 26—*continued*

Year	Foodstuffs and Livestock		Raw Materials and semi-manufactured Goods			Manufactured Goods			Weighted average of Total Trade			Sauerbeck Index
	Imports	Exports*	Imports	Exports*	Turnover†	Imports	Exports*	Turnover†	Imports	Exports*	Turnover†	
1876	122	92	105	78	101	112	100	103	113	97	107	112
1877	131	97	101	72	97	105	96	98	113	93	106	110
1878	119	93	95	67	91	106	93	96	106	89	100	103
1879	113	94	90	62	86	106	88	92	102	85	95	97
1880	117	91	97	68	92	112	92	100	107	88	100	103
1881	118	93	95	65	89	111	87	92	106	85	97	100
1882	119	99	94	65	89	107	88	92	105	85	97	99
1883	114	95	91	64	87	107	86	90	103	84	95	97
1884	105	89	89	62	84	106	83	88	98	81	91	90
1885	98	87	83	60	79	100	80	84	92	77	86	84
1886	92	83	77	57	74	99	76	81	86	74	81	81
1887	91	82	77	58	74	95	76	80	86	73	80	80
1888	93	84	81	61	77	97	77	81	88	75	83	83
1889	95	89	81	70	79	98	77	82	89	78	85	84
1890	92	88	81	83	82	98	82	85	88	82	86	84
1891	97	88	78	80	79	98	82	86	89	82	86	84
1892	93	83	75	74	75	97	79	83	86	78	83	80
1893	92	84	75	69	74	92	78	82	85	77	82	80
1894	83	80	69	71	70	88	74	78	78	74	76	74
1895	80	80	66	78	66	88	72	76	75	72	74	73
1896	79	77	71	62	69	88	74	78	77	73	76	72
1897	80	81	70	63	69	86	73	77	77	72	75	73
1898	83	80	67	68	67	85	72	76	77	72	75	75
1899	81	88	73	77	74	86	76	79	79	77	78	80
1900	82	90	84	108	89	91	85	87	85	89	86	88
1901	84	89	79	90	81	87	84	85	82	85	83	83
1902	85	90	77	81	78	88	80	82	82	81	82	81
1903	85	88	81	80	81	90	82	84	84	82	84	81
1904	84	81	83	78	82	92	84	87	85	83	84	83
1905	87	84	82	80	81	94	85	87	86	84	85	84
1906	87	89	91	85	90	94	89	91	90	89	89	91
1907	91	88	95	94	95	96	94	95	94	94	94	94
1908	93	86	85	88	86	97	93	94	90	91	91	86
1909	96	90	86	82	85	98	90	92	92	88	91	87
1910	98	92	100	86	97	110	93	94	99	92	96	92
1911	97	96	96	86	94	98	96	96	97	94	96	94
1912	102	97	96	93	95	98	97	97	98	96	97	100
1913	100	100	100	100	100	100	100	100	100	100	100	100
1914	107	100	95	96	95	100	100	100	101	99	100	100
1915	131	114	100	116	103	110	106	107	114	108	112	128
1916	154	143	145	158	147	143	132	135	148	137	144	160
1917	209	181	195	181	192	187	168	173	199	170	189	206
1918	242	244	242	211	237	226	241	235	239	236	238	226

* Home Products.   † Excluding Re-exports.

Table 26—*continued*

Year	Foodstuffs and Livestock		Raw Materials and semi-manufactured Goods			Manufactured Goods			Weighted average of Total Trade			Sauerbeck Index
	Imports	Exports*	Imports	Exports*	Turnover†	Imports	Exports*	Turnover†	Imports	Exports*	Turnover†	
1919	250	253	241	285	247	228	296	274	243	292	257	241
1920	282	286	292	404	308	290	370	346	288	368	316	291
1921	202	225	158	194	164	214	293	271	186	272	212	187
1922	157	201	134	144	136	171	217	204	149	199	167	154
1923	149	183	141	173	149	161	195	184	148	189	163	153
1924	151	189	155	167	157	161	196	185	154	190	166	165
1925	156	192	157	151	156	148	193	177	155	185	164	159
1926	148	184	131	143	133	151	179	169	141	174	151	149
1927	143	178	125	137	128	143	166	158	136	161	144	144
1928	141	180	126	126	126	145	165	158	136	159	144	141
1929	139	169	122	123	122	141	163	155	133	155	140	134
1930	121	158	99	137	102	131	157	147	115	148	125	113
1931	99	139	73	103	78	118	141	130	93	133	103	97
1932	92	128	70	100	75	108	128	121	86	122	95	95
1933	85	129	71	101	76	104	124	117	82	119	92	93

* Home Products.
† Excluding Re-exports.

INDEX

Acts of Parliament, Consolidation of Duties (1787), 7; Corn Laws (1815-1846), 60-1, 111
Actual Current Values, 17, 18ff., 24ff.
Africa, South. *See* Union of South Africa; South-West. *See* S.W. Africa; West, *see* Cameroons, Gold Coast, Nigeria
Alcoholic Drinks, 66, 97. *See* Beer
America, 35, 79, 81. *See* Canada, U.S.A., etc.
America, North (British), 111. *See* Canada
Ammonia, Sulphate of, 72, 104
Anglo-Egyptian Sudan. *See* Sudan
Arms, 20
Asia, 93. *See* India, Malay States, Straits Settlements, etc.
Australia, 90, 93, 94, 104
Austria-Hungary, 35 (n), 81

Bacon, 62, 113
Balance of Payments, 31, 33
Bar Iron, 12
Bark, Peruvian, 72
Barley, 57, 111
Beans, 20
Beef, 63, 113
Beer, 71 97
Belgium, 37, 81
Bermudas, 35, 90
Bloom (Iron), 12
Bolivia, 6
Books, 20, 104
Booms. *See* Trade Cycle.
Boracic Acid, 67
Bounties, 7
Breweries, 71
Bristles, 20
Brussels Register, 10-12, 28
Budgets, 1842, 67, 111-113; 1853, 67, 113; 1868, 68, 113
Bulls, 112
Butter, 20, 63-4, 66, 70 (n), 71, 113

Cameroons, 94
Campion, H. *See* Daniels
Canada, 90, 93-6, 104.
Candles, 20
Capital Goods, 57
Cattle, 111, 112
Cereals, 58, 59 (n). *See* Maize, Oats, Wheat
Ceylon, 96
Chalmers, George, 4, 30
Cheese, 63-4. 70 (n), 71, 111
Chemicals, 67, 73, 97

Chocolate, 71
Civil War, American, 54
Clocks, 66
Clover Seeds, 20
Coal, 13, 19, 55, 56, 72, 75, 104
Cochineal, 72
Cocoa, 19
Coffee, 17, 19, 66
Coke, 75
Commons, House of, 4
Commonwealth. *See* Empire (British)
Confectionery, 71
Consumption Goods, 57
Continent (Europe), 68, 82, 87
Copper, 57, 72
Corn, 70 (n), 111
Corn Laws, 60-1, 111
Cotton, Piece Goods, 7, 20, 67, 72; Raw 16, 19, 21, 89, 96; Waste, 72; Famine, 54, 77, 89
'Country of Consignment,' 6-7
'Country of Destination,' 6
Crisis, Commercial. *See* Depression
'Crisis Exports,' 46, 77
Crops, 59
Crowther, G. *See* Layton
Culliford, 3 (n)
Current Values. *See* Actual Current Values
Custom House (London), Fires (1718, 1814) ... 3, 5, 6, 33 (n)
Cutlery, 20
Czecho-Slovakia, 35 (n)

Dairy Products, 19
Daniels, G. W., Calculation of 'Export Proportions,' 76-7 (n)
Depression (1929-33), 51, 75, 79
Distilleries, 71
Dominions (1938). *See* Canada, etc.
Drugs, 19, 72
Dyes, 19, 20, 32 (n), 72. *See* Indigo, Cochineal, Madder, etc.

Eggs, 63-4
Egypt, 93
Eire, 37, 38
Electrical Engineering. *See* Engineering, electrical
Embroidery, 17
Empire (British), 66, 88 ff, 97 ff. *See* Dominions, India, etc.
Engineering, 72, 97; Electrical, 57, 73, 75; Machinery, 75
Europe, 79, 81; Central, 35, 81, 83, 90; Industrial, 35, 81, 83, 87

— 179 —

— 180 —

Expansion of British Industry. *See* Hoffman, W.
'Export-Proportions,' 75 ff
Fertilisers, 72
Fish, 66, 71
Flour, 38
Fluctuations, Trade. *See* Trade Cycle
Food, 10, 19, 28, 38, 59, 66, 71, 75, 98, 99, 111. *See* Wheat, Oats, Meat, etc.
France, 42, 81, 83
Free Trade, 43, 59, 63, 64, 67, 68
Fruit, 28, 66, 71
Furs, 67, 73. *See* Pelts

Germany, 69, 81; Colonies, 93, 94
Gladstone, W. E., 67
Glass, 20
Gold Coast, 94
Goods, Capital. *See* Capital Goods; Consumption. *See* Consumption Goods
Grain. *See* Wheat, Oats, Maize
Haberdashery, 17
Ham, 38, 62, 113
Hardware, 20
Hides, 72
Hoffmann, W. 42, 50, 56 (n), 57
Holland. *See* Netherlands
Hungary, 35 (n), 81 (n)
Imlah, A. H., 33–4 (n)
Index, Industrial Output. *See* Hoffmann, W.; Prices. *See* Jevons, Sauerbeck, Layton, Silberling
India, 93, 96, 97, 104; Cotton, 89
Indigo, 72, 96
Industrial Revolution, 18
Inspector-General (Customs), 3, 4
International Register. *See* Brussels Register
Ireland, 5, 16, 17, 29, 37
Irish Free State. *See* Eire
Iron, 12, 28, 67, 72, 97, 104
Italy, 81, 83

Japan, 81 (n)
Jevons, W. S.; Price Index, 24–6, 31–2
Jute, 96, 98

Lace, 20
Lambs, 112
Layton, W. T., Cost of Living Index, 94 (n), 65 (n)
Lead
Leather, 28, 67, 73, 97, 98
Linen Yarn, 20
Livestock, 10, 28, 62–3
Luxemburg, 35 (n), 81
Luxuries, 64, 66

Machinery, 17, 67, 75, 97
Madder, 72
Maize, 20

Malay States, 96
Marshall, J.; *Digest*, 6, 29, 30, 33
Meal, 70 (n)
Meat, 19, 28, 63, 65, 66, 70 (n), 71 *See* Beef, Pork, etc.
Metals, 28, 72, 73. *See* Iron, etc.
Mexico, 35
Millinery, 17
Moreau, C., 4, 5, 9, 15–16 (n)
Motor Vehicles, 57, 73, 75, 97, 104

Napoleonic Wars, 33, 34 (n), 41, 42, 48
National Debt, 43
National Income, 47 ff
Nauru, 94
Needlework, 17
Netherlands, 81
Newfoundland, 96
Newsprint, 98
New Zealand, 90–4
Nigeria, 94
North American Dominions. *See* Canada, Newfoundland
Oatmeal, 20
Official Values, 3, 8, 15 ff
Oil, Cake, 96; Mineral, 56, 57; Vegetable, 72
Oranges, 17
Ores, 28
Ottawa Agreements, 89
Output, Industrial. *See* Hoffmann, W.
Oxen, 112

Palestine, 93
Paper, 20, 57, 67, 73, 75, 97
Parcel Post Goods, 10
Peel, Sir Robert, 67
Pelts, 72
Peruvian Bark, 72
Pickles, 71
Pitt, Wm. (Younger); Consolidation of Duties Act (1787), 7, 8
Porcelain, 73
Pork, 63, 113
Portugal, 43
Potash, 67
Pottery, 73
Prices. *See* Jevons, Sauerbeck, Layton, Silberling, etc.
Printed Matter, 104
Processed, Cotton Waste, 72; Foodstuffs, 71, 75
Production, Industrial. *See* Hoffmann, W.
Protection, 63, 68, 82, 89

Rags, 20
Railways, 90
Raw Materials, 10, 11, 28
Real Values. *See* Actual Values
Re-Exports
Refineries, 71

Refrigeration, 65
Repeal of Corn Laws, 111
Rice, 19, 28, 66
Rubber, 57, 72, 75, 96

Samoa, Western, 94
Saltpetre, 67
Sauerbeck, A., Price Index, 24–6, 31–2
Sawmills, 19
Scandinavia, 42
Scotland, 5, 16, 17
Scrap, 28, 71
Sheep, 62, 111, 112
Shipping, 8, 9
Silberling, N. J., Cost of Living Index, 49 (n)
Silk, 19, 20, 67, 72
Skins, 73
Sliding Scale (Corn Law), 111
Slumps. See Trade Cycle
Smuggling, 7, 8
Soap, 104
South Africa. See Union of South Africa
South West Africa, 94
Spain, 43; Spanish Wool, 16 (n)
Spices, 19
Spirits. See Alcoholic Drinks
Statutes. See Acts of Parliament
Steam Navigation, 65
Steel, 67, 104
Straits Settlements, 96
Sudan, 93
Sugar, 70 (n), 71, 96
Sulphate of Ammonia, 72, 104
Switzerland, 6, 37

Tanganyika, 93
Tea, 38, 66, 96, 105
Terms of Trade, 78
Textiles, 13, 19, 21, 22, 28, 57, 72, 73, 96, 97, 104. See Cotton, Linen, Silk, Wool, Jute

Timber, 19, 20, 94, 105
Tin, 72, 96
Tobacco, 10, 20, 67, 97, 105
Togoland, 94
Trade Cycle, 43, 46, 75
Transit Trade, 71
Tropical Products, 19, 66
Turkey, 93
Tyres, Rubber, 75

'Unenumerated' Articles, 11, 12, 98
Union of S. Africa, 90, 93, 94, 104
United States of America, 43, 68, 81–3, 87–90

Vegetables, 28
Vehicles. See Motor Vehicles
'Volumes', Calculation of, 26 ff; On 'Price-Basis', 28–29, 32–33; On 'Value-Basis', 28–29, 32–33
Wages, 65
Wales, 5, 16
War, 41, American Independence, 41; Napoleonic, 33, 34 (n), 41, 42, 48; American Civil, 54, 77, 89, 90; Franco-Prussian, 90; First World, 41, 43, 48–50, 54, 56, 57, 70, 72, 73, 75, 76, 77, 79, 81, 83, 85, 88, 93, 96, 98
West Africa. See Nigeria, Gold Coast, Cameroons, etc.
West Indies, 97. See Bermuda.
Wheat, 60–2, 70 (n), 96, 111
Whitworth, Sir Charles, 4, 30, 31
Wine, 105
Writing Materials, 17
Wood, G. H., Cost of Living Indiex 49 (n)
Wool, Raw, 16, 19, 72, 94, 96; Yarn and Goods, 7, 20, 67, 72; Worsted Yarn and Goods, 20

Zinc, 67